Nuggets of Destiny

2024 EDITION

365 Days
Of Daily Devotion

PLUS One Year
Bible-Reading Plan

JOHN K. WILLIAM

Unless otherwise indicated,
All Scripture references are taken from the Holy Bible, New International Version (NIV). Copyright © 1973, 1978, 1984 by the International Bible Society. Used with the permission of the International Bible Society.

Nuggets of Destiny

Copyright © 2023
By
John K. William

ISBN: 978-9914-9630-8-3
All Rights Reserved:

Contents and/or cover may not be reproduced in whole or in part in any form without the express written consent from the publisher, except for brief excerpts in published reviews.

Printed in the Republic of Kenya

Published by
Brook Publishers Ltd
P.O. Box 14185 - 20100, Nakuru, Kenya.
Tel. +254 722 344360, +254 799 573310
Email: brookpublishers@gmail.com

Acknowledgment

When God gives us a new year, it marks a new season of walking with Him. It is not only a privilege but a special blessing which we should greatly thank Him for. God is ready to walk with us yet again. We really honour Him for His greatness and are assured that "He crowns the year with His goodness and His paths drip with abundance" Psalm 65:11 (NKJV).

I thank my loving wife Rev. Naomi for her great support and companionship. You are an inseparable part of my life and ministry. I love you.

I extend my personal and heartfelt gratitude to the entire publishing team. Truly, you are a great team and may the Lord bless and make your generations great.

The Kingdom Seekers Fellowship Family and MBCI partners and friends, for your prayers and support

The Lord greatly bless you.

Dedication

To all members of the Body of Christ whose zeal for God has kept growing. May you have a fresh anointing every day of this year even as God continues shaping your destinies for His own glory.

Preface

Destiny refers to the position that God ordained for you to attain or occupy in life. It is what you were intended for, the plan that existed concerning you before you were born. It consists of all that God wanted you to become, have and dispense. God is a Master Planner who declares the end from the beginning. He planned for your life from the beginning to the end, long before you came to existence.

Nuggets of Destiny is a collection of brief, word-packed, spirit-stirring, destiny-oriented devotional pieces whose aim is to inspire, uplift, encourage, challenge and enlighten the reader on a daily basis to help them remain focused on pursuing their God-ordained destinies. This book can be used as a daily devotional resource because the content is designed to cover every day of the year.

The reader is encouraged to read and reflect on the content together with the day's Scripture to allow the Holy Spirit speak to your heart. It also has a daily prayer that you need to pray alongside with the help of the Holy Spirit. Set aside some time each day to confess what you believe God is speaking to your heart.

How to Read Nuggets of Destiny

This devotional serves as a tool to deepen your intimacy with God every day of the year. Its purpose is to enhance, not replace, your time with God.

Read the daily Scripture in your Bible, using a version you find find easy to understand and stay open to the leading of the Holy Spirit. Consider the daily verses within their context to grasp their intended meaning. As you read, invite the Holy Spirit to help you understand how to implement these teachings in your life. Keep a notebook and pen handy during your devotions to jot down directions, insights, and applications revealed as you engage with His word and prayer.

Reflect thoughtfully on how the daily Scripture and inspirational message relate to your journey towards your God-given destiny. Incorporate Scripture memorization into your reading for spiritual growth. Regularly pause to assess your life, recognizing any missteps or detours, and take prompt corrective action. Daily, seek God's assistance to cultivate a humble and teachable spirit, remaining receptive to the Holy Spirit's transformative power.

As this devotional is systematically organized for each day of the year, read one entry daily to fully benefit from the Scriptures, reflection thoughts, and prayer prompts. The Bible-reading plan at the bottom of each page aims to guide you through the entire Bible in one year. Adhere to this plan as closely as possible, maintaining consistency until year's end.

Nuggets of Destiny

1st January

Cherish the Presence of God

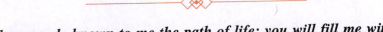

"You have made known to me the path of life; you will fill me with joy in your presence, with eternal pleasures at your right hand" (Psalm 16:11).

The presence of God is the most important treasure every believer should seek. It cannot be compared with any amount of wealth or privilege. God's intention in creating man was fellowship. The Garden of Eden where man was placed after creation was full of God's presence. When Adam and Eve sinned, they were banished from the Garden and from the presence of God. However, through the death and resurrection of Jesus, man's relationship with God was restored. Through faith in Jesus, all believers are now reconciled with God and empowered by the Holy Spirit to carry His presence.

God desires that we have an intimate relationship with Him. As we relate closely with Him, we learn His ways and become increasingly transformed until we attain His full stature. His presence gives divine backup and strength to possess the promises of God. In addition, it makes the possibilities in Christ a reality in the lives of all who approach Him by faith.

God's presence is the most conducive environment for a man to thrive in. Make it your goal this year to walk in God's presence. This will make your life impactful and your ministry effective as you devote quality time each day to fellowship with God.

Further Reading: Exodus 33:13-15; Luke 5:17
Prayer for the Day: Oh God in the name of Jesus, I pray that your presence will go with me today and forever. Amen

Genesis 1-3

Day 1

2nd January

Our Sufficiency Comes from God

"Not that we are sufficient of ourselves to think of anything as being from ourselves, but our sufficiency is from God" (2 Corinthians 3:5 NKJV).

The word of God commands us to have a sober assessment of ourselves. Doing so helps us acknowledge that we are weak, limited in knowledge, have inadequate wisdom, and need understanding to live as God would desire. However, when the Holy Spirit is in and with us, we become confident as He empowers us in our walk with God.

God does not call the qualified in His sovereignty and for His glory. Instead, He qualifies all He calls by apportioning them grace, wisdom, and the anointing they need to complete their assignments.

Since God requires that we walk by faith and not sight, He never calls us to do what we can by ourselves. Instead, He gives us assignments we are guaranteed to fail in unless with His help. To effectively accomplish what God has called us to, we must learn how to depend on Him. This also helps us have a fruitful walk with Him. Fervently seeking His face causes us to express our dependence on God even as we serve Him. That way, we show our submission to His power and receive the strength we need to make progress towards our destinies.

Further Reading: Philippians 4:13; John 16:13; John 14:16

Prayer for the Day: Lord God, I pray that you will help me depend on your strength which is sufficient at all times. I pray in Jesus' name, amen.

Day 2 | Genesis 4-7

3rd January

Respond to the Call of God

"Before I formed you in the womb I knew you, before you were born I set you apart; I appointed you as a prophet to the nations." "Ah, Sovereign LORD," I said, "I do not know how to speak; I am only a child" (Jeremiah 1:5-6).

Before the foundation of the world, God knew each one of us and predestined us for greatness in this life and through eternity. He has called us to make a lasting impact in different areas including ministry, business, media, the arts, education, governance, and family. We have a divine duty to discover and actualise the fullness of the deposits God has placed in us.

Scripture documents the words God spoke to Jeremiah when He called him as a prophet to the nations. Feeling weak and timid, Jeremiah resisted. He tried to make excuses not to serve God by claiming he was a youth.

Like Jeremiah, many people feel weak and inadequate when given assignments by God. However, God desires that they depend on Him for strength, wisdom, insight, and utterance. Those who rely on God do great exploits and leave a lasting legacy because God backs them up with His unlimited power to display His glory.

Instead of despising ourselves, we should seek to understand and respond to the call of God. Failure to do this hinders the fulfillment of the purposes of God. Your response to God's call is needed today.

Further Reading: Ephesians 2:10; Romans 11:29
Prayer for the Day: Father in the name of Jesus, I ask You to help me respond to Your call so that I may rise to the peak of my destiny. Amen.

Genesis 8-11

Day 3

4th January

Listen to the Voice of Your Destiny

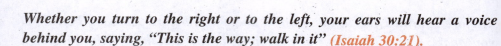

Whether you turn to the right or to the left, your ears will hear a voice behind you, saying, "This is the way; walk in it" **(Isaiah 30:21).**

Modern automotive technology has greatly improved enhancing efficiency and mobility. Drivers unfamiliar with new places benefit from navigators installed in vehicles. These devices help them get to their desired destinations with ease. In the same way, dependence on God's guidance will help us arrive at our destination.

God's wisdom and knowledge predate technology. He has a spiritual navigation system, which He gives to those who commit themselves wholeheartedly to Him. He guides and leads them daily through His gentle, still, and small voice.

The above scripture states that God's voice guides those who are attentive to Him. It reveals the route they should follow and the specific directions they need to take in order to connect with their breakthroughs. The Holy Spirit is a master teacher and guides believers into all truth. He is all-knowing and has the blueprint of our destinies. As we walk with Him and yield to His leadership, He reveals the specific paths we should walk through to accomplish everything God ordained for us. Each one of us should strive to not only hear but also obey the voice of our destiny

Further Reading: John 16:13; Jeremiah 10:23
Prayer for the Day: **Oh God, help me hear and obey the voice of my destiny that your name may be glorified. Amen.**

Day 4 | Job 1-5

5th January

Grace Empowers Us to Do Great Exploits

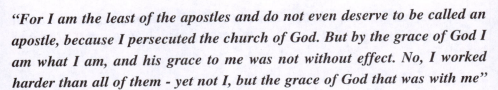

"For I am the least of the apostles and do not even deserve to be called an apostle, because I persecuted the church of God. But by the grace of God I am what I am, and his grace to me was not without effect. No, I worked harder than all of them - yet not I, but the grace of God that was with me" (1 Corinthians 15:9-10).

We have the privilege of believing God to give us strength and grace to do great things. The more we acknowledge our weakness and depend on God's mighty power, the more effective we become in fulfilling our divine mandate.

Apostle Paul knew the secret of relying on divine strength to fulfill His calling. He acknowledged that he was the least among the apostles and did not even deserve to become an apostle, because he had previously opposed the gospel by persecuting believers. However, after his encounter with the Lord on the road to Damascus, his life was transformed. He became a passionate preacher of the gospel of God's grace. With God's empowerment, he was able to do more than all the other apostles.

The grace of God empowered him to witness, pray, fast, endure and glorify God effectively. God desires to manifest His mighty power through the saints. As we align ourselves with His will, He helps us walk in signs, miracles and wonders (Mark 16:17-18).

Further Reading: Daniel 11:32b (NKJV); Ephesians 3:10; Titus 2:11-14
Prayer for the Day: Holy Spirit, fill me with divine strength to do great exploits in the name of the Lord.

Job 6-9

6th January

Emulate the Lord Jesus in Everything You Do

"And whatever you do, whether in word or deed, do it all in the name of the Lord Jesus, giving thanks to God the Father through him" (Colossians 3:17).

The will of God is that all disciples of Jesus would have godly character and walk in His footsteps. He desires that His children have Christ-like lives both in private and in public.

Our speech, character, conduct, purity and lives should be modelled on Jesus Christ. Before acting on an issue, we should take time to reflect and ask what Jesus would do or say in the same situation. Many people are in trouble as a result of actions they undertook and words they spoke that were against God's word. We can avoid that by obeying the teachings in the Scripture above.

When we read and meditate on the word of God continually, we understand the mind of God concerning our thoughts, actions and words. The disciples in the early church were described as Christ-like because they acted like Him. We too should be distinguished from unbelievers by abiding in the word of God and allowing it determine what we do and speak.

God is glorified and honoured when His children emulate the character of His only begotten Son. He died to deliver us from the world so that we may be zealous to do good works. Our speech and actions must therefore reflect Him.

Further Reading: 1 Corinthians 11:1; Mark 1:17

Prayer for the Day: My God and my father, help me emulate Jesus in every aspect of my life. In the name of Jesus, I pray. Amen

Day 6 — Job 10-13

7th January

Seek to Know and Represent God

"After that whole generation had been gathered to their fathers, another generation grew up, who knew neither the LORD nor what he had done for Israel. Then the Israelites did evil in the eyes of the LORD and served the Baals" (Judges 2:10-11).

God's purposes are cross-generational. In every generation, He looks for people who can align themselves with His purposes. God's greatest desire is for mankind to know Him. Throughout history, He has used diverse ways to reveal Himself. In the Old Testament, He spoke to His people through different prophets. In the New Testament, He has revealed Himself to us through His Son Jesus Christ (see Hebrews 1:1-2). The lifestyle, teachings and example of our Lord form a pattern we should emulate to attain our destinies and glorify God.

Our scripture highlights the danger of failure to propagate the knowledge of God from one generation to the other. After the death of Joshua, there emerged a generation in Israel that did not know God or His great deeds in Israel. As a result, Israel forsook God and turned to the worship of idols.

As believers, we have a two-fold calling. First, God desires that we may have a personal relationship with Him. We initiate this the moment we become born again and grow it by walking in the Spirit. Second, we have been called to make God known to the world. We do this by faithfully witnessing through preaching the gospel and living in accord with its teachings.

Further Reading: Deuteronomy 6:4-6; Ezekiel 22:30; Luke 17:20-21; 1 Corinthians 4:20

Prayer for the Day: Father, in the name of Jesus Christ, I pray that You will enable me become a faithful ambassador of Your kingdom on earth in all my endeavours. Amen.

Job 14-16

8th January

Commit Yourself to Your Divine Assignment

"Be diligent in these matters; give yourself wholly to them, so that everyone may see your progress" **(1 Timothy 4:15).**

As a follower of Jesus, you have a divine calling and a specific assignment. This is only possible when you identify the purpose for which God created you for and offer yourself wholeheartedly to do what God has set out for you.

Some are called to minister through preaching the gospel; others to serve believers through spiritual gifts while others are divinely empowered to make wealth so that they can sponsor the preaching of the gospel. We also have areas where we are called to be partakers, irrespective of the service we offer in our churches or to God such as prayer and living holy lives.

The nature or magnitude of our assignment notwithstanding, God requires us to be fully committed to His purposes. Our progress will be determined by how much we offer ourselves unreservedly to God. All our energies, efforts, and gifts should therefore be fully dedicated to discerning and doing the will of God. The word of God assures us of noticeable progress if we wholeheartedly commit ourselves to our divine assignment.

In the process of serving God, we encounter opposition. Nevertheless, we can overcome all hindrances by keeping our eyes on the goal the same way Jesus fixed His attention on the Father and endured the shame of the cross for our salvation.

Further Reading: Colossians 3:23; Jeremiah 29:11
Prayer for the Day: Dear God in the name of our Lord Jesus Christ, do help me offer myself wholly to fulfill the assignment You have given me. Amen.

Job 17-20

9th January

Strive to Capture Spiritual Highways

"And a highway will be there; it will be called the Way of Holiness. The unclean will not journey on it; it will be for those who walk in that Way; wicked fools will not go about on it" (Isaiah 35:8).

Just as natural highways exist, there are spiritual highways on which the godly walk as they journey towards their earthly and eternal destinies. Those who walk on them do so in righteousness with an aim of pleasing God. There are different highways in the kingdom of God. Our creator desires that we reclaim all the highways the enemy has stolen from the church and especially signs, miracles, and wonders. The enemy hinders us from capturing spiritual highways because he is aware that we can cause massive destruction in his kingdom by walking in them.

God's people perish for lack of knowledge (Hosea 4:6). In the spirit realm, there are many invisible things that adversely affect our lives in diverse ways. The word of God offers us light and direction so that we can walk in His ways (Psalm 119:105). The knowledge of the word of God we possess determines our effectiveness in possessing the promise of capturing our spiritual highways.

To capture more spiritual highways, we need to increase our activities in the spirit realm. Sadly, few believers understand how to capture spiritual highways for many walk in the flesh. Such are unable to bear lasting spiritual fruit because their paths to fruitfulness are blocked.

Further Reading: *Isaiah 58:12; 2 Corinthians 4:4; Ephesians 6:12-18*
Prayer for the Day: *Lord God Almighty, grant me the wisdom and strength I need to capture every spiritual highway. In Jesus Name I pray. Amen.*

Job 21-23

10th January

Brace Yourself to Win Spiritual Battles

"For our struggle is not against flesh and blood, but against the rulers, against the authorities, against the powers of this dark world and against the spiritual forces of evil in the heavenly realms" **(Ephesians 6:12).**

The life of a believer is a battlefield, not a playground. Evil spiritual forces are determined to limit our effectiveness and fruitfulness, or to destroy us. We need knowledge on spiritual warfare to resist and overcome these forces.

The enemy is an experienced schemer. If you are not keen to resist him steadfastly in accordance with the word of God, he can destroy your life. He can allow you be a good Christian, filled with the Holy Spirit and prayerful, but hinder you from accessing spiritual wealth that God has ordained to catapult you to your destiny. That would make God's enemies mock and discredit Him as weak because His people have failed to fulfill their purpose and attain their destinies.

As we walk with Christ, we have to engage in spiritual warfare. We ought to emulate the example of our God who described Himself as a man of war (Exodus 15:3). We also need a militant spirit to resist all the devices the enemy can use to sabotage the purposes of God for our lives. In addition, we need spiritual insight on the material and spiritual inheritance God has secured for us through the cross of Christ and guard them jealously for God's glory.

Further Reading: 2 Corinthians 11:13; Daniel 10:12-13

Prayer for the Day: Oh God in the name of Jesus, I pray that You may grant me victory whenever I engage in spiritual battles. Amen.

11th January

Be Proactive in Pursuing Your Destiny

"For we are God's fellow workers; you are God's field, God's building" (1 Corinthians 3:9).

To fulfill His purposes God partners with human agents. He is loving and delights in working with and through those committed to ensuring that His will is done on earth as it is in heaven. God requires us to be proactive in pursuing the destinies He has given us. This means that we cannot attain everything He desires if we do not actively participate in the process of transformation into His likeness so that we can become like Him.

Besides being God's fellow workers, we are His field and building. In the same way, farmers tend crops to maturity and fruit-bearing, God provides everything we need for life and godliness to enable us to attain our destinies. We need to yield to His grace to be transformed until we become like Him. We are living stones that He is working on so that we become His dwelling. Apostle Peter encourages us to allow Him to build us into a spiritual house that can offer holy sacrifices (1 Peter 2:5).

To attain our destinies, we need to partner with God who is able to strengthen us and execute the assignment He gave us. We may be weak and lacking in charisma but as we surrender to God, He leads us towards our destinies. With Him on our side, we can overcome every form of opposition until we become all God intended us to be.

Further Reading: Isaiah 41:11-15; 2 Corinthians 6:1
Prayer for the Day: Father in Jesus name, today I pray that you may enable me to pursue my destiny without faltering. In Jesus' Name I pray. Amen.

Job 29-31

12th January

Exercise Authority Over the Enemy

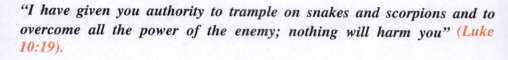

"I have given you authority to trample on snakes and scorpions and to overcome all the power of the enemy; nothing will harm you" (Luke 10:19).

To succeed in life and attain our destinies, we need to be militant. Successful Christian living is a spiritual battle for which we must be fully armed to secure victory. As believers, God has called us to exercise dominion over all creation including the kingdom of the evil one. The world is not only populated by human beings, but also evil spiritual forces that resist God's people hindering them from becoming what they were predestined to be.

Through the anointing of the Holy Spirit who is our Helper, we can remove all the obstacles the enemy places on our path. The snakes and scorpions mentioned in the anchor verse represent powers in the kingdom of darkness. God has called and given us the mandate to destroy all the works of the enemy. Jesus commissioned His disciples instructing them to heal the sick, raise the dead, cleanse lepers, and deliver the oppressed.

To exercise authority over all the power of the enemy, we need to be bold and courageous. We also need to walk by faith in God. When we trust God with all our hearts, we gain confidence and believe the promises of God until we attain the level of success He has ordained for us. Do not fear; arise and resist all the works of the evil one.

Further Reading: 1 John 4:4; Matthew 28:18-20; Acts 1:8 4:4; Matthew 28:18-20; Acts 1:8

Prayer for the Day: Lord God in the name of Jesus, help me exercise authority over all the power of the enemy. Amen

Day 12 — Job 32-34

13th January

The Treasure of Divine Revelation

"Where there is no vision, the people perish: but he that keepeth the law, happy is he" *(Proverbs 29:18 KJV).*

We cannot manifest the seed of greatness in our lives if we are unaware of how God works. We therefore need to treasure divine revelation because it holds the key to our breakthroughs and blessings. God delights in revealing His ways to those who seek and desire to please Him. He regards highly those who reverence His word and tremble at it (Isaiah 66:3). His word says that His greatest interest in our lives is to know and do His will.

Our strength as God's children lies in seeking spiritual insight. As such, we need to desire the leadership of the Holy Spirit who knows the password to spiritual resources in Christ. As we strive to walk with God, we need to delight ourselves in the word of God. As we study and meditate on His word, we become wiser and knowledgeable in serving God's purposes.

A good indicator of spiritual health is the desire to learn from God and walk closely with Him. Vision is different from sight. Sight is physical and it helps us to behold temporary things while vision is spiritual and enables us to perceive eternal things. We should daily seek God for spiritual insight so that we may walk with Him in a worthy manner.

Further Reading: **Ephesians 1:17-18; Isaiah 33:6 (NKJV)**
Prayer for the Day: **Father, open my inner eyes that I may be able to behold the treasure of divine revelation. Amen.**

Job 35-37

14th January

You Have a Gift from God

"I wish that all men were as I am. But each man has his own gift from God; one has this gift, another has that" **(1 Corinthians 7:7).**

Before releasing products to the market, most manufacturers exercise due diligence to ensure that quality is of the expected standards. In the same way, God created us uniquely and gave us different spiritual gifts to enable us bear spiritual fruit. He expects us to identify and make the most of those gifts.
As a believer, you owe it to God and the church the responsibility of identifying your gift and fanning it to flame. Spiritual gifts are meant to be utilized in meaningful kingdom work and cannot be subjected to negligence. For this reason, we must exercise them so that they can flourish as God intended.

With the awareness that our time on earth is limited, we should make the most of each day. Scriptures encourage us to make the most of every opportunity. When we discover our spiritual gifts and talents early in life, we have more time to polish them to their perfection for God's glory. We thus encourage the youth to identify and develop their gifts when they are still energetic and vibrant. This helps them to perfect what God has freely given them.

Spiritual gifts fanned to flame cause great destruction in the kingdom of darkness. Therefore, we should resist forces of darkness that fight to cripple our spiritual capabilities.

Further Reading: 1 Corinthians 12:7-10; Romans 12:6-8
Prayer for the Day: Father Lord in the Name of Jesus Christ, today, I pray that You will help me activate my gift and use it to serve the church to the glory of your Holy Name. Amen.

Job 38-39

15th January

Build Your Spiritual Momentum

"And we, who with unveiled faces all reflect the Lord's glory, are being transformed into his likeness with ever-increasing glory, which comes from the Lord, who is the Spirit" (2 Corinthians 3:18).

Walking with God requires that we build and maintain spiritual momentum. It takes inner strength to remain in faith and believe in God for the fulfillment of the promises He has made. Walking with God is a lifetime commitment that requires one to be intentional and determined. The word of God commands us not to lack in zeal (Romans 12:11) but to have a passion for spiritual things since the only way we can walk in the Spirit is by devoting ourselves fully to God's ways.

To build our spiritual momentum, daily commitment to prayer and regular fasting, walking in holiness, and devoting ourselves to reading the word of God, loving Him and His people wholeheartedly is a necessity. Those who do these things are spiritually healthy, bear spiritual fruit, and glorify God.

When we build momentum in our walk with God, we overcome demonic forces that could distract us from our faith and lead us to backsliding. Every believer must be cautious not to lose faith in God and return to the world, by keeping the spiritual lamp burning at all times.

To thrive in our walk with God, we must also deal with spiritual laziness and walk closely with the Holy Spirit who empowers us and aids us in moving towards our divine destinies.

Further Reading: *Isaiah 40:28-31; Luke 18:1*
Prayer for the Day: *Oh LORD, I pray that You will help me maintain spiritual momentum that I may overcome demonic forces in my walk with You. In Jesus' Name I pray. Amen.*

Job 40-42

16th January

Lasting Legacies are Built through Knowledge

"By wisdom a house is built, and through understanding it is established; through knowledge its rooms are filled with rare and beautiful treasures" (Proverbs 24:3-4).

Scripture compares the life of a believer to a house. It states that houses are built by wisdom and established through understanding. Knowledge empowers believers to access spiritual treasures that beautify their lives in this life and through eternity.

As we walk with God and trust Him to help us attain our destinies, we need to daily ask Him for spiritual wisdom. This helps us make the right decisions concerning our short and long-term goals. We also need to seek the establishment of our lives through knowledge. Knowledge is the antidote to ignorance, which is a weapon the enemy uses to destroy the destinies of God's people.

As we move closer to the end of this age, God is committed to releasing spiritual wisdom and knowledge to His people. The Holy Spirit will release great manifestation of His power as He is poured richly on all flesh (Acts 2:17-18). Therefore, as His chosen vessels to manifest God's glory, let's seek His hidden wisdom and knowledge so that we can partake of the banquet God has prepared for us in these last times.

We can impact our generation powerfully through the gospel if we allow God's wisdom to teach and impart us with spiritual knowledge and wisdom. Our legacy is secure if we allow divine wisdom to daily guide us.

Further Reading: Proverbs 1:7; Isaiah 33:6
Prayer for the Day: My Father and my God, help me build my life through wisdom and knowledge that I may impact my generation powerfully, to the glory of Your Holy Name. Amen.

Day 16 — Genesis 12-15

17th January

Depend on God to Rise to the High Places

"The Sovereign LORD is my strength; he makes my feet like the feet of a deer, he enables me to go on the heights" *(Habakkuk 3:19).*

God's desire is for His children to rise to the peak of their destinies. We can only rise to where He intends us to reach if we rely on His empowerment. Unfortunately, many people depend on themselves and not God. Such people fail to accomplish divine assignment because the arm of flesh they rely on is limited. They take the grace of God in vain and fail to attain their destinies.

We express our dependence on Him by acknowledging our weakness, walking in humility, and submitting to His power and will. God is a caring father and delights in helping His children when they seek Him.

In His grace, God has given us the Holy Spirit to not only dwell in us and help us discern His will but also to empower us for our divine assignment. Since He is all-knowing, the Holy Spirit has the blueprint of our destinies. He is also omnipotent and has all the power we need to move towards our destinies. Jesus promised His disciples that the Holy Spirit would endue them with dynamic power to be His witnesses to the ends of the earth (Acts 1:8).

Further Reading: **Exodus 15:2; Isaiah 40:28-31; Psalm 28:7; 118:14**
Prayer for the Day: **Oh God, help me rise to the high places of my destiny in Jesus' name. Amen.**

Genesis 16-18

18th January

Take Great Care of Your Spiritual Health

"Dear friend, I pray that you may enjoy good health and that all may go well with you, even as your soul is getting along well" (3 John 2).

Many people take great care of their bodies. They are immunized against communicable diseases, visit the dentist every six months, have regular medical checkups and buy insurance policies. However, few take adequate care of their souls, which are more valuable than physical bodies. Some live carefree lives and miss the blessings they could have received if they were spiritually healthy.

To take good care of our spiritual health, we need to ensure that we feed our spirits on the balanced doctrine of the word of God. This entails not only accepting the portions of Scripture that promise blessings but also those that warn, rebuke, correct and instruct. It also implies subjecting the desires of the sinful nature to the Holy Spirit who indwells us and helps us become more like God.

Another aspect of a healthy spiritual life is exercising our faith. We must put our faith to work just as we do physical workouts to tone our muscles and increase blood circulation.. This involves taking the word of God for what it is and doing what it commands. We should pray for the sick, believe God for breakthroughs, provision, increase and establishment. As we do so, His power manifests in us making us fruitful believers.

Further Reading: 1 Corinthians 9:26-17; 1 Peter 2:24
Prayer for the Day: My God and my Father, help me take care of my spiritual health through studying your word and allowing it shape me into being more like You. Amen.

Day 18 | Genesis 19-21

19th January

Make the Holy Spirit Your Best Friend

"You adulterous people, don't you know that friendship with the world is hatred toward God? Anyone who chooses to be a friend of the world becomes an enemy of God. Or do you think Scripture says without reason that the spirit he caused to live in us envies intensely?" (James 4:4-5).

God is generous to His people. Besides giving us Jesus to die for our sins, He sent us the Holy Spirit to abide in us forever and help us do His will. God desires that we cultivate friendship with His Spirit daily until we become His close friends. When we are intimate with Him, He can share with us things that matter most to Him the same way close friends confide in one another.

Scripture indicates that those who become friends with the world become enemies of God. It also says that the Holy Spirit's desire is for us to do the will of God at all times. The Lord describes Himself as jealous (Exodus 34:14). He does not want us to be devoted to other things at His expense. As such, we must safeguard our relationship with God.

We need to grow our intimacy with the Holy Spirit because of the multiple roles He does in our lives. He is our intercessor and helper (John 14:16). He guides us into all truth (John 16:13). He also gives us access to the Father (Ephesians 2:18).

Further Reading: 2 Chronicles 20:7; Isaiah 41:8
Prayer for the Day: Oh God today, I pray that You will help me become a close friend of the Holy Spirit, that He may guide, teach and lead me into all truth. Amen.

Genesis 22-24

20th January

Depend on the Holy Spirit's Guidance in Your Prayers

"In the same way, the Spirit helps us in our weakness. We do not know what we ought to pray for, but the Spirit himself intercedes for us with groans that words cannot express" *(Romans 8:26).*

The strength of every believer is measured by his or her prayer life. Those who pray persistently and consistently receive inner strength to resist temptation, fulfill their mandate, and attain divine destinies. On the other hand, those who hardly pray are spiritually weak, fall easily into temptation, and face the risk of becoming casualties in spiritual warfare.

To secure our lives from destruction and spiritual weakness, God has given us His Spirit to help us in prayer as the anchor verse says. The word of God described Him as the Spirit of grace (Hebrews 12:29). Grace is the divine enablement to do the will of God and pursue divine purpose while resisting all forms of ungodliness. When the Holy Spirit rests on us, He strengthens us with might (Isaiah 11:2). He also helps us know the mind of God and thus discern the perfect will of God for our lives. Armed with this knowledge, we can make targeted prayers that help us make progress toward our destinies.

Many people pray amiss or lack the strength to pray because they depend on themselves instead of relying on the Spirit of God. This is why the word of God encourages us to be dead to self so that we can pray in the will of God.

Further Reading: Matthew 27:51; Romans 8:27
Prayer for the Day: Holy Spirit of the living God, I ask You this day to guide me in my prayers always, that I may never pray a miss but be in tune with God's will. Amen.

Day 20 — Genesis 25-26

21st January

Recovering and Manifesting Full Potential Takes Time

"We do not want you to become lazy, but to imitate those who through faith and patience inherit what has been promised" (Hebrews 6:12).

Many people go through painful and trying wilderness experiences similar to the one Israel had in the desert before they inherited the Promised Land. Some become casualties because they are unable to keep going and wait on God to fulfill His purpose. Those who are patient, humble, and submissive receive God's grace and peace, which carry them through the process of discovering, recovering, and manifesting their God-ordained destinies. In the fullness of time, they receive all the promises of God and live abundant lives for God's glory.

It is imperative to understand that recovery of one's divine identity takes time. The fulfillment of God's promises requires faith and patience. To recover our identity, we need to be consistent in pursuing our purpose and calling. Since God is faithful, He helps those who trust Him to attain their full potential. The recovery process must be complete for one to manifest.

We need to have a strong resolve and be purposeful to attain everything God has in store for us. It took Joseph more than ten years to recover and manifest his greatness. David did not rise to the throne as king over all of Israel immediately after Samuel anointed him. He progressed from being ruler over part of God's people until he exercised authority over all of Israel. Do not give up even if God appears to be taking too long to help you recover and manifest your identity. Persistence wears out resistance.

Further Reading: Luke 18:1, 7-8; Exodus 23:29-30
Prayer for the Day: Oh God, my humble prayer today is that, You may help me remain persistent until I manifest my greatness. This I pray in the name of our Lord Jesus Christ. Amen.

Genesis 27-29

22nd January

We Become Valuable through Divine Moulding

"...can I not do with you as this potter does?" declares the Lord. "Like clay in the hand of the potter, so are you in my hand" (Jeremiah 18:6).

In His wisdom, God has chosen to partner with man to carry out His purposes on earth. Since man shares in Adam's sinful nature, he must be regenerated, transformed and divinely empowered to co-work with God in advancing His kingdom. To achieve this objective, God graciously made a way for man to be saved, renewed and equipped to become a carrier of His divine nature.

The Bible depicts God as a potter and His people as clay. Before going through the hands of a potter, clay is of little value. However, after being moulded into a vessel, its value increases and must be handled with care lest it gets damaged. Before God uses a man to do great exploits, He first moulds them into usable vessels. He desires to make the best from each of them on condition that they let Him work in every aspect of their lives - their spirits, hearts, souls, minds and emotions.

It should be every believer's desire to personally witness the Biblical truth that all things work together for good for those who love God and are called according to His purpose (Romans 8:28). I believe that the world is yet to see what God can do through a man who is fully yielded to His moulding. May this revelation trigger a divine turnaround in your life.

Further reading: Isaiah 48:10; Ezekiel 36:25-27
Prayer for the day: Oh LORD in the name of Jesus, I pray that you may grant me a heart of flesh. A heart that is willing to yield to you always as You make the best of me through the moulding process.

Genesis 30-31

23rd January

A Life of Exploits Comes at a Cost

"Although he was a son, he learned obedience from what he suffered and, once made perfect, he became the source of eternal salvation for all who obey him and was designated by God to be high priest in the order of Melchizedek" (Hebrews 5:8-10)

The will of God is that His children yield to His moulding in order to create a conducive environment for Him to co-work with them. He desires that believers bear the fruit of the Spirit, grow in knowledge and walk in obedience to His word at all times. For this to happen, He first shapes, teaches, instructs, rebukes and sharpens us through His word, power and the circumstances He allows our way.

Living a life of extraordinary exploits demands that believers fully understand the word of God. In many cases, getting a personal and intimate knowledge of God occurs when men go through difficult circumstances that call for divine intervention. The Spirit of God guides believers to the word of God and His mighty power makes a way for them.

Jesus set the perfect example that every believer should emulate. Although He is the Son of God, He was led by the Holy Spirit to undertake forty days and forty nights of prayer and fasting so that He could be equipped for ministry. He demonstrated self-denial and endured long days and nights away from the comfort of His heavenly home. At the end of that period of prayer and fasting, He was endued with the power of the Holy Spirit. Consequently, He became effective and His ministry made a lasting impact.

Further Reading: *Isaiah 48:10; Philippians 2:6-11*
Prayer for the Day: *My Father in the name of Jesus, I pray for grace, to be able to pay the cost that will enable me live a life of exploits. Amen.*

Genesis 32-34

24th January

Understand the Secret of Following Christ

"Come, follow me," Jesus said, "and I will make you fishers of men" **(Mark 1:17)**.

In His grace and wisdom, God can take a person who has no qualifications and make him evidently successful. He only requires wholehearted dependence on Him and total submission to His authority. His gracious hand causes men and women to become great and influential notwithstanding the circumstances that surround their lives, backgrounds, or their academic credentials.

Jesus instructed His disciples to follow Him and He would make them soul-winners. His disciples were ordinary men but through the power of the Holy Spirit, they turned their world upside down with exploits. The secret of becoming what God intended us to be is in the process of following Him. God expects us to respond to His call by walking intimately and willingly submitting to His guidance. This makes Him release His power, wisdom, and grace.

God is all-knowing; He declares the end from the beginning and has a record of the vessels He intends us to become. However, there is a process one has to undergo before becoming the vessel God intends of which, all of us are at different stages. In the different stages, all of us are in, we ought to be grateful to God for the growth that has taken place in our lives. We should acknowledge God's sovereignty and cooperate with Him so that He can mould us to reflect His glory. The more submissive and cooperative we are, the faster we manifest the fullness of His plan for our lives.

Further reading: Isaiah 46:10; Genesis 17:1-2
Prayer for the day: Oh God, help me follow and cooperate with You as You make me become the vessel You destined me to be. Amen.

25th January

God Can Permit Suffering in Your Life

"I consider that our present sufferings are not worth comparing with the glory that will be revealed in us" *(Romans 8:18).*

Suffering is an experience many would not desire to go through. However, it is an integral part of the process of transformation, which God in His sovereignty chooses to take His children through, to make them vessels of honour. Believers should derive joy in the fact that the suffering they go through is temporal. It is a tool of shaping their hearts in order to be what God desires. He tests them through the furnace of affliction to see if they qualify for His glory. Through suffering, refining takes place and those who endure the process are proved worthy to manifest His glory (Isaiah 48:10).

God-ordained suffering results in glory and reveals His divine power. It is a prelude of the eternal glory that believers will share when Jesus is revealed, as they partake in His nature.

Jesus Christ was born to die to save humanity. He learnt obedience through the things He suffered (Hebrews 5:7-8). He yielded to God's will for His life and was consequently given the highest place at the Father's right hand. We are called to follow in His example and thus, we must yield to the will of God. We need to live in the awareness of the truth that God uses adversity, pain and other undesirable circumstances to mould us into vessels He can use to reveal His power, love and glory.

Further reading: 2 Corinthians 4:17; Romans 8:29
Prayer for the day: Thank You Lord for allowing me go through suffering for these sufferings produce steadfastness in me. Amen.

Genesis 38-40

26th January

The Lord Our God is a Potter

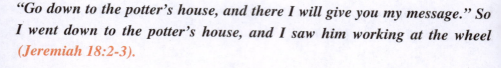

"Go down to the potter's house, and there I will give you my message." So I went down to the potter's house, and I saw him working at the wheel (Jeremiah 18:2-3).

God transforms believers so that they can manifest His power to humanity. His topmost agenda for man is to advance His kingdom on earth. The moulding process is important for both believers and unbelievers as God uses it to raise believers through whom He manifests His glory on earth. God speaks to man through ordinary things and experiences. Jesus illustrated His teachings using common examples that His hearers could readily identify with (Matthew 13:34). In the above Scripture, God wanted Prophet Jeremiah to see how the potter works so that He could give Him a message for Israel.

The potter represents God who takes men through a process of moulding to make them what He desires. The process through which God takes His beloved bears similarities with what potters subject clay to as they make different articles. The church is God's workshop where He calls His people, transforms, and commissions them to serve His purposes. With this knowledge in mind, we should not become benchwarmers in the house of God. Rather, we should dedicate ourselves to God so that He can fashion us into noble vessels that He can use for every good work. Every time you go to the house of God, desire to meet the potter. Always cultivate a desire for a divine encounter with Him and you will never be the same again.

Further reading: Isaiah 64:8; 2 Corinthians 3:16-18, Ephesians 3:10-12
Prayer for the day: O Lord, I pray for a divine encounter with You, so that my life may be transformed so that I may serve Your purposes here on earth. In the name of Jesus I pray Amen.

Day 26   Genesis 41-42

27th January

We are Like Clay in the Hands of a Potter

"Yet, O LORD, you are our Father. We are the clay, you are the potter; we are all the work of your hand" (Isaiah 64:8).

Clay is the basic raw material in a potter's house. In a vision, Jeremiah saw literal clay in the potter's house but metaphorically, God's people are the clay He works on to make vessels for different uses. Clay is not useful until it goes through the hands of a potter. Similarly, our lives cannot be useful in God's kingdom until He transforms us. The potter is at liberty to make any vessel he wishes and reserves the right to determine the sort of vessel he wishes. None of us is special since we originated from the same lump of clay-Adam. We need to cultivate humility and gladly accept the roles assigned to us by God.

One of the greatest qualities of clay is malleability. This is the ability to be shaped without breaking or cracking. This makes it take the desired shape. God detests the hardness of the heart and releases judgment on those whose hearts refuse to submit to Him. The Bible gives us an example of Jeremiah at the potter's house where the vessel the potter was making was marred (Jeremiah 18:4) but the potter quickly shaped it into another one as he desired. Hardness of heart causes us to become marred vessels in the hands of the potter and forces Him to reshape us into something else.

Further Reading: **Romans 9:21; 2 Corinthians 4:8-9**
Prayer for the Day: **Father, in the Name of Jesus Christ, I pray that you help me be malleable so that I can withstand the pressure subjected to me as You mould me into a vessel of honour.**

Genesis 43-45

28th January

God's Fire Refines Us for Greatness

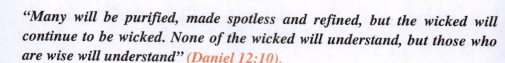

"Many will be purified, made spotless and refined, but the wicked will continue to be wicked. None of the wicked will understand, but those who are wise will understand" *(Daniel 12:10).*

After moulding and drying up at room temperature, vessels of clay in a kiln are subjected to very high temperatures for hours, to harden them. God uses a similar process to harden and prepare believers for ministry. Daniel saw the end times and prophesied as recorded in Scripture. I believe God is releasing an anointing of the potter's touch because we are living at a time of great spiritual awakening that has a great move of God. It is revival time!

When God allows us to go through fiery trials and tests, we should not be scared. Our transformation clearly manifests when we emerge from the fiery trials. We should not be bitter, resentful or take offence. We should cooperate with the potter, with full awareness that the prevailing circumstances are not permanent. God uses those who endure His moulding process to work great exploits. He also uses them to be an encouragement and bring healing and restoration to others. He turns them into vessels of honour. He gives them favour and opens doors for them, using them to display His glory and draw men to Himself.

The potter, the clay and the wheel work in sync to serve God's purposes, and to execute His will on earth. It is a great privilege for God to allow us to partner with Him, and this should encourage us to wholeheartedly yield to Him.

Further Reading: Isaiah 48:10; Malachi 3:1-4
Prayer for the Day: O God, I pray for the grace to withstand the furnace experience and come out refined, having been made a vessel of honour. Amen.

Genesis 46-47

29th January

Put Your Past Where it Belongs

"But whatever was to my profit I now consider loss for the sake of Christ. What is more, I consider everything a loss compared to the surpassing greatness of knowing Christ Jesus my Lord, for whose sake I have lost all things. I consider them rubbish, that I may gain Christ" **(Philippians 3:7-8).**

The experiences we have had in the past can affect our lives if we are not careful. Wrong choices, shame, pain, or the lack we have faced in the past can be stepping stones to the fulfillment of God's purpose. The will of God is that we make progress in every aspect of our lives.

Apostle Paul understood that God had a special purpose for his life. He knew that he was set apart from his mother's womb to declare the good news to the Gentiles (Galatians 1:15-16). However, as a Judaist, he was zealous in persecuting believers. He sought and imprisoned them with the approval of religious leaders. When he was converted, he became a zealous preacher of the gospel and attained his destiny. Like Paul, we should not allow our wrong past to affect the glorious future God has planned for us.

God prepared a special work for each one of us. He has rescued us from accidents, pain, hardship, diseases, and other calamities because His desire is for us to do the work He pre-ordained (Ephesians 2:10). Do not get stuck in your past. Arise and advance in the special purpose for which you were created. Walk in the newness of God.

Further Reading: Isaiah 43:18-19
Prayer for the Day: Oh Lord God, do help me to forget the past and enable me walk in the newness of life. I ask this in name of Jesus, Amen.

Genesis 48-50

Day 29

30th January

Strive to Complete Your Divine Assignment

"However, I consider my life worth nothing to me, if only I may finish the race and complete the task the Lord Jesus has given me - the task of testifying to the gospel of God's grace" (Acts 20:24).

The idea that one can miss the original purpose and fail to fulfill his divine duty makes me tremble. Paul made it clear that no matter the situation, he had a duty to complete the work God assigned him. Unlike us, God has nothing to lose when men disregard His assignment. He replaces rebels immediately and His work goes on. Aside from being substituted, rebels perish alongside their families.

To avoid such, we need to ensure that we finish the work God has assigned us despite its demands. We partner with God in doing any work assigned to us by relying on His grace and obeying the instructions given. Although God had appointed Saul as the first king of Israel, Saul rebelled against the Lord. This led to the premature ending of his reign (1 Samuel 13:13-14).

It is painful for God to tell a person that He has sought another to replace him or her. Besides replacing the rebellious, God does not allow them to go scot-free. He leaves them vulnerable to their enemies. Saul was replaced as king and subjected to torment by an evil spirit. The latter days of his life were full of trouble, misery, and pain. Those who abscond their calling and original purpose subject themselves and their offspring to judgment.

Further Reading: 2 Timothy 4:7-8; Colossians 4:17, John 4:34, John 17:4, Acts 13:25, Acts 13:36

Prayer for the Day: Father in the name of Jesus, I pray for the grace to fight a good fight and finish my assignment that I may receive my reward. Amen.

Exodus 1-3

31st January

God Elevates Us to Serve His Purposes

"And who knows but that you have come to royal position for such a time as this?" (Esther 4:14).

God has placed some people in positions of influence to serve His purpose. The purpose can only be known through discernment. Esther was elevated and given access to the king to save her Jewish race from annihilation. She became queen but nobody knew the reason for her rising except Mordecai – his cousin – who cautioned her that she was in her position to serve a divine agenda.

Protocol in the Persian kingdom demanded that no one could approach the king without being summoned. However, when the Jews were in danger of extermination, Esther was their only hope because she was in a position where she could safeguard their lives. Had she not intervened, her people would have been killed. Mordecai her cousin told her that she had to act fast lest God rescued the Jews through another person to the detriment of her family.

Aware of God's expectations, Esther was willing to die for her people to be preserved (Esther 4:15). We too should take risks and make good use of the positions, skills and privileges God has accorded us. He has given us grace, strength, revelation and understanding so that we can partner with Him to serve our divine mandate. Your career, position, gift and locality carry God's hidden purpose. You are not where you are by accident.

Further Reading: Ephesians 2:10; Proverbs 25:2
Prayer for the Day: Oh God, I pray that You will enable me to not only discern Your hidden purpose for me, but also fulfill it for Your glory. In the mighty name of Jesus I pray, Amen

Exodus 4-6

1st February

Be Careful Not be Found Wanting

"You have been weighed on the scales and found wanting" *(Daniel 5:27).*

In the pursuit of our destiny and service to God, the Lord occasionally weighs us on His scales to determine our progress. His scales are His standards and expectations over our lives. Before you rejoice and rush into service or calling, first seek to know God's standards, so that you can adhere to them.

Belshazzar, a grandson of Nebuchadnezzar, was aware that his grandfather was punished for breaking God's law. Nebuchadnezzar was given the mind of a beast for seven years. Despite knowing this, Belshazzar used consecrated utensils to take wine. While in the act of desecrating the consecrated utensils, a hand appeared and wrote God's judgment against him. He died the same night he was found wanting (Daniel 5:25-31).

Losing one's original purpose renders a person useless. It causes someone to lose protection. Our value in life and in the kingdom of God is dependent on the purpose we serve. The way we discard the things we have outlived is the same way God does away with those who fail to live by His standards. That is why it is important to know the standards God has set specifically for us and abide by them in areas such as giving, prayer, fasting, commitment, and righteousness as we serve Him. In measuring our usefulness in His Kingdom, God takes note of everything we do or fail to do. Just like Saul and Belshazzar, a person found wanting is replaced immediately by another.

Further Reading: *1 Samuel 15:26; 1 Samuel 2:30*
Prayer for the Day: *My Father and my God, I pray that I will be able to meet Your standards by Your grace, that I may not be found wanting. In Jesus' Name I pray, amen.*

Exodus 7-9

2nd February

Pursue Godly Character

Do not be misled: "Bad company corrupts good character" *(1 Corinthians 15:33).*

God attaches a high premium to character. He desires that we have good character and walk in humility, obedience, love, compassion, generosity, and holiness. Scriptures instruct us to make an effort to reinforce our faith with spiritual virtues so that we are fruitful and effective. These spiritual virtues amount to a believer's character. A person with a good character is likely to be fruitful in their service to God.

Good character preserves gifts and talents. Many people who were great or could have become great were ruined by bad characters. A gift or talent opens great doors for people, but only character can sustain them.

The heart is the seat of character and we should strive to make it align with the will of God. We should therefore work on our character as this attracts God's reward. The company we keep influences our character greatly. A man is known by the kind of company he keeps. Surrounding oneself with good or bad people can influence a person positively or negatively. As such, one should choose the right relationships because this will have a great impact on their character.

Further Reading: 2 Peter 1:5-8; Matthew 7:15-20
Prayer for the Day: Dear Lord, help me refine my character by the help of the Holy Spirit. In Your Name's sake I pray, Amen.

Exodus 10-12

3rd February

Guard Your Heart with All Diligence

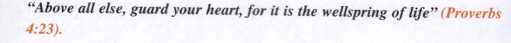

"Above all else, guard your heart, for it is the wellspring of life" (Proverbs 4:23).

Solomon highlighted the centrality of the heart by pointing out that all the issues of life emanate from the heart and that if it is not protected, destruction is inevitable. We should therefore diligently watch over our hearts above all other things.

The human heart is deceitful and desperately wicked. It must be trained to yield to God so that He can search and cure it. A man by himself cannot be able to do this. Only God can. A yielded heart is able to serve God with ease and walk in the fullness of His purpose.

Jesus knocks at the door of our hearts with a desire to enter and dine with us. However, evil things also strive to gain access. These include bitterness, unforgiveness, pride, adultery, fornication, and the lust of the flesh. No matter how much evil strives to gain access to our hearts, we must not give them room. All forms of evil come from the heart and make people unclean. We should therefore guard against the entry of sin into our hearts and allow God mould our character to resemble His.

Further Reading: Jeremiah 17:9-10; Mark 7:20-23

Prayer for the Day: Dear God, help me guard my heart against all manner of evil and reveal and discard everything that is not of You. I pray this in the name of Jesus, Amen.

Day 34 | Exodus 13-15

4th February

Set and Observe Godly Boundaries

"No one is greater in this house than I am. My master has withheld nothing from me except you, because you are his wife. How then could I do such a wicked thing and sin against God" (Genesis 39:9).

To walk with God, we need to set godly boundaries. These include what we can or cannot do, where we can or cannot go, the words we can let fall from our lips and those we cannot. Boundaries are necessary because they enable us stay away from sin, and everyone who commits sin is a slave to sin. We should strive to leave no room for sin to creep into our lives.

The word of God outlines the values believers need to commit to because they enable us to set godly boundaries that glorify our Maker. For instance, it prohibits believers from engaging in fornication, adultery, bearing false witness, and dishonouring parents. Every person who desires to please God must identify what glorifies God and shun evil.

God preserved Joseph because he was a man of character. He set godly boundaries and this enabled him to rise to the peak of his destiny in a foreign land. He was committed to living in sexual purity even when Potiphar's wife severally seduced him to commit fornication. He knew the consequences of sin and refused to indulge in anything that would go against God's laws. He kept his boundaries by respecting Potiphar's wife as her boss.
God is committed to helping all those who walk on the narrow path and He helps them attain their destinies.

Further Reading: Ephesians 5:3-7; Acts 6:2-4
Prayer for the Day: My Father and my God, I ask You to help me set and adhere to godly boundaries, as it is in Your word. In Your mighty Name I pray. Amen.

Exodus 16-18

Day 35

5th February

Desire to Become a Vessel of Honour

"In a large house there are articles not only of gold and silver, but also of wood and clay; some are for noble purposes and some for ignoble. If a man cleanses himself from the latter, he will be an instrument for noble purposes, made holy, useful to the Master and prepared to do any good work" (2 Timothy 2:20-21).

In every generation, God desires to raise men of purpose, distinction and zeal with whom He can co-work to glorify Himself. He moulds individuals, families, cities and nations who respond to His call to become vessels of honour. He transforms them from the common and ordinary and makes them extraordinary and honourable.

In a house are articles of clay, wood, silver or gold. Apostle Paul draws an analogy between the vessels found in large houses and believers. Believers are the articles God uses for His service. It is worth noting that although all these vessels are in use, some are reserved for noble use while others are for ignoble. Scriptures teach that one becomes a vessel of honour by cleansing himself from ignoble things. This implies setting oneself apart for God so that He can transform and prepare you for fruitful kingdom service.

As we seek to do the will of God, we need to aspire to become vessels of honour. That way, He can use us to do His will and manifest His glory to the nations.

Further Reading: Ephesians 2:10; Isaiah 41:15-16
Prayer for the Day: Father in the Name of Jesus Christ, I ask You to make me a vessel of honour for noble work in Your House. Amen.

Exodus 19-21

6th February

Live a Disciplined Christian Life

"No, I beat my body and make it my slave so that after I have preached to others, I myself will not be disqualified for the prize" (1 Corinthians 9:27).

Discipline is critical in the life of every person who desires to attain and maintain greatness. It aids a person to be orderly and to exercise self-control in a bid to focus on set goals.

To serve God's purposes, one must be disciplined in prayer, fasting, and reading the word of God. This helps keep the body and its fleshly desires in check because if the flesh is not subjected to the spirit, it can make one its slave. Believers who are not disciplined enough to practice Christian virtues make little progress or suffer stagnation in their walk with God. They are unable to attain their destiny and accomplish their God-given mandates.

Apostle Paul observed that although he was a minister of the gospel, he could easily miss the prize if he failed to subject his body to the perfect will of God. He beat his body and tamed its appetites in order to keep in line with God's expectations of Him. Many believers have lost much in their lives because of failure to play their individual roles in ministry. They lack discipline and therefore fail to move to the levels God intended for them. This does not glorify Him.

Further Reading: 2 Timothy 1:6; 1 Timothy 4:15
Prayer for the Day: Dear God help me have discipline so that I may rise to the level You intended for me. I pray this in the name of Jesus, Amen.

Exodus 22-24

7th February

Doubt and Unbelief Hinder Progress

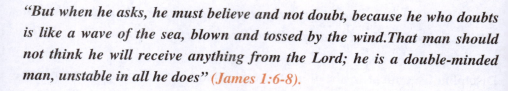

"But when he asks, he must believe and not doubt, because he who doubts is like a wave of the sea, blown and tossed by the wind. That man should not think he will receive anything from the Lord; he is a double-minded man, unstable in all he does" **(James 1:6-8).**

Doubt and unbelief make God's people unfruitful. Doubt is the lack of trust in God. It is a suspicion that somebody is not trustworthy or sincere about what he claims to be or does. A person who is doubtful feels unconvinced or uncertain about God and what He can do. On the other hand, unbelief is a lack of belief; the mental attitude that is opposed to faith and therefore inclined to reject spiritual truths.

Those who are doubtful hardly benefit from God. Instead of responding to divine instructions by faith, they ask numerous questions and fail to take the steps of faith that God requires. Unbelief and doubt cast aspersions on God's character and hinder Him from working in the lives of His people. A person who doubts God neither receives anything from Him nor makes progress because he is double-minded and unstable in the things of God.

On the other hand, faith helps us understand all things because creation is best understood through faith (Hebrews 11:3). Whenever we hear the voice of God, we should respond by faith. Do not fail to walk into the promises of God as a result of doubt. Walk by faith because His promises are true.

Further Reading: Hebrews 3:7-12; Mark 11:23-24
Prayer for the Day: Oh God this day I pray that You may increase my faith in You, that I may experience progress in the name of Jesus. Amen.

Day 38 | Exodus 25-27

8th February

Understand Times and Seasons

"...men of Issachar, who understood the times and knew what Israel should do **(1 Chronicles 12:32a).**

God has set times and seasons for everything on earth. Those unable to discern times and seasons cannot partake the divine nature. The greatness of a man is usually tied to a particular time and season set by the heavens. . When the time comes for a person to be elevated, he should be ready and willing to be aligned to the season for the manifestation to be realized.

The sons of Issachar prospered because they were aware of the demands of the times they were living in. Although they were few, they ruled over the house of Israel because they knew what Israel needed to do at any given time. The people in the city of Jerusalem on the other hand perished because they did not understand the time of God's visitation and deliverance (see Luke 19:41-44).

God has a set time for every believer and He desires that we align ourselves to His will. We need to know the seasons and their demands because it can lead us to destruction. God has set timeframes to determine when each of us should be ushered into greatness for His glory. He causes all things to prosper in the season He has divinely set. Thus, we should do everything in our power not to miss our season.

Further Reading: Psalm 102:13; Ecclesiastes 3:11; Luke 19:41-44
Prayer for the Day: Father, in the Mighty name of Jesus, I ask You to enable me to discern the times and seasons of my life. I pray this in Jesus' Name. Amen.

Exodus 28-29 — Day 39

9th February

Lay Down Your Life for a Noble Cause

"I tell you the truth, unless a kernel of wheat falls to the ground and dies, it remains only a single seed. But if it dies, it produces many seeds. The man who loves his life will lose it, while the man who hates his life in this world will keep it for eternal life" (John 12:24-25).

Walking with God and becoming a noble vessel requires that we be selfless and ready to give up our rights for the benefit of others. Selfish people cannot accomplish God's purposes. Selflessness demands that believers allow Christ to be preeminent in their lives. Apostle Paul confessed to having been crucified with Christ and to no longer have his life since that of Christ lived in him (Galatians 2:20).

To become worthwhile disciples, we must die to self. Selfishness prevents a person from seeing the beyond self, resulting to failure to submit to God's moulding which is meant to transform an individual into a vessel He desires. Jesus set a perfect example for us by laying down His life. Through His death on the cross, God's purpose was accomplished because we were reconciled to Him.

Those who refuse to allow God to fashion them into stewards of His blessings cannot fulfill His purposes, because the kingdom of God requires selflessness. Will you lay down your life for the sake of God's purposes?

Further Reading: Luke 9:23-26; Luke 12:16-21
Prayer for the Day: My Father and my God, today I pray that You may help me deal with every form of selfishness in my life, so that I may live for You. Amen

Day 40 | Exodus 30-32

10th February

We Carry Treasures in Jars of Clay

"But we have this treasure in jars of clay to show that this all-surpassing power is from God and not from us" (2 Corinthians 4:7).

The treasures of the kingdom of God are borne by human beings who are jars of clay. God has put the treasures of His kingdom in ordinary men made from the dust of the earth, but have eternal souls. He does this to make it clear that this power has originated from Him and not us. None of us can take credit for the things God does in and through us.

Vessels become honourable by virtue of the treasure deposited in them. Believers are honourable because they are chosen to carry God's power, grace, authority and anointing. God gives divine enablement and power to those who admit they are inadequate and acknowledge their dependence on Him, but resists the proud. Humble people acknowledge their need of God and allow Him to mould them to serve His temporal and eternal purposes. Scriptures instruct us to approach the throne of grace with confidence so that we may receive mercy and find grace to help us in times of need (Hebrews 4:16).

God is pleased to partner with believers in propagating His kingdom. To accomplish this, He delegates power and authority to them for service because His kingdom cannot advance or be effective without His power. The spiritual deposits of power, grace, authority and anointing of the Holy Spirit God has put in us are His treasures to empower us serve His purpose.

Further Reading: **1 Corinthians 3:9; Ephesians 2:10**
Prayer for the Day: **LORD, in the mighty name of Jesus, I pray that You may make me into Your choice vessel by releasing spiritual deposits into my life.**

Exodus 33-35

11th February

Be Joyful in Times of Testing

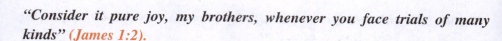

"Consider it pure joy, my brothers, whenever you face trials of many kinds" (James 1:2).

Believers are bound to face diverse trials and challenges as they walk with God. Going through trials is not always easy, as one gets overwhelmed or demoralized. Some people fail the test when tried, sometimes giving in to discouragement and departing from the faith.

Scriptures contain many examples of people who were severely tested. Joseph was sold as a slave in Egypt by his brothers. He was falsely accused of sexual impropriety by his master's wife and was jailed for years. Through all these hardships, God prepared a way for his promotion. The word of God had to be tested through him for his dream to become a reality.

God's word admonishes us to receive seasons of trials with joy no matter how hard they become. During such times, the Lord transforms and makes us His vessels. Trials are an integral part of God's ugly process of making. The Lord is closest to us at such times because of His desire for us to remain steadfast and His purposes for our lives to be fulfilled. The greater the trial, the greater the testimony. As believers, we should face trials with confidence because God assures us that He will always be on our side.

Further Reading: Psalm 105:17-19; Psalm 34:19
Prayer for the Day: *Dear Lord, I pray that You will help me persevere in times of testing and fill me with joy as You refine and transform me. Amen.*

Day 42 — Exodus 36-38

12th February

Wait on the Lord Patiently

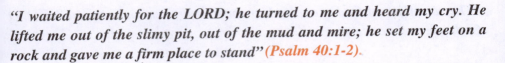

"I waited patiently for the LORD; he turned to me and heard my cry. He lifted me out of the slimy pit, out of the mud and mire; he set my feet on a rock and gave me a firm place to stand" (Psalm 40:1-2).

We live in a fast world where technological innovations have transformed how things operate, greatly increasing their speed and efficiency. Most of these operations are done with just the click of a button. As a result, much time is redeemed and people enjoy the services of these operations in the comfort of their homes. This has its advantages, but it has also caused the detriment of others.

In the walk of faith, patience is a virtue and those who fail to be patient may never fulfill great things in the kingdom of God. David waited patiently for the Lord until He heard his cry and was saved from trouble. Before the Lord makes you the praise of the nations by doing wonders in your life, you must pass the test of patience.

Impatience paves the way for discouragement, which gives birth to sin. Those who yield to discouragement abort their dreams and visions and fail to fulfill God's purposes. The impatient hardly rise to the peak of their destinies as God works on His own timetable, which is different from ours.

Believers should develop the virtue of patience in everything. Though God may tarry, He eventually remembers us for He is faithful. None of His promises fails, and He never speaks what He does not intend to perform.

Further Reading: James 1:3; Galatians 6:9
Prayer for the Day: Father in the Name of Jesus, help me wait on You patiently even when I go through testing as this develops perseverance. In Jesus' Name I pray, amen.

Exodus 39-40 — Day 43

13th February

Brokenness is Critical in Accessing God's Mercy

"The sacrifices of God are a broken spirit; a broken and contrite heart, O God, you will not despise" (Psalm 51:17).

Brokenness is a prerequisite for receiving God's mercy. The heart of man is naturally proud and rebellious towards God. As we seek God, we should activate the key of brokenness because God does not despise broken and contrite hearts. We cannot serve God if our hearts are not broken before Him. Our God is sovereign and He decides whom He will have mercy upon. The Lord is also a great judge. When He releases His verdicts, we should accept them and petition Him for mercy. God's mercies are not only dependent on His sovereignty but He has given us avenues through which we can access them.

Although God is merciful, gracious and compassionate, some people fail to access His mercy because they do not cultivate the inner brokenness. It is unfortunate that even though some people go through intense misery and suffering, they are unable to access divine mercy.

Arrogance and pride hinder God's mercy and grace. We need to guard our hearts against them and continually renounce them so that we can access divine mercy. Aside from that, we need to have repentant and humble hearts so that we can align ourselves with the will of God. Our achievements, wealth, education and comforts of life can harden our hearts if we are not watchful.

Further Reading: Matthew 9:13; Romans 9:16-18
Further Reading: Father, in the mighty Name of Jesus, a broken and contrite spirit, thou shall not reject. This is what I ask for today in Jesus' Name. Amen.

Day 44 — Leviticus 1-4

14th February

Contend Against Little Foxes

"Catch for us the foxes, the little foxes that ruin the vineyards, our vineyards that are in the bloom" **(Songs of Solomon 2:15).**

As we walk with Christ, we increasingly understand the gravity of sin and its impact. Little foxes in this context mean the sins we trivialize and think they do not affect our relationship with Christ. These include anger, bitterness, unforgiveness, envy, or gossip. These traits seem harmless but go a long way in affecting our relationship with God.

Scripture admonishes us to identify and deal with the sins that ultimately destroy our relationship with God and hinder us from harvesting what God has in store. We should destroy the enemies who seek to weaken us. In short, before aiming for great things, we should deal with these first.

As believers, we should always read the word of God and use it as a mirror to check our lives. Anything that goes against the word of God should be dealt with lest it make us fall. Taking time to fellowship with the Holy Spirit in prayers helps us identify these sins and with His help, overcome them.

Further Reading: Revelation 21:21; Matthew 15:13
Prayer for the Day: Oh Holy Spirit, I pray that you may help me identify every sin in my life. I also repent of every sin of commission and omission, in the Name of Jesus. Amen.

Leviticus 5-7

Day 45

15th February

Discover the Good Works God Ordained for You

"For we are God's workmanship, created in Christ Jesus to do good works, which God prepared in advance for us to do" (Ephesians 2:10).

God predestined each of us for exploits. This is only attainable through divine revelation. When God reveals our purpose, we understand the course He designs for us, which helps us commit to fulfilling our divine purpose with understanding. Ordinary education systems do not teach us to discover the purpose for which God created us. Rather, we enlist the help of the Holy Spirit who holds the blueprint of our lives.

Our destinies are unique and God preordained them before we were born. Through Christ's redemptive work, He foresaw the works we would do to advance His kingdom and in His wisdom and sovereignty, He customized us for this season.

When we discover our purpose, we need to pursue it passionately for the grace of God is available to each of us, empowering us to live for Him. As such, we should never take for granted the issues for which God allows us to have a burden for. They are an integral part of the reason we live.

When we understand that other people might not necessarily share the burdens we carry, it helps us avoid comparing ourselves with them. This motivates us to run our race. God provides all spiritual and material resources required for the advancement of His kingdom. We are His co-workers.

Further Reading: Jeremiah 29:11; Jeremiah 1:4-9
Prayer for the Day: Dear God, I pray that You may grant me divine knowledge to fulfill my destiny in the Name of Jesus Amen.

Leviticus 8-10

16th February

Do Not Fight Aimlessly

"Therefore, I don't run like a man running aimlessly; I do not fight like a man beating the air" *(1 Corinthians 9:26).*

The life of a believer is characterized by spiritual warfare against different ranks of forces and principalities in the kingdom of darkness. Matthew 11:12 states that the kingdom of heaven suffers violence and the violent take it by force. This violence is not physical but spiritual.

Our anchor verse draws our attention to the importance of knowing exactly what we wrestle against so that we do not throw blows in the air. We ought to have this understanding and not be ignorant of the schemes of the devil (2 Corinthians 2:11). Many have become casualties as they engage in warfare while ill-prepared or at the wrong time. Failure to know this can make us easy targets of the kingdom of the enemy.

To avoid being outwitted in spiritual warfare, we ought to take time in prayer and fasting as well as meditating on the word of God always, for we cannot fight a full-time devil by being part-time Christians. By enlisting the help of the Holy Spirit, we understand when and how to fight. David, whom the Scriptures describe as a man after God's own heart, made a lifestyle of enquiring from the Lord every time before he went out to war. Consequently, he always emerged as the winner. This should be our secret weapon and battle strategy against our adversary.

Further Reading: Ephesians 6:12; 1 Corinthians 10:3-5
Prayer for the Day: *Father, in the Name of Jesus, I pray for strategies for battle and the grace to win all my battles. In the mighty name of Jesus, Amen.*

17th February

Humility Attracts God's Mercy

"But the tax collector stood at a distance. He would not even look up to heaven, but beat his breast and said, 'God, have mercy on me, a sinner' (Luke 18:13).

We can neither achieve anything nor attain our destinies without the mercies of God. Our secret for rising to the peak of our divine destinies in God is in learning to seek God's help and yielding to His guidance.

The word of God teaches that human effort is irrelevant in causing people rise to positions that are God ordained. It teaches that while we may have a desire to be exalted and make great achievements, we can only rise to the level that the mercies of God allow (Romans 9:16-17). This is why humility is critical in walking with God towards one's prophetic destiny.

The tax collector received God's mercy because he was humble and had a contrite spirit. He acknowledged his shortcomings and sought God's forgiveness from a genuine heart and his request was granted.

Knowing God's merciful character can encourage us to seek Him with all our hearts (see Ephesians 2:4). Prophet Habakkuk admitted that he was amazed by God's deeds in past generations and knew that He could do greater things in his generation (Habakkuk 3:2). When we walk in rebellion against God and defy His word, we deserve judgment. However, His mercies cause Him to withhold his judgement so that we can have time to amend our ways.

Further Reading: Lamentations 3:22; Micah 7:18
Prayer for the Day: Oh God, may Your mercies that are new every morning be upon my life. In Jesus' name, Amen.

Day 48 | Leviticus 14-15

18th February

God's Mercy Breaks Protocols

"But for that very reason I was shown mercy so that in me, the worst of sinners, Christ Jesus might display his unlimited patience as an example for those who would believe in him and receive eternal life" **(1 Timothy 1:15).**

Mercy is God's greatest attribute but many people rarely acknowledge this. Most people know God as a healer, provider, banner of victory, and the almighty God. Few people fully understand His merciful nature and that His mercies are new for us every morning (Lamentations 3:22-23).

The mercies of God cause Him to transform our lives daily. We have come this far because of His mercies. Our salvation is a product of the mercy and grace of God. We did nothing to deserve the redemptive work of Christ. We are different from the hardcore drunkards, prostitutes, drug addicts, and thieves because God has been merciful to us.

As demonstrated in the life of Apostle Paul, mercy transforms the vilest of sinners into the most zealous ambassadors of Christ.

God demonstrates his mercy by releasing His grace and favour to a person through empowerment in a particular area in life where stagnation is broken and breakthroughs are achieved. When God's appointed time to visit His people comes, He releases the abundant riches of His mercy.

Further Reading: *Jonah 4:1-2; Psalm 145:8-9*
Prayer for the Day: *My God and my Father, I thank You for Your mercies which are new every morning upon our lives. Receive all adoration and thanksgiving. Amen.*

Leviticus 16-18

Day 49

19th February

Seek Divine Knowledge on Your Boundaries

"My people are destroyed from lack of knowledge. "Because you have rejected knowledge, I also reject you as my priests; because you have ignored the law of your God, I also will ignore your children" **(Hosea 4:6)**.

Information about your life is in the hands of God. Unfortunately, many people only know what they learned in school and what they hear others say about them. This ought not to be the case because God desires that we receive knowledge through Him. He made us and designed our destinies. Revelation knowledge comes from God and helps us understand the principles of His kingdom, which we use to receive the inheritance God has for us. When we know the boundaries set by God, we are able to receive grace to apply these principles.

Divine knowledge includes a clear understanding of our identity. It enables us to embrace our assignment, mandate, and purpose. The enemy of our divine boundaries works through distorted knowledge to hinder God's people from becoming everything He intended. God is full of love, is sovereign, and can transform us in spite of our backgrounds. Our past should not dictate our future. We depend on God for help to empower us to attain the fullness of our destinies.

Further Reading: *Exodus 23:31; Judges 11:1-3*
Prayer for the Day: *Oh God, grant me the revelation knowledge of my divine boundaries, that I may understand the principles of Your kingdom hence, receive the inheritance You have for me. In Jesus' Name I pray, Amen.*

Day 50 — Leviticus 19-21

20th February

Wage Warfare for Your Divine Boundaries

"Timothy, my son, I give you this instruction in keeping with the prophecies once made about you, so that by following them you may fight the good fight" (1 Timothy 1:18).

The spiritual realm controls the physical. Having this understanding is critical as it can help us wage warfare so that we are able to manifest the seed of greatness God has deposited in us. Some influential people visit altars that include graves because this has a spiritual dimension, which they seek in order to achieve the greatness they so much desire.

It's important to note that things do not just happen; they are made to happen through different forms of power. We need this divine power to progress to our destinies. God reveals our divine boundaries through visions, prophetic words, and dreams. In the anchor Scripture, He revealed Timothy's divine boundaries as a minister of the gospel through prophecy where Timothy was required to wage spiritual warfare to possess the promise of God.

We too can make progress towards our destinies despite great opposition from the kingdom of darkness. Satan fights us because of the potential we carry to impact the lives of those who believe the message of the gospel we proclaim. To succeed in spiritual warfare, we need to create a conducive environment for God in our lives through holy living and living within the bounds of Scripture.

Further Reading: Proverbs 21:31; 2 Kings 21:9
Prayer for the Day: Father in the mighty Name of Jesus, today I pray that You will help me wage spiritual warfare until I attain everything ordained for me. Amen.

Leviticus 22-23

Day 51

21st February

Prepare for Your Divine Boundaries

"For we are God's workmanship, created in Christ Jesus to do good works, which God prepared in advance for us to do" (Ephesians 2:10).

Preparation is an integral part of God's agenda for our destinies. In the same way farmers prepare their land before sowing seed, God prepares our lives and hearts before empowering us to fulfill our divine purpose. When Jesus Christ called the twelve disciples and assigned them the apostolic duties, He instructed them to spend time with Him so that he could equip them (Mark 1:17).

Similarly, when David was anointed king, he did not begin reigning over God's people immediately. When Joseph had a prophetic dream revealing that he would become great, he went through many challenges including imprisonment in Egypt. God uses our seasons of preparation to mould and equip us for the task ahead.

We therefore ought to make the most of every opportunity. God gives us adequate time to prepare for our assignment so that when He opens doors for our greatness to manifest, we are ready for the responsibility. The more we submit to God for equipping and empowerment during our season of preparation, the more impact we are likely to make in the long run.

Further Reading: Psalm 102:13; Revelation 3:7
Prayer for the Day: LORD, in the mighty Name of Jesus, grant me the grace to submit to You during the preparation process towards my destiny. Amen.

Day 52 | Leviticus 24-25

22nd February

Strive to Pass the Test of Trust

"Whoever can be trusted with very little can also be trusted with much, and whoever is dishonest with very little will also be dishonest with much. So if you have not been trustworthy in handling worldly wealth, who will trust you with true riches? And if you have not been trustworthy with someone else's property, who will give you property of your own?" (Luke 16:10-12).

God seeks trustworthy people to become carriers of His power and to advance His kingdom on earth. He works with and through faithful stewards whom He puts in charge of His possessions. Everything we have including the positions we occupy, our careers and ministries do not belong to us but to Him. We need to make sure that we pass the test of faithfulness for God to entrust more to us.

Our father of faith Abraham possessed God's promise after passing His test. God swore by Himself
that He would surely bless Abraham when he willingly laid down his only son.

You may have had prophetic words spoken to you, but you must first pass the test God subjects you to, before you possess your promise. It is a Biblical principle that one must prove faithful with little, in order to be entrusted with much. You must be faithful with worldly mammon to be trusted with the true riches of the kingdom of God, which are spiritual in nature.

Further Reading: 1 Samuel 15:10-28; Genesis 22:1-17
Prayer for the Day: Dear God, help me to be trustworthy in what You have entrusted to me. In the name of Jesus I pray, Amen.

Leviticus 26-27

23rd February

Train Yourself to Hunger and Thirst for God

"Blessed are those who hunger and thirst for righteousness, for they will be filled" (Matthew 5:6).

When we approach God, He responds in proportion to our spiritual hunger and thirst. The intensity of the hunger and thirst we have in this kingdom determines what we receive from God.

Spiritual complacency is one of the main reasons the church is unable to walk in the power and glory of God. Many believers do not seek God and His kingdom as intensely as they ought. The measure of our spiritual hunger for God is an indicator that we are alive and healthy.

In 1 Peter 2:2, Apostle Paul likens the spiritual hunger of a Christian to that of a baby. Healthy babies crave breast milk throughout the day and it helps them grow. In our walk with God, we need to crave the spiritual milk of the word of God, to be spiritually healthy.

One of the greatest gifts you can receive from God is spiritual hunger. When God gives you this gift, you yearn for righteousness and desire to walk in holiness. We cannot walk in revival unless we are desperate for God. We need to long for God so that He can give us spiritual gifts to manifest His glory to all the nations of the earth.

Further Reading: *Psalm 42:1-2; John 7:38-39*
Prayer for the Day: *Loving Father in the Name of Jesus, help me hunger and thirst for righteousness that I may be filled. Amen.*

24th February

Fix Your Eyes on the Reward

"The king will give great wealth to the man who kills him. He will also give him his daughter in marriage and will exempt his father's family from taxes in Israel" (1 Samuel 17:25b).

When Christians face challenges, most of them only consider the pain they go through. Few consider the reward they will get afterward. This should not be the case, as we ought to have a long-term vision to avoid getting discouraged in paying the cost of greatness.

The Philistines attacked Israel but unfortunately, there lacked a man who could stand against Goliath - the representative of the Philistines, until David rose to the challenge of facing the enemy of God's people. God gave him success and he was rewarded alongside his family. He was motivated to fight by fixing his eyes on the reward.

Our motivation should come from the rewards that await us when we are victorious at the fullness of time. As we walk with God, we should be determined to discard the desires of the flesh lest they hinder us from receiving our great reward from God. We should emulate Christ, who endured the cross because of the joy set before Him (Hebrews 12:1-2). By faith, we are going to receive every reward God has in store.

Further Reading: Romans 8:18; Philippians 3:14

Prayer for the Day: Father in Jesus' Name, I pray that You may help me to fix my eyes on the reward You have set before me, even through difficult times that may come my way. Amen

Numbers 3-4

25th February

Give Every Matter the Weight it deserves

"If anyone comes to me and does not hate his father and mother, his wife and children, his brothers and sisters - yes, even his own life - he cannot be my disciple. And anyone who does not carry his cross and follow me cannot be my disciple" **(Luke 14:26-27).**

Following Jesus requires sacrifices including relegating to the background critical family relationships so that we can do the will of God. God demands the first place in our lives. We therefore cannot claim to be followers of Christ if we attach more value to other relationships.

Most people are unable to secure victory because they are not wholeheartedly committed to doing the will of God. In the area of prayer, many are casual resulting in mediocre results. In the kingdom of God, only those who are fully committed realize great results. Jesus told the multitude that followed Him that each person should take up his cross and follow Him, to become His disciples.

As followers of Jesus, we should endeavour to take spiritual matters seriously. Our ability to stand firm for the purposes of God will influence the lives of many future generations, and we should therefore take it with the gravity it deserves.

Further Reading: Luke 14:28-31
Prayer for the Day: Oh Lord, help me to take every matter with the weight it deserves, that I may influence my generation and those to come in Jesus' name. Amen.

Day 56 — Numbers 5-6

26th February

Desire to Manifest the Grace of God

"But by the grace of God, I am what I am, and his grace to me was not without effect. No, I worked harder than all of them - yet not I, but the grace of God that was with me" **(1 Corinthians 15:10).**

Every aspect of our lives as believers is a product of the grace of God. Each of us is apportioned a measure of grace according to the generosity of Christ (Ephesians 4:7). The will of God is for us to identify, honour and manifest the grace He has deposited in us. This is so because it is possible for someone to be endowed with grace but fail to manifest it if he does not recognise it, and take the necessary steps to actualise it.

Grace is a kingdom investment that requires kingdom returns. God requires us to be faithful with the measure of grace He has given each of us. He invests His power into our lives with the intention that we will bear lasting fruit to glorify Him.

The grace of God expresses itself in different ways. As such, we ought to ensure we allow it to manifest in our lives. The word of God warns us not to take it for granted because doing so exposes us to the danger of being cut off (Isaiah 5:2-7). We need to show sincere appreciation for the grace God has deposited in us as we glorify Him.

Further Reading: *1 Timothy 1:16; 2 Corinthians 6:1*
Prayer for the Day: *My God in the Name of Jesus, help me identify, honor and manifest Your grace in my life, that I may bear lasting fruits that glorify You. Amen.*

Numbers 7

Day 57

27th February

God Desires to Raise Deliverers

"But when they cried out to the LORD, he raised for them a deliverer, Othniel son of Kenaz, Caleb's younger brother, who saved them" (*Judges 3:9*).

It is a biblical pattern that God raises a deliverer, when His people are spiritually or politically oppressed. He expresses His sovereignty by showing mercy. His word says that He has mercy on whom He wants to have mercy. He decides who to elevate, bless, promote and anoint for exploits.

Deliverers rescue people from oppression, exploitation and suffering. God chooses whom to raise in a family and the individual doesn't have to be a firstborn. When we call on His name when we are suffering under the yoke of oppression, He raises deliverers. We therefore need to co-work with Him so that deliverers can arise in all the seven mountains of influence. Our prosperity and establishment depends on the men and women God raises as deliverers.

As believers, we should celebrate and pray for all the people He has called in His service. We must avoid being jealous or competitive towards those God has raised to fulfill His purposes in our generation. When God anoints us as deliverers, we need to pray that He will help us be bold so that we can stand for His purpose despite the great opposition.

Further Reading: Judges 3:15; Hosea 13:9-13
Prayer for the Day: *My God and my Father, today I pray that You will raise many deliverers in Your vineyard and endow them with boldness that they may fulfill Your purpose in Jesus' Name, Amen.*

28th February

You Can Access God's Light through Thanksgiving

"For with you is the fountain of life; in your light we see light" **(Psalm 36:9).**

When we approach God in prayer and thanksgiving, He loads our lives with many benefits. The anchor Scripture mentions light twice. The first light mentioned is the light of God that we encounter when we enter His presence. When we behold that light, it illuminates and helps us see our own light. That light makes it possible for us to possess the possibilities in Christ which include the ability to access the gates of our destinies.

Heartfelt thanksgiving ushers us into the presence of God. The word of God commands us to thank God in all circumstances (1 Thessalonians 5:18). Our prayers are incomplete if they are not accompanied by thanksgiving.

The Bible contrasts light and darkness. Darkness stands for gloom, suffering, sickness, oppression whereas light stands for progress, increase and breakthrough. We need to strive to walk in the light of God because it has the power to transform and make us the vessels God intended us to be.

Light is an emblem of all the blessings that come from God. When we approach our heavenly Father with gratitude, we access the blessings God has in store for us. That way, our lives are transformed to reflect more of Christ's glory, until we attain the fullness of His stature in the fullness of time.

Further Reading: *1 Samuel 7:12; John 1:4; Acts 16:25-36*
Prayer for the Day: *Dear God, I pray that You may enable me access Your light through the power of thanksgiving. Amen.*

29th February

God is Committed to Protecting His Reputation

"he restores my soul. He guides me in paths of righteousness for his name's sake" **(Psalm 23:3).**

God cares about His reputation among men and guards it jealously. Since He has revealed Himself as gracious, compassionate, loving and just, He protects His identity zealously lest His name is dishonoured.

Scriptures teach that God desires that we become victorious for His name's sake. He guides, leads, and provides for us so that His name can be revered (Psalm 23:1-2). This means that if we fail, His name is likely to be mocked. God also forgives us when we fail for the sake of His name (Psalm 25:11). We should therefore depend on His grace to live in a manner worthy of His name and be careful how we walk because God's forgiveness is not an excuse for recklessness.

The Psalmist testified that God led and guided him for His name's sake (Psalm 31:3). God hates it when the ungodly mock and blaspheme His name due to our failure to live according to His standards. As such, we should live in a manner worthy of our calling so that His name can be honoured by all. The unregenerate can revere the name of God if we live as God desires. When this happens, He draws close to us and manifests His glory through us.

Further Reading: Psalm 79:9; Isaiah 48:9; Ezekiel 20:44
Prayer for the Day: Oh God, I thank You for always keeping Your promises to me, for Your Name's sake. Lord be hallowed and honoured for this. In Jesus' Name I pray. Amen.

1st March

Morning Prayers Give Access to Divine Strength

"Very early in the morning, while it was still dark, Jesus got up, left the house and went off to a solitary place, where he prayed" (Mark 1:35).

God desires to have the preeminence in the life of every believer. We should always start with God in everything so that He takes His rightful place and guides us all the way. Seeking Him early is a demonstration of dependence upon Him for help and guidance through all we undertake to do, including the day, month or year.

During His ministry, our Lord Jesus spent quality time with God in prayer. Through communing with God, He was effective in ministering to the needs of the people (see Acts 10:38). Jesus would have His prayers early in the morning. Morning prayers give you inspiration and divine strategies to win battles. They equip and empower you as a believer.

God fills us with great wisdom and knowledge as we devote ourselves to seeking Him daily early in the morning. Praying in the morning enables us to seek His counsel, which leads us to making wise decisions and maximizing our day. The Holy Spirit helps us plan our day and cancel every appointment that is not in God's perfect will. Through these prayers we invite God to order our steps in accordance to His word.

Rise up early to pray and you will experience great miracles and breakthroughs. Cultivate the discipline of spending quality time with God in prayer every morning.

Further Reading: Psalm 59:16; Psalm 5:3
Prayer for the Day: Father in the name of Jesus Christ, I ask for grace to be consistent in my morning prayers. Amen.

Numbers 14-15; Psalm 90

Day 61

2nd March

Offer God a Sacrifice of Thanksgiving

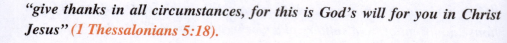

"give thanks in all circumstances, for this is God's will for you in Christ Jesus" (1 Thessalonians 5:18).

It pleases God to have a mature relationship with Him. Spiritual maturity is assessed by examining the content of our prayers. In God's design, prayer is not just meant to be an avenue to present our needs but a channel of conveying our gratitude to Him. Our prayers must be accompanied by thanksgiving at all times as scripture commands us to thank God in all circumstances.

In His sovereign power, God works in our lives in stages. In all the stages, He desires that we give Him thanks. When this principle is applied, God is pleased and He takes us to the next level.

Jesus healed ten lepers. However, only one returned to tell him thank you. As a result of his thanksgiving, he was made whole (see Luke 17:19). Many people are not whole because they do not take time to sincerely thank God for the far He has brought them.

Ingratitude causes stagnation in the lives of many believers. When gratitude ceases, we get grounded. At times, when we go through failure, we find it difficult to thank God. This should not be so, for failure is not final. It is not the opposite of success but rather a part of the journey to success and wholeness.

Further Reading: Romans 8:28; Luke 17:11-19
Prayer for the Day: Dear Lord, I pray that You may grant me a heart that freely expresses gratitude to You every day.

Day 62 — Numbers 16-17

3rd March

The Graces that Ignite Revival

"And God is able to make all grace abound to you, so that in all things at all times, having all that you need, you will abound in every good work" (2 Corinthians 9:8).

The grace of God is multifaceted. We need to understand how it expresses itself so that we can be partakers of it.

The church needs different dimensions of graces to birth and sustains revival. One of the graces we need for revival is intense prayer. To accomplish His mission, Jesus prayed in the garden of Gethsemane until His sweat turned into drops of blood (Luke 22:44). To pray effectively, we need to depend on the Holy Spirit to help us pray frequently, at length and in-depth. With these components, our prayers will be effective in birthing a move of God.

The second grace necessary for birthing revival is faith. Scriptures say that without faith, we cannot please God (Hebrews 11:6). Nothing is impossible to the man who has faith (Mark 9:23). As we serve God and seek Him, we have a guarantee to find Him if we have faith and do not faint. We can accomplish great exploits through faith in the name of Jesus Christ.

The third grace responsible for revival is purity. Since our God is holy, He requires us to emulate His character and walk in holiness so that we can enjoy revival. Through walking in purity, we become vessels God can use for noble purposes (Titus 2:11-12).

Further Reading: Hebrews 11:6; 1 Kings 17:12-22
Prayer for the Day: My God and my Father, today I pray that You may connect me with the graces that activate revival, In Jesus' name, Amen.

4th March

Recognize Your Time of Visitation

"They will dash you to the ground, you and the children within your walls. They will not leave one stone on another, because you did not recognize the time of God's coming to you" **(Luke 19:44).**

God has called us in the household of faith to operate beyond the physical realm. Our focus should rise above the temporal to the eternal. For this to happen, we need to cultivate an intimate relationship with God and be connected to what He is doing in the spiritual realm.

Jesus mourned the misfortunes that would befall Jerusalem. Unfortunately, the inhabitants of the city were spiritually blind and did not recognise the time of their visitation that could have brought their salvation. Instead of seeking the Savior, the inhabitants of the city went about their business as usual in oblivion of the looming destruction. Therefore, they did not seek God's mercy and help.

As believers, we ought to walk in understanding and discern the things that are happening in the spiritual realm. The Holy Spirit can help us know the times and seasons when certain things are bound to happen so that we can prepare adequately. We need to be careful not to miss our times of visitation by investing time in seeking God in prayer, fasting, studying and meditating in the word, and walking in the Spirit.

Further Reading: Matthew 22:37; Colossian 3:2
Prayer for the Day: *O Lord in the Name of Jesus Christ, help me discern your time of visitation in every aspect of life. Amen.*

5th March

Refuse To Be Defeated by Infirmities

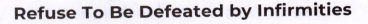

"How then could I do such a wicked thing and sin against God? And though she spoke to Joseph day after day, he refused to go to bed with her or even be with her" *(Genesis 39:9b-10).*

Infirmity is the state of being weak in health or body; it is the state of frailty. However, from a spiritual perspective, it means weaknesses in the flesh as a result of our fallen nature. The human race was sold to sin when Adam and Eve sinned. Sin opened a door for mankind to suffer.

Joseph refused to sin with Potiphar's wife despite her use of persuasive words to lure him into fornication. As a handsome and healthy young man, Joseph could have engaged in sin, but because he feared God, he did not want to do anything that could grieve the Lord. He already had a divine revelation of the greatness of his destiny and knew that sexual sin could have hindered him from attaining it. He therefore stood firm and resisted the allure of this infirmity that would have destroyed his life.

This example demonstrates that we should be firmly rooted in Christ. When we do so, we are able to resist the devil and stand firm in the face of temptations. The same way Joseph stood firm because of the fear of God, is how we too should resolve not to yield to temptation however attractive or enticing.

Further Reading: Colossians 2:7; Galatians 5:16
Prayer for the Day: Holy Spirit my help and my teacher, today I ask You to give me strength to overcome all temptations. In Jesus' name I pray, Amen.

Numbers 23-25

6th March

Seek God's Will for Your Life

"For this reason, since the day we heard about you, we have not stopped praying for you and asking God to fill you with the knowledge of his will through all spiritual wisdom and understanding" *(Colossians 1:9).*

Our lives have a solid foundation when we understand the will of God. Failure to align our lives to God's purposes can make us unfruitful in His kingdom. It is unfortunate that many people spend a lot of energy and time pursuing what God never intended for them.

To avoid this, every believer ought to be filled with the knowledge of God in all spiritual wisdom and understanding. Apostle Paul often prayed that the recipients of his epistles could have this privilege. He knew that when they partner with Him and pursue what God intended them to become, they could attain their divine purpose. Those with this kind of understanding pray in the perfect will of God and receive answers.

Scriptures command us to walk circumspectly and to understand the will of God, which is the secret to our growth and prosperity. We must daily rely on the Holy Spirit to empower us to walk in truth. We are bound to receive favour, breakthrough, increase, and blessings if we walk with understanding and spiritual wisdom.

Further Reading: *Ephesians 1:17; Ephesians 5:15-17*
Prayer for the Day: *Oh Lord in Jesus' Name, help me understand Your perfect will and fill me with Your wisdom and understanding. Amen.*

7th March

Serve Your Original Purpose

"For he chose us in him before the creation of the world to be holy and blameless in his sight. In love, he predestined us to be adopted as his sons through Jesus Christ, by his pleasure and will" **(Ephesians 1:4-5).**

When God created us, He already knew everything concerning our lives. He declares the end from the beginning (Isaiah 46:10). God created everything and every man for a specific purpose. Along with this, He provides all the spiritual resources we need to fulfill that original purpose. Satan opposes the purposes of God by using craftiness, deception, and lies to seduce God's people from the path He has ordained for them. We have a divine duty to fight against Him and resist all his wiles lest he perverts our lives and hinder us from serving our original purpose.

It is critical to note that even though God has a plan for our lives, He does not impose His will on any man. He invites us to willingly partner with Him through making the right choices and decisions until we become what He intended us to be.

Unfortunately, many people do not live according to God's plans for their lives. They imitate others and fail to manifest the peculiarity God intended them to have in order to impact the world. To ensure that we do not miss the path God ordained for us, we need to learn the art of making enquiring prayers so that God can guide us as we make choices in life. Through His help, we can discover, recover and manifest our original purpose.

Further Reading: *Psalms 139:16; Jeremiah 29:11; Psalm 148:2-14*
Prayer for the Day: *Father in the Name of Jesus, today I pray that You will help me serve my original purpose as I discover, recover and manifest it. Amen.*

8th March

Sin is a Hindrance to Divine Purpose

But they will reply, 'It's no use. We will continue with our plans; each of us will follow the stubbornness of his evil heart.'" Therefore this is what the LORD says: "Inquire among the nations: Who has ever heard anything like this? The most horrible thing has been done by Virgin Israel" *(Jeremiah 18:12-13).*

The word of God defines sin as the transgression of the law (1 John 3:4). Some people commit sin by the things they do while others break God's law by what they fail to do. In doing this, they commit the sins of commission and omission. As believers, we need to walk in the light of the word of God and avoid breaking His holy law.

Many people defy God's law and rebel against His instructions at will. In so doing, they suffer losses and disgrace by failing to attain their destinies. Israel defied God's word and followed the stubbornness of their hearts. Although God sent them His messengers to lovingly draw them back to Himself, they refused to heed His word and this eventually led to their destruction.

Like Israel, many people do not serve their purpose because they lend themselves to committing sin. God does not let us go free when we refuse to fulfill His purpose. Our disobedience can lead to the suffering of many, and He chastises and discipline us so that we may return to His ways. To walk with God, we need to turn our backs on the flesh and refuse to gratify the desires of the flesh.

Further Reading: James 4:17; Luke 12:47-48
Prayer for the Day: Father in the Name of Jesus, grant me the power to overcome sin in my life that I may not be hindered from attaining my destiny. Amen.

9th March

Take Responsibility for Your Life

The man said, "The woman you put here with me gave me some fruit from the tree, and I ate it." Then the LORD God said to the woman, "What is this you have done?" The woman said, "The serpent deceived me, and I ate" *(Genesis 3:12-13).*

Responsibility is one of the keys to success and greatness. Irresponsibility is a foundational problem in mankind as many prefer to shift blame from themselves to others. God desires to see His children taking control of their destinies. To do exploits, therefore, demands that we take responsibility for our lives, own up to our past mistakes and the wrong decisions we have made. We should also avoid bitterness and trust God to help us turn our lives around by making the right choices.

Jabez went through much suffering and pain. However, instead of resigning to his predicament, he took responsibility and called on the Lord to bless him and enlarge his territory (1 Chronicles 4:9-10). This is an indication to all of us that, God can transform our lives no matter the challenges we have faced. We may not have control over what happened to us, but we can decide how to respond to the things that happened to us without blaming others. It is important to always take charge of our lives by not entertaining things that would destroy our physical and spiritual man. We should learn to ignore our enemies since paying too much attention to them is likely to trouble our hearts.

Further Reading: Exodus 32:22-24; 1 Kings 20:38-40
Prayer for the Day: Oh Lord, I pray that You may help me take responsibility for my life, in Jesus' name, Amen.

Numbers 33-34

10th March

Arise and Take Territories for Christ

"And he called his ten servants, and delivered them ten pounds, and said unto them, Occupy till I come" **(Luke 19:13 KJV).**

God has given the responsibility of taking territories for Jesus to the church. This is occupying and taking charge. The government of the kingdom of darkness is territorial in nature and the devil rules by assigning different territories to forces of darkness to control them. This should not be the case for the church ought to be in control of the territories.

When The Church fails to take territorial control, it becomes irrelevant. . Erecting structures and worshipping in them is not enough. We should identify the powers that control territories, pray and renounce their authority. Jesus came to establish a kingdom and spiritual government that will increase and advance. We are supposed to advance the dominion of His kingdom on earth, as we take control of our territories and communities for Jesus.

The devil likes religion; he can be a member of a religious church. He only has a problem with a Church that understands its authority and power. The will of God is for us to take responsibility. Jesus said that He would build His Church, 'on this rock- Christ Jesus who is the founder of the church,' and the gates of hell shall not prevail over it.

We must arise as watchmen over our territories. A watchman does not allow the enemy to enter the gate when he is in charge. You have power and authority over your community. Do not just watch hopelessly.

Further Reading: Ephesians 6:12; Mark 5:12
Prayer for the Day: Oh Lord in the Mighty name of Jesus, grant us the strength we need to take our communities and territories for Jesus. Amen.

Day 70 | Numbers 35-36

11th March

The Holy Spirit Yearns for Us Jealously

"Or do you think the Scripture says without reason that the Spirit He caused to live in us envies intensely?" *(James 4:5).*

God expresses Himself to His people in different ways: as a father who lavishes His love on us, as a lover, who expresses great affection and loves His bride- the church, deeply. In the same way, a bridegroom jealously longs for his bride, Christ loves His bride intensely. He expects the church to reciprocate similar devotion and love.

God dwells in the saints through the Holy Spirit, who overshadows us with great love and creates in us a sense of belonging, in the presence of God. Through His indwelling presence, we experience the fullness of God's love. He expects us to reciprocate this love by walking in holiness and not allowing anything to stand between Him and us. We cultivate intimacy with Him when we understand what He expects of us and commit ourselves to doing it. This greatly pleases Him.

As God's lovers who desire to walk intimately with Him, creating quality time daily to build a strong relationship with Him, is of paramount importance. We should avoid anything that is likely to divert our attention or interfere with our time with God. In addition, we should not provoke God's jealousy because it is like a consuming fire, which has two dimensions – releasing a blessing or bringing judgment.

Further Reading: Deuteronomy 4:23-24; Romans 8:14; Zechariah 1:14
Prayer for the Day: My God and my Father, I desire greater intimacy with You. Help me to spend quality time with You daily in prayer. Amen.

Deuteronomy 1-2 | Day 71

12th March

You Can be Trapped by Your Words

"if you have been trapped by what you said, ensnared by the words of your mouth, then do this, my son, to free yourself, since you have fallen into your neighbor's hands: Go and humble yourself; press your plea with your neighbor!" (Proverbs 6:2-3).

The words we speak can make or break our lives. Carelessness can lead us to say things that trap and destroy us. Careless speech can land us in trouble with God and fellow men.

Many people have made costly mistakes by making careless utterances. To avoid being trapped by the words we speak, we should only speak words that build others. Our speech should be full of grace, as we submit to the leadership of the Holy Spirit.

The sins of the tongue likely to ensnare a person include gossip, tale-bearing, slander, lies, and abusive language. Some people speak words to demean, undermine, and hurt others. This should not be the case for those who profess faith in God. Our speech should be godly, graceful and worth emulating by other people.

An untamed tongue is a restless evil that can destroy life. We therefore need to exercise self-control in our speech so that we can always use our tongues to glorify God. We can build our destinies by devoting ourselves to prayer and building our fellowship with God, instead of misusing the power given to us in our tongues.

Further Reading: Matthew 12:36-37; James 3:2, 6-12; Colossians 4:6
Prayer for the Day: *Dear God give me the ability to use my tongue to bless others, and to free myself from every trap of negative words spoken against my life. Amen.*

Day 72 | Deuteronomy 3-4

13th March

Understand the Power of Your Tongue

"The tongue has the power of life and death, and those who love it will eat its fruit" (Proverbs 18.21).

The words we speak have great power to direct our lives. To enjoy our lives and attain our destinies, we need to be careful with the words we utter. We should strive not to act in a manner that provokes others to utter negative and potentially destructive words against us.

Unfortunately, many people have killed and destroyed their destinies by their confessions knowingly or unknowingly. Scriptures indicate that even though the tongue is a small organ, it carries great power. Almost all the troubles in our societies today are a result of words spoken against the will and purposes of God; words that enforced evil covenants and curses uttered by people in authority. Such can only be dealt with by renouncing and reversing them through the authority in the name of Jesus our Lord.

When you receive a revelation concerning your life, use the power in your tongue to agree with God's plan. The Bible promises us that we shall decree a matter and it shall be established (see Job 22:28-29).

At creation, God made decrees over the earth and what He declared came to pass. Similarly, the kingdom of darkness employs the power of the tongue to program destinies with a view to destroying them.

Further Reading: Genesis 1:1-8; Hebrews 11:3; Ecclesiastes 8:4; Matthew 12:36-37
Prayer for the Day: Oh God, today I have learnt about the power of the tongue. Help me use my tongue wisely. In Jesus' name I pray, Amen.

Deuteronomy 5-7

14th March

Keep Yourself Pure from Worldly Corruption

"These are those who did not defile themselves with women, for they kept themselves pure. They follow the Lamb wherever he goes. They were purchased from among men and offered as first fruits to God and the Lamb" **(Revelation 14:4).**

The word of God admonishes us to keep ourselves pure. Purity has great value both in this life and in eternity. Nothing impure or corrupt will find its way into the New Jerusalem. For this reason, we should wholeheartedly allow the Lord to enable us to walk in purity.

Scripture talks of saints who do not defile themselves by women. This expression encompasses physical and spiritual unfaithfulness to God through sexual immorality and the worship of idols. God desires we have a close relationship with Him that is free from worldly lusts and corruption.

As children of light, we need to know that God has put a treasure in us. He has also given us the power to escape the things that defile us. Unfortunately, that defilement has infiltrated the lives of many people including some believers.

As we walk with God, let us ensure that we uphold righteousness by emulating His purity in every aspect of our lives. The blood of Jesus shed at Calvary made us to be reconciled with the Father by faith. Through the work of the cross, we can devote ourselves to God and live in a manner that pleases Him in spirit, soul and body.

Further Reading: Revelation 14:15; Jeremiah 13:1-11
Prayer for the Day: Dear God, I desire to uphold righteousness in my life and today, I pray that You may enable me not to defile myself by shunning all forms of impurity. Amen.

Day 74 — Deuteronomy 8-10

15th March

Guard against All Forms of Defilement

"Reuben, you are my firstborn, my might, the first sign of my strength, excelling in honor, excelling in power. Turbulent as the waters, you will no longer excel, for you went up onto your father's bed, onto my couch and defiled it" (Genesis 49:3-4).

God has deposited a seed of greatness in every believer. He requires that we abide in His word so that we can manifest His glory. If we align ourselves with His plan and purposes, we will have a great impact and those who witness His doings will hold His name in high regard.

Reuben was destined for greatness but defiled himself by having sexual relations with his father's concubine. Consequently, he lost his position and power as a first-born of Jacob and inherited a curse.

The enemy releases a wave of defiling spirits to attack, oppress, entice and corrupt as many people as possible to hinder them from attaining their destinies. Physical, moral and spiritual corruption makes the glory God intended His people to manifest fly away like a bird. We must therefore be careful and watchful against doctrines, company, actions and behaviours that contradicts the word of God. The enemy sometimes takes advantage of legitimate human desires and appetites to propel people down the road of destruction when they seek gratification outside the parameters God has prescribed. We must allow the Holy Spirit do His sanctifying work in our lives.

Further Reading: Hosea 9:9-13; Ezekiel 9:9-11
Prayer for the Day: My God and my Father, today I pray that You may enable me to guard against every form of defilement, in Jesus' name, Amen.

Deuteronomy 11-13

16th March

Appropriate the Grace of God to Be Effective

"But by the grace of God I am what I am, and His grace toward me was not in vain; but I labored more abundantly than they all, yet not I, but the grace of God which was with me" **(1 Corinthians 15:10).**

God created us unique but many have lost their originality by copying the callings of others. They imitate the lifestyles of other people and end up as failures because God never intended them to be copyrights but to be original. The Bible teaches us that the easiest person to become is yourself. This is because although we might have good and successful role models, the intention is not to be their carbon copies.

Apostle Paul was successful and impactful in his generation because He discovered and manifested his true identity and calling as an apostle. He testifies on numerous occasions that he became impactful by appropriating and making good use of the grace God released into his life. This grace made him stand out from the other apostles, including the twelve who were with Jesus in His earthly ministry.

Many people fail because they live other people's lives and do not appreciate or maximize the grace God has given them. An immediate prayer those who have strayed from God's purpose can make is for restoration to their original purpose. When we ask for divine intervention to receive and put the grace we receive from God to meaningful kingdom work, He will help us rise to the peak of our divine destinies.

Further Reading: *Judges 4:19-22*
Prayer for the Day: *Dear God, I thank You for Your grace upon my life. Help me put it to work for Your glory. Amen.*

17th March

Praising God is the Password of Our Establishment

With praise and thanksgiving they sang to the LORD: "He is good; his love to Israel endures forever." And all the people gave a great shout of praise to the LORD, because the foundation of the house of the LORD was laid" **(Ezra 3:11).**

We can compare our lives with a building. For a building to be complete, it needs a foundation, walls and a roof. God is a master builder who spiritually and physically develops the lives of His people until they reflect the glory of Christ.

As we walk with God and allow Him to build our lives, we need to cultivate grateful hearts that give praise to His name at all times. God taught Israel this secret and they made use of it when they were building the temple. The priests led the people to praise and thank Him when they laid the foundation of the temple.

The word of God teaches that God dwells in the praises of His people (Psalm 22:6). Those who make a lifestyle of praising and thanking God in and out of season greatly experience His workings in their lives. He releases His mighty power, which results in signs, miracles, and wonders.

When we thank God out of a sincere heart, He perfects His work in us. The Samaritan who was among the ten lepers Jesus cleansed knew this secret and returned to thank Him for his cleansing. Scriptures record that after thanking Jesus, he was made whole (Luke 17:19). When we thank God, we create an atmosphere for Him to do more for His glory.

Further Reading: *2 Samuel 3:39*
Prayer for the Day: *My God and my Father, today I give You thanks for all You have done. I praise and thank You Lord, for You are good and Your mercies endure forever. Amen.*

Deuteronomy 17-20

18th March

Know the Holy Spirit and His Work

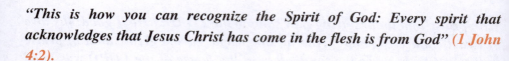

"This is how you can recognize the Spirit of God: Every spirit that acknowledges that Jesus Christ has come in the flesh is from God" **(1 John 4:2).**

In His unsearchable wisdom and knowledge, God is aware that without His supernatural help, we cannot align ourselves with His will. For this reason, He has given us the Holy Spirit to be our Helper. We need to know Him and His ways, to successfully walk with Him. The Holy Spirit is the Spirit of truth that reveals the power and work of the Father. He helps, empowers, and guides us to walk in the will of God. He also helps us to pray since we do not know how we ought to pray (Romans 8:26). The Holy Spirit also transforms us so that we can become more like Christ.

Once we are born again, our greatest need should be to be filled with the Holy Spirit. More importantly, we should learn how to maintain His presence for God desires to transform us into vessels of honour to advance His kingdom.

Spiritual knowledge is paramount in the attainment of destiny. As followers of Christ, we should daily depend on the power of the Holy Spirit to attain our destinies. With Him on our side, we can weather any storm and overcome every resistance.

Further Reading: Malachi 3:2-3; Colossians 1:9
Prayer for the Day: Holy Spirit, I pray that You may fill me with divine power, grace and knowledge of the will of God, In Jesus' name, Amen.

19th March

Jesus is a Merciful High Priest

"For we do not have a high priest who is unable to sympathize with our weaknesses, but we have one who has been tempted in every way, just as we are - yet without sin" *(Hebrews 4:15).*

A high priest is a preeminent authority of a movement or doctrine. In ancient times, a high priest was the chief religious functionary who entered the Holy of Holies to offer sacrifices on behalf of the people. When Jesus was resurrected, He became the great high priest of all believers, and His ascension to heaven set Him as the first perfect man who was glorified and sat at the right hand of God (Hebrews 12:2b).

The Lord Jesus was both God and man. He went through life as a man although the fullness of the Godhead dwelt in Him. Since He was tempted in every way as we are, He understands the pain we go through. As such, He is able to help us when we are tempted (Hebrews 2:17-18). He knows what it is like to suffer and be rejected and sympathizes with our weaknesses.

As believers, we need to walk with the revelation that when we call on Him in our troubled moments, He understands and intercedes for us (Romans 8:34). We should therefore be confident and call on Him always. He is the ever-present help in times of trouble and guides our ways when we depend on Him.

Further Reading: Isaiah 53:3; 1 Peter 3:22
Prayer for the Day: Today, I pray that I may have faith in the Lord Jesus and access God through Him as my high priest. Amen.

20th March

You Must be a Strong Fighter

"If you falter in times of trouble, how small is your strength!" **(Proverbs 24:10)**

We need a certain degree of forcefulness to walk with God and attain our destinies. The world does not only have God and the holy angels; it also has the devil, demonic principalities, powers, and rulers in the heavens. To become successful Christians, we must deploy spiritual weapons to defeat all forms of opposition.

As a matter of principle, the enemy does not fight success; he fights potential. He sees the greatness within us in the spiritual realm before it manifests, and rallies evil powers to resist, frustrate, and oppose thus hindering us from becoming all that God intended. The enemy pursues us with the intention of derailing us from the path of destiny. We therefore have no choice but to fight for life, not for the weak. We must also be strong in the Lord, and understand that our warfare is not carnal.

Unfortunately, many people give up in the face of battle. Their strength is limited and fails them when they need it most. As wise children of God, we need to be bold and fight for our destinies with zeal. We need to be firm in pursuing God's plan because our prosperity is in doing the will of God.
The kingdom of God is a kingdom of warriors. Cowards have no chance of succeeding because the enemies who oppose us are strong and vicious. Strive to emulate the Lord who is a man of war (Exodus 15:3).

Further Reading: *Ephesians 6:11; 2 Corinthians 10:3-5*
Prayer for the Day: *Oh Lord, I ask for strength as I engage in warfare against the enemy. I ask this in Jesus' name, Amen.*

Day 80 | Deuteronomy 28-29

21st March

Your Destiny is intertwined with Leadership

"Be strong and courageous, because you will lead these people to inherit the land I swore to their forefathers to give them" (Joshua 1:6).

Leaders determine the rise or fall of people. We need domestic, political, and spiritual leaders to attain our divine destinies. God ordained leadership to guide His people from one level to another. We cannot make progress in the kingdom of God in the absence of leadership. This clearly demonstrates that our destinies are intertwined with the leadership God has given us.

Without Joshua's leadership, Israel would not have inherited the Promised Land. God took time to mould Joshua to be a selfless leader by serving Moses for the better part of his ministry. Joshua learnt the virtues of prayer, dedication, humility, selflessness and faith, by watching how Moses walked with God as he led Israel from the land of bondage to the Promised Land (Exodus 33: 11).

Apart from Joshua, Israel had other leaders who were appointed as spies to go ahead of the people and inspect the land God had promised to give their fathers. Ten of them brought a negative report to Israel. However, Joshua and Caleb believed God would help Israel conquer the inhabitants of the land and dispossess them. All the people who did not believe God's promise perished in the wilderness because they displeased God.

As believers, we owe our nation a patriotic duty to pray for leaders in all sectors.

Further Reading: Exodus 32:19-22; Romans 13:1-3; 1 Timothy 2:1-4
Prayer for the Day: Dear God, help me to always honour those in positions of leadership and always pray for them as commanded in your word. Amen.

Deuteronomy 30-31

Day 81

22nd March

Be Diligent and Committed in Everything You Do

"Whatever your hand finds to do, do it with all your might, for in the grave, where you are going, there is neither working nor planning nor knowledge nor wisdom" (Ecclesiastes 9:10).

Success is always the product of keen application of certain principles. For instance, businesspeople need to apply financial best practices to succeed. Ministers of the gospel need to live by the word of God in order to succeed. Living a prosperous life and attaining one's destiny requires one to cultivate virtues. One needs to be diligent and committed. Scripture teaches that we need to do everything we set our eyes on, with all our might. Half-hearted efforts and wavering commitment can only lead to failure or dismal results.

Those who succeed pursue the fulfillment of their divine mandate with zeal and unflinching commitment. The Lord Jesus, our ultimate role model, did His redemptive work by being focused on His assignment. He did not consider available options because that would have been detrimental to God's plan.

Like Jesus, we need to be ready to count the cost and pay the price of our assignment. He did not shy away from death on the cross even though it was painful and humiliating. Commitment and diligence are indispensable components of living successfully and fulfilling our destinies.

Further Reading: Proverbs 12:24; Proverbs 24:33-34
Prayer for the Day: Father in the Name of Jesus Christ, today I ask You to help me exercise commitment and diligence in all I do. Amen.

Day 82 — Deuteronomy 32-34; Psalm 91

23rd March

Mortify the Deeds of the Flesh

"For if you live according to the sinful nature, you will die; but if by the Spirit you put to death the misdeeds of the body, you will live" **(Romans 8:13).**

The old man in us desires to indulge in worldly pleasures that resist God's plan for us to walk in the Spirit, and thereby put to death the works of the flesh.

The phrase "put to death" means "to mortify" which means to practice self-denial of one's body and appetites. It also means to hold within limits and control. The flesh finds great fulfillment in deeds such as immorality, greed, lust, foolishness, coarse jokes, bad company and witchcraft. However, these deeds lead to the corruption of the human soul and ultimately to death. On the other hand, the Spirit of God delights in holiness, purity, uprightness and righteousness. When we yield to Him, we bear spiritual fruit (see Galatians 5:22-23) to the glory of God.

To please God and receive His help to attain our destinies, we need to crucify every ungodly desire. We must renounce and turn away from engaging in the deeds of the flesh, which not only corrupt men but also make them enemies of God. God resists sin and abhours sinfulness. He lives in holiness and His presence cannot coexist with the works of the flesh because He is a consuming fire.

Further Reading: **Colossians 3:1-5; Galatians 2:20**
Prayer for the Day: **Dear God I pray that You may help me mortify all dead works and live by the Spirit, in Jesus' name, Amen.**

Joshua 1-4

24th March

Be Cautious in Forming Friendships

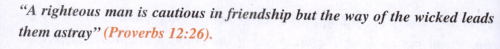

"A righteous man is cautious in friendship but the way of the wicked leads them astray" (Proverbs 12:26).

Man is a social being. An old adage holds that no man is an island. We need family members, friends and destiny helpers to attain the fullness of God's plan.

The word of God commands us to be cautious in forming friendships. No matter how helpful we think people can be to us, we should be aware that not all people are valuable friends. Some of the people around us can expose us to harm and destruction if we are not careful.

Jesus set an example we should emulate in the area of choosing and making friends. He loved all people without exception but only made friends with a chosen few. He chose the twelve disciples to be His close associates. However, three of them namely James, Peter and John stood out as His closest associates. This teaches us that friendship is in levels. As we relate with those we consider friends, we should know how close we should be with them. We risk hurting our lives and destinies if we make friendship with unworthy people who are likely to betray us.

As we choose friends, we need to consider their moral uprightness. We also need to choose those who fear God because associating closely with the ungodly is an avenue of engaging in wicked ways.

Further Reading: Proverbs 18:24; 1 Corinthians 15:33
Prayer for the Day: My Father and my God, since bad company corrupts good morals, I ask You to grant me the blessing of godly friends, in Your Name's sake I ask, Amen.

25th March

Become a Friend of Christ

"I no longer call you servants, because a servant does not know his master's business. Instead, I have called you friends, for everything that I learned from my Father I have made known to you" *(John 15:15).*

A lesson all believers need to learn is that Jesus looks for friends from among the sons of men. Since He is a Person, He delights in relating closely with other people. By His nature, the Lord is relational. This is why He is a triune being, comprising the Father, the Son and the Holy Spirit.

Besides offering the warmth of love, a true friend confides in someone. This is the message Jesus shared with His disciples. He made known the secrets and mysteries of the heavenly kingdom to His committed followers.
By His redemptive work and teachings, Jesus has made it possible for us to know God and the mysteries that govern His kingdom. He has made known to believers truths that are concealed to those who have no relationship with Him.

Sadly, many people have no genuine friends. Loneliness has reached the level of a pandemic and many have harmed themselves and others because they had nobody to share their challenges, experiences and weaknesses. This need not be the case as the Lord is willing and able to be our friend and connect us with godly friends.

To be friends of God, take great care not to grieve His Holy Spirit.

Further Reading: 2 Chronicles 20:7; John 15:15
Prayer for the Day: *Oh God I pray that I may be among those You consider as friends and not only servants and also grant me the gift of genuine friends, in Jesus' name, Amen.*

Joshua 9-11

Day 85

26th March

Submit Your Life to God

"Submit yourselves, then, to God. Resist the devil, and he will flee from you" **(James 4:7).**

The spirit realm is responsible over everything that happens in the physical realm. God created the universe and He is supreme, having dominion and authority over everything on earth and in heaven. When we accept Christ as Lord and Saviour and live under his authority, He seats us with Christ in the heavenly places (Ephesians 2:6). From that position, we are able to have dominion over all other powers.

To attain victory over all forces of darkness, God requires us to submit to Him as a matter of priority. We have no power of our own and the only way we can receive it is by Him delegating it to us. Jesus told His disciples that all power and authority had been given to Him, and he instructed them to align the world to the will of the Father through the proclamation of the good news (Matthew 28:18-20).

When divine power works in us, we are able to resist the devil. Our being steadfast in our position against his wicked schemes and machinations makes him flee. He is a defeated foe whose power is constrained and limited. For us to exercise our spiritual power legitimately, we must perfect our obedience to God's plan and will. The secret of our ability to exercise divine power lies in our wholehearted submission to God.

Further Reading: 2 Corinthians 10:3-5; 2 Chronicles 30:8; Job 22:21
Prayer for the Day: Oh God, help me subject every aspect of my life to Your will. In Jesus' name I pray, Amen.

27th March

Develop a Teachable Spirit

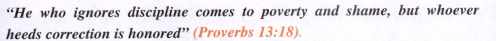

"He who ignores discipline comes to poverty and shame, but whoever heeds correction is honored" (Proverbs 13:18).

As disciples of Christ, we must acknowledge that we have limited knowledge and understanding. We need to submit to the master teacher Jesus, so that we can learn the ways of God and walk in them.

Solomon received wisdom and understanding from God when he offered an acceptable sacrifice., He consequently wrote words of counsel and instruction to teach us. He states that those who heed correction are honoured. Accepting correction is an implication of humility and willingness to learn. A person with a teachable spirit admits that he is limited in knowledge and needs to increase it through learning and instruction.

Those who hate instruction end up in destruction. Their advancement in life becomes hampered and it takes long for them to prosper. Their decisions may fail to be well-informed, which is likely to lead them to destruction.

The word of God is His breath and is aimed at teaching, correcting, rebuking and training us in righteousness (2 Timothy 3:16-17). We need to delight ourselves in the law of the Lord and meditate on it day and night in order to be prosperous (Joshua 1:8). The Holy Spirit, who abides in every genuine believer, is a teacher. He reveals to us the deep mysteries of the kingdom of God as we yield to His leadership. He instructs us in the ways of our God.

Further Reading: Proverbs 12:1; 1 Corinthians 2:13-14; Proverbs 9:9
Prayer for the Day: Today I have learnt that whoever heeds correction is honoured. Oh God, grant me a teachable spirit that I may be successful. Amen.

Joshua 16-18

28th March

Strive to Grow in Faith

"Consequently, faith comes from hearing the message, and the message is heard through the word of Christ" **(Romans 10:17).**

Our spiritual lives bear many similarities with our physical lives. The same way we are born weak and helpless in the natural, is the same as when we are regenerated because we are spiritually weak and uninformed. To attain spiritual maturity and bear lasting fruit in the kingdom of God, we need to feed on spiritual milk. When we are consistent and persistent, we grow to spiritual maturity and handle the deep truths of the word of God.

Our faith begins at the infant stage and only grows as we feed and nurture it by applying the principles of the word of God. Faith comes from hearing the proclamation of the word of Christ which must be unadulterated for our faith in God to be authentic and fruitful.

Growing in faith and walking in God should be a lifestyle. It is however so sad that many believers are weak and unfruitful because they only walk with God on Sunday mornings. The rest of the time, they do little or nothing to build their faith. As a result, they are defeated by the circumstances of life. These people paint a negative picture of their faith in God since it has no meaningful impact. After accepting Christ as Lord and Saviour, we must strive to grow in faith until we attain maturity.

Further Reading: *Mark 9:23; Romans 1:17*
Prayer for the Day: *Dear Lord, I pray that my faith in You will grow to maturity and bear much fruit. Amen.*

29th March - Good Friday

The Death of Christ Defeated Satan Completely

"having canceled the written code, with its regulations, that was against us and that stood opposed to us; he took it away, nailing it to the cross. And having disarmed the powers and authorities, he made a public spectacle of them, triumphing over them by the cross" (Colossians 2:14-15).

The death of Jesus is the most significant and meaningful event in human history. It marked the end of hostility between God and man provided that man repents and believes in Christ's redemptive work. When Christ was crucified, a man who was separated from God by sin was given an opportunity to relate intimately with God just as was the intention from the beginning.

As an enemy of God's purposes, the devil accuses believers of all manner of sin (Revelation 12:10). By the work of the cross, Jesus canceled the arrest warrant that was issued against us and disarmed the enemy by making a public spectacle of his destructive work. He defeated him completely and as long as we fully submit to God, He keeps us safe by imputing righteousness on us by faith.

As He hung on the cross, Jesus declared, "It is finished" (John 19:30). By this He meant that He had made a way for man to be reconciled with God. We can triumph over Satan and his armies by understanding our new position as God's beloved children and walking in obedience to the terms of the new covenant that the blood of Jesus sealed for us.

Further Reading: *John 19:30; Hebrews 10:10*
Prayer for the Day: *Thank you, God, for through the death of Your son, 'Jesus' You have given me total victory over all the works of the enemy, in Jesus' name. Amen.*

Joshua 22-24

30th March - Easter Saturday

Dying to Self is the Key to Successful Christian Living

"I tell you the truth, unless a kernel of wheat falls to the ground and dies, it remains only a single seed. But if it dies, it produces many seeds" **(John 12:24).**

The life of a genuine believer entails a deliberate denial of oneself and total submission to the will of God. In His teachings, Jesus commanded His disciples to lay down their lives for Him and assured them that He would be with them. He also taught the futility of pursuing selfish interests which lead to loss and destruction.

Jesus set for us an example of what self-denial is. Even though He is equal to God, He humbled Himself to the lowest level possible – becoming as a slave for the salvation of mankind (Philippians 2:7-11). This pleased the Father, who exalted Jesus, giving Him the name that is above all other names. In the same way, if we live in line with God's perfect will and lay down our lives for His sake, He has promised to elevate us and reward us both in time and in eternity.

As our anchor Scripture indicates, a grain of wheat must first fall to the ground and die to bear fruit. As followers of Jesus, we must die to every form of selfish ambition so that God can have the preeminence in our lives. This pleases God. Our lives would be futile if all we do is strive to meet our selfish goals and ambitions, while we have been given the noble duty of being God's witnesses on earth.

Further Reading: Luke 9:23-26; Galatians 2:20
Prayer for the Day: Oh Lord, help me lay down every aspect of my life for Your glory, Amen.

31st March - Easter Sunday

Christ's Death Atoned for Our Sins

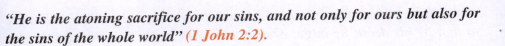

"He is the atoning sacrifice for our sins, and not only for ours but also for the sins of the whole world" **(1 John 2:2).**

The Lord our God is a just judge. He punishes the guilty and defends the cause of the guiltless. In the Old Covenant, He demanded life for sin. He has not changed and requires a holy sacrifice to atone for sins. This sacrifice could only be offered by Christ who was sinless. John the Baptist recognized Jesus as the Lamb of God who would take away the sins of the world (John 1:29). Atonement refers to the act of making amends for a wrong or injury. Through His self-sacrificing death on the cross, Jesus shed His innocent blood that satisfied the justice of God. He vindicated Christ by raising Him from the dead preparing a way for all believers to share in the eternal life that is only found in Him.

Those who are in Christ have been purified and justified. However, they continue living on earth where they are tempted in different ways and sometimes commit sin. The blood of Jesus is powerful and effective, sanctifying and making them like Christ. As we walk with God, we should show our reverence for Him by avoiding all forms of ungodliness and through repentance. God promises to be gracious to us, forgiving us so that we are able to walk in freedom from sin, and to attain our destinies.

Further Reading: *Hebrews 9:22; John 3:16*
Prayer for the Day: *Oh God, may the truth of the atonement of my sin become a daily reality in my life, Amen.*

Judges 3-5 | Day 91

1st April - Easter Monday

You Can Overcome the Fear of Death

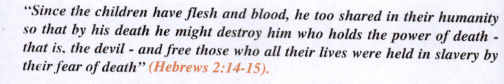

"Since the children have flesh and blood, he too shared in their humanity so that by his death he might destroy him who holds the power of death - that is, the devil - and free those who all their lives were held in slavery by their fear of death" (Hebrews 2:14-15).

One of the greatest fears many people face today is that of death. Many are uncertain of what will become of their lives once they die, and greatly dread the day they depart from earth. However, this need not be the case, especially for those who have accepted Jesus as Lord and Saviour. The fact that He triumphed over death and rose again should encourage us and give us peace because we shall be like Him.

God has made provision for us to overcome not only the fear of death but also death itself. Our anchor Scripture indicates that Satan holds the power of death and holds many people captive through the fear of death. As genuine believers who believe in the word of God, we should not fear because Christ in us is greater than the enemy who is in the world (1 John 4:4). During His earthly ministry, Jesus raised several people from the dead. He also made strong statements on His power over man's greatest enemy. He said that He is the resurrection and the life, that those who believe in Him shall never die (John 11:25). Like God the Father, the risen Christ has the power to give life to whomever He pleases (John 5:21).

Further Reading: *1 Corinthians 15:56; Revelation 14:13; Revelation 21:4*
Prayer for the Day: *Thank you God that through the cross, You have given me dominion over death, in Jesus' name, Amen.*

Day 92 | Judges 6-7

2nd April

How You Handle Finances Impacts Your Faith

"Whoever can be trusted with very little can also be trusted with much, and whoever is dishonest with very little will also be dishonest with much. So if you have not been trustworthy in handling worldly wealth, who will trust you with true riches?" (Luke 16:10-11).

The topic on money is quite sensitive both in church and generally. Believers need not be caught up in the confusion of material wealth since the earth and everything in it belongs to God (Psalm 24:1).

God's will is that His people should seek first His kingdom and His righteousness. He promises to add everything else to those who do so (Matthew 6:33). On the contrary, due to the commercial nature of the world, many people seek money first and God second. This is a misnomer because it contradicts the word of God.

We were created in the image and likeness of God and are both spiritual and physical beings. Scripture states that God requires us to be faithful with little before He can entrust us with much. Aside from that, faithfulness is one of the key virtues expected of disciples of Jesus Christ.

Scriptures teach that our ability to receive and handle true riches such as spiritual gifts depends on our ability to handle money faithfully. Many believers have disqualified themselves from receiving spiritual wealth because of the way they handle material wealth, which is in an unworthy manner. The way you handle money may or may not qualify you to receive spiritual gifts.

Further Reading: Haggai 2:7-8; Psalm 50:10; 1 Timothy 6:10

Prayer for the Day: Father, I ask You to grant me the wisdom needed in handling financial resources in accordance to Your word, for Your Name's sake, Amen.

Judges 8-9

3rd April

God Desires to Prosper the Saints

"Dear friend, I pray that you may enjoy good health and that all may go well with you, even as your soul is getting along well" (3 John 2).

The church of Jesus Christ comprises of believers from diverse backgrounds brought together by His redemptive work to serve God's purposes on earth. God's will is to prosper every saint physically and spiritually. A prosperous church is a great asset and touches the world with the mighty power of the gospel by winning souls and disciplining believers.

According to the third epistle of John, it is the perfect will of God for saints to enjoy good health and for all to go well with them. God's desire is for the souls of all saints to prosper as they grow and mature in their relationship with Christ.

God owns everything in the universe. He has blessed us with every spiritual blessing with Christ in the spiritual realm (Ephesians 1:3). However, since spiritual blessings are intangible, He desires us to partner with Him so that they can be a reality. We also need to apply the principles of His word by faith so that all possibilities in Christ can become reality in our lives.

The abundant life Jesus promised His disciples (John 10:10) is for all saints in all dispensations as a fulfillment of the promises God made to the patriarchs.

Further Reading: Ephesians 4:11-12; 1 Corinthians 12:12-26; Psalm 35:27

Prayer for the Day: My God and my Father, today, I pray that divine prosperity will fill every area of my life, in Jesus' name, Amen.

Day 94 | Judges 10-12

4th April

Our Fullness is in Christ

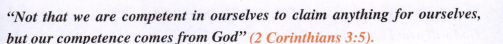

"Not that we are competent in ourselves to claim anything for ourselves, but our competence comes from God" (2 Corinthians 3:5).

Before creation, the earth was formless and void. The Bible records that darkness hovered over the surface of the deep (Genesis 1:1). The same is true of our lives. Before we come to Christ for salvation, we live as unregenerate sinners who are separated from God and doomed to destruction. However, once we acknowledge and confess the Lordship of Jesus and live in line with His word, we become new creatures and God brings order into our lives.

Apostle Paul writing to the saints in Corinth stated that he could not claim anything for himself. The power, grace and anointing that enabled him to serve God and be effective in ministry came from God. This is the admission we need to make so that God's power can be revealed in and through us. Those who do not believe in God face the challenge of being self-sufficient and leaning on their own understanding. This contravenes God's word which warns us against doing anything without His involvement (Proverbs 3:5-6). The more a person tries to attain his destiny without God, the more frustrated he gets because God opposes such people and frustrates their self-confident efforts.

Like Apostle Paul, we need to lay aside every claim of self-sufficiency and surrender to the Holy Spirit who divinely empowers us to fulfill our mandates and destinies.

Further Reading: *John 15:4; Jeremiah 10:27*
Prayer for the Day: *My God, my humble prayer today is that You may help me to be sufficient in every good work, in Jesus' name, Amen.*

Judges 13-15

5th April

The Righteous Avoid All Extremes

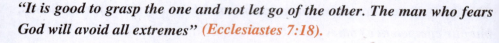

"It is good to grasp the one and not let go of the other. The man who fears God will avoid all extremes" (Ecclesiastes 7:18).

The enemy uses imbalanced doctrines to deceive and mislead people from the straight and narrow path of true doctrine. Almost all cults and sects have some degree of truth in them, except that it is not tempered by the balance of the word of God.

As believers, we need to avoid all extremes. Scriptures state that the devil masquerades as an angel of light (2 Corinthians 11:14). To mislead many, he releases doctrinal attacks to cast aspersions on God's word to cause people to doubt it. Ministers of the gospel and believers in general need to watch their teachings closely and avoid making doctrines from cherry-picked scripture. The saints in Berea (Acts 17:11) were diligent students of the Scriptures. We too must be diligent students of the word of God. We need to interrogate and reason through the teachings we receive lest we be misled into believing wrong doctrines. We also need the spirit of discernment lest we are ensnared by deceiving spirits.

Biblical doctrine advocates for balance in one's spiritual, financial, and social life. False prophets, Christs, and teachers are on the rise, but they cannot deceive those whose doctrine is balanced.

Just as vehicles require wheel alignment, believers need to align themselves with the word of God by constantly checking the spiritual diet they take.

Further Reading: 2 Timothy 2:15; 1 John 4:1
Prayer for the Day: Dear Lord, grant me a balanced life both spiritually and socially always, in Jesus' name, Amen.

Day 96 — Judges 16-18

6th April: Good Friday

Enter Strict Training to Perfect Your Faith

"Therefore I do not run like a man running aimlessly; I do not fight like a man beating the air. No, I beat my body and make it my slave so that after I have preached to others, I myself will not be disqualified for the prize" (1 Corinthians 9:26-27).

Spiritual living is compared to a wrestling match (Ephesians 6:12). This sport requires strength and tenacity to defeat one's opponent. It also requires alertness since a momentary loss of focus can cost one his victory. The same is true of our spiritual lives. We are in a wrestling match against forces of darkness and they can use every possible tactic to wrestle us to the ground.

Believers are compared to athletes and boxers. Apostle Paul indicates that for one to be a successful athlete, he needs to cross the finish line. In the same way, a boxer needs aim his blow towards the opponent with the intention of hitting him. As followers of Jesus, we have a duty to identify the spiritual forces that resist and oppose us so that we can direct our efforts into fighting and defeating them. Without clarity and focus, we can easily become casualties.

Spiritual clarity can only be achieved by subjecting oneself to strict spiritual training. Christ's intention is for us to be more than conquerors and this can only be attained when we allow Him to train us as soldiers in His army.

Further Reading: 1 Timothy 4:7-8; 2 Timothy 2:2-3
Prayer for the Day: Oh God, I pray that You may empower me to engage in strict spiritual training to perfect my faith, Amen.

Judges 19-21

7th April: Easter Saturday

Learn to Offer Acceptable Sacrifices to God

"But Abel brought fat portions from some of the firstborn of his flock. The LORD looked with favor on Abel and his offering, but on Cain and his offering he did not look with favor. So Cain was very angry, and his face was downcast" (Genesis 4:4-5).

The spirit realm dictates what happens to the natural realm. The Bible teaches that sacrifices are an indispensable part of worship both in the kingdom of light and of darkness.

Nonetheless, we should be aware that not all sacrifices men offer to God are acceptable. He reserves the right to either accept or refuse an offering. To ensure that out sacrifices are acceptable in His sight, a standard is needed, so that what we offer is proportional to the blessings, grace and revelation He has given.

Acceptable sacrifices speak for those who offer them, and are taken seriously. The highest sacrifice offered on earth was that of Jesus Christ at Calvary. He defeated the devil and death on our behalf (Hebrews 2:14).

As we approach God with our sacrifices, we should know that His Spirit is ready and willing to help us discern the good, pleasing and perfect will of God (Romans 12:1-2). When we rely on His guidance and help, we are able to offer God sacrifices that delight Him and cause Him to bless, secure and increase us for His glory.

Further Reading: Hebrews 13:15; Revelation 5:8; 2 Samuel 24:24
Prayer for the Day: Dear Lord in Jesus' name, I pray that You will help me offer acceptable sacrifices to You always, Amen.

Day 98 — Ruth 1-4

8th April: Easter Sunday

Stick to the Pattern God Has Given

"See that you make them according to the pattern shown you on the mountain" (Exodus 25:40).

Believers are spiritual builders. God has called us to emulate Him by doing what He does. His word prescribes the way we should follow so that we can become what He intended from the beginning. God has a pattern He desires us to follow so that we can attain our destinies.

He has also assigned us different responsibilities as we partner with Him in building the body of Christ. The different responsibilities fall into the fivefold ministry offices meant to equip saints for the work of the ministry (Ephesians 4:11-13).

As we build our lives in God, we need to be careful to stick to the pattern He has given us. The same way Moses had to make the tabernacle in the exact way God showed him, is how we should build our lives and destinies in the way God desires. As part of God's building, we are increasingly being transformed into His likeness. Christ is the chief cornerstone of the church and God expects us to model our lives alongside His. His lifestyle and teachings form the basis of our character.

As disciples, we must follow Him faithfully until we attain our temporal and eternal destinies. To do this, we need to humbly accept His word and live as He instructs us in every aspect of our lives.

Further Reading: Exodus 25:9; Philippians 3:17; 2 Timothy 1:13; Hebrews 8:5

Prayer for the Day: My God in the Name of Jesus Christ, help me exercise fidelity to the pattern of the vision You have given me, in Jesus' name, amen.

1 Samuel 1-3

9th April : Easter Monday

Use Your Spiritual Gift for the Common Good

"Now to each one the manifestation of the Spirit is given for the common good" (1 Corinthians 12:7).

Generosity is one of the most outstanding attributes of God. He freely gives all good things to those who love Him to glorify Himself. He has given us diverse graces and gifts to propel us towards our destinies. We need to identify the gifts we have and put them to good use for the benefit of other saints. That way, we shall bear fruit that will glorify God.

Everyone has a valuable spiritual gift that should be used to build others up. Just like reputable companies ensure they package high quality products for their clients, God packages us with great talents, potential and abilities which we should discover and maximize for the benefit of the body of Christ.

God blesses us and gives us spiritual gifts with His kingdom in mind. It is a travesty of His will and wisdom for any saint to use his spiritual gift for personal gain. Since He is a generous and purposeful giver, He desires to see us put priority in advancing His kingdom with every spiritual gift He has given us.

Spiritual gifts include speaking in tongues, interpretation of tongues, healing, faith, working of miracles and discernment of spirits. Every recipient of these heavenly treasures should walk in the awareness that God has given them to us for the common good, not as medals of honour or for selfish use.

Further Reading: Romans 12:6-8; 1 Corinthians 1:7; 1 Corinthians 14:1
Prayer for the Day: Oh God in the name of Jesus, I pray for the infilling of the Holy Spirit that we may be able to use our gifts to benefit others, in Jesus' name, Amen.

Day 100 — 1 Samuel 4-8

10th April

God Answers Prayer According to Our Faith

When he had gone indoors, the blind men came to him, and he asked them, "Do you believe that I am able to do this?" "Yes, Lord," they replied. Then he touched their eyes and said, "According to your faith will it be done to you" (Mark 9:28-29).

We can only access the limitless resources God possesses through the means He has prescribed in His word. Prayer and faith are key necessities of accessing God and receiving from Him. As we approach God in prayer for our needs, we need to do so with the awareness that our needs can only be met by divine resources only in proportion to our faith. During His earthly ministry, Jesus often made it clear to those who sought divine intervention from Him that their ability to receive from God depended on the faith they had in Him. The more faith one has, the more He receives from God.

The Scriptures teach that the just shall live by faith (Romans 1:17). Faith offers solutions to all problems as nothing is impossible to the man who has faith (Mark 9:23). The quality and impact of our lives depends on the amount of faith we have in God. We thus need to ensure that we have genuine faith in who God is and what He can do.

Faith is paramount in our lives and in our prayers just as the Scriptures teach that everything that is not of faith is sin (Romans 14:23b).

Further Reading: Mark 11:24; James 1:6-8
Prayer for the Day: Oh God, grant me the ability to believe in Your power to answer prayers whenever I pray. In Jesus' name I pray, Amen.

1 Samuel 9-12

11th April

Strive to Walk in God's Power

"No one calls on your name or strives to lay hold of you; for you have hidden your face from us and made us waste away because of our sins" (Isaiah 64:7).

The spirit realm requires a certain degree of forcefulness with which to relate. Jesus taught that the kingdom of God suffers violence, and that the violent take it by force (Matthew 11:12). The kingdom of God is established in heaven and He has appointed believers as ambassadors on earth to represent Him and advance its interests. He commanded His disciples to always pray that His will be done on earth as it is done in heaven (Matthew 6:10).

Our fruitfulness in the kingdom of God as believers is dependent on how intensely we plug ourselves into God's power. We need to strive to connect ourselves with God so that His purposes can be fulfilled in our lives. God has obscured His power and might from men, only revealing and manifesting these to those who fervently seek to access them.

As believers and servants of God, we need to grasp the truth that training for ministry is good but connecting oneself with the Holy Spirit is more important. Mere knowledge without spiritual power to back us up is not beneficial.

In this regard, we must strive to receive divine power through diligently seeking God. This is the only way our service to Him can be authentic.

Further Reading: Luke 24:49; John 15:4-7
Prayer for the Day: Oh God, fill me with the Holy Spirit, that I may be able to manifest Your power, in Jesus' name, Amen.

Day 102 | 1 Samuel 13-14

12th April

Take Responsibility for Your Destiny

"Also, seek the peace and prosperity of the city to which I have carried you into exile. Pray to the LORD for it, because if it prospers, you too will prosper" (Jeremiah 29:7).

God preordained and predestined us to fulfill our destinies with His help and guidance. However, since He respects our choices, He does not force anyone to become what He designed him or her to be. Rather, He gives us the opportunity to make choices on the path we wish to follow. We may choose to rebel and disobey or to humble ourselves and obey Him wholeheartedly.

God desires we take personal responsibility for our destinies. Whether we fail or succeed, we need to own up to our choices, decisions and mistakes for God to help us. Unfortunately, many people avoid taking responsibility and choose the treacherous path of blaming others, thereby aborting their destinies. To avoid this, we must make personal decisions to pursue our destinies and become everything God meant us to be. We must also not create room for irresponsible behaviour because God will hold us accountable for everything we do or fail to do (Romans 14:12).

It is unfortunate that many people are irresponsible for their lives and destinies. Instead of seeking to know God's plan for them, they waste time on comparison. Apostle Paul commanded Timothy to pray and wage warfare until every word God spoke to him when he was consecrated for ministry became a reality (1 Timothy 1:18).

Further Reading: Luke 12:47-48; Revelation 22:12
Prayer for the Day: Oh God, help me take responsibility over every area of my life, in Jesus' name, Amen.

1 Samuel 15-17

Day 103

13th April

Understand the Weight of Your Destiny

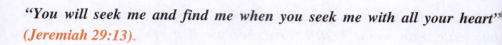

"You will seek me and find me when you seek me with all your heart" (Jeremiah 29:13).

God has availed all the resources of heaven and earth to man. With this understanding, we are able to commit ourselves to seeking God with all our strength and might. He only promises to reveal Himself to those who seek Him zealously.

Finding God and accessing the resources at His disposal is conditional and dependent on our seriousness and commitment in pursuing Him. Those who are devoted and focused on seeking His face find Him. The halfhearted and the noncommittal receive nothing because they operate outside His revealed will (James 1:6-8). We cannot attain our destinies and manifest the seed of greatness which God has deposited in us if we are not convinced of His good plans for our lives.

Our destinies should be taken into serious consideration. This can be a testament of our walking in the perfect will of God. Our Lord and Saviour Jesus understood the reason why He was born, and became willing to pay the price of dying on the cross. It was neither easy nor convenient for Him to face death as a criminal but He endured it for our redemption. We too, must be willing to pay the price.

Further Reading: Hebrews 12:1-3; Philippians 2:5-9
Prayer for the Day: Dear Lord, in the name of Jesus, I ask You to help me focus on my ultimate goal of seeking and finding God in my life, in Jesus' name, Amen.

Day 104 — 1 Samuel 18-20; Psalm 11, 59

14th April

Our Destinies are Intertwined

"For if you remain silent at this time, relief and deliverance for the Jews will arise from another place, but you and your father's family will perish. And who knows but that you have come to royal position for such a time as this?" (Esther 4:14).

God created the human race from one man and decided the time and place where each man would live (Acts 17:26-27). The purposes of God are multifaceted and trans-generational. He works in and through every generation to fulfill what He intended from the beginning.

Our destinies are intertwined. The success of other people depends on ours. For instance, the success of a teacher's career is intricately tied to the students he teaches and vice versa. Ministers of the gospel thrive if their congregants are enjoying success.

We are not meant to live selfish and shallow lives. As we walk with God and have faith in His purposes for our lives, we should learn to rely on His grace to propel us forward as we get deep in our understanding of His ways. Our disobedience can cause the suffering of other people whom we are meant to impact in diverse ways. Although Esther lived a comfortable life in the king's palace, had placed her there as an instrument of salvation for the Jews from annihilation. Her uncle's cousin Mordecai cautioned that if she failed to play her part, she and her family would perish and God would still seek a substitute for her.

Further Reading: 2 Timothy 1:5-6; Genesis 18:18-19
Prayer for the Day: Father in Jesus' name, I ask for the tenacity to pursue my destiny until it comes to pass, as my destiny affects many others. I pray this in Jesus' name, Amen.

1 Samuel 21-24

Day 105

15th April

Know Your Part in Fulfilling Destiny

"Timothy, my son, I give you this instruction in keeping with the prophecies once made about you, so that by following them you may fight the good fight" **(1 Timothy 1:18)**.

Most believers are discouraged and weak because even though they know what God intends them to become, their lives remain miserable and wretched. They do not manifest His glory even though He is all-powerful and all His promises are true. This happens because many do not know what they need to do to fulfill their destinies.

According to Scripture, a prophetic word is not an end in itself. It is a call to prayer and spiritual warfare because evil spiritual powers remain determined to abort God's plans for His people. We are co-workers with God and He is ready to grant us victory if we align ourselves with Him.

Attaining destiny is not for the naïve. We need to know the magnitude of our calling and the level of commitment and sacrifices we need to offer to become what God intended for us. We must know how best to live and walk with God so that He can empower us to attain our destinies.

Our spiritual formation and growth determine how successful we become. This calls for us to strive and understand the formula God uses to elevate and bless His people (Psalm 103:7). To rise to the peak of our destinies, we need to grow in virtue – love, purity, godliness, mutual love, brotherly affection and spiritual perfection (2 Peter 1:5-9).

Further Reading: Acts 17:26-27; Luke 14:26-33
Prayer for the Day: Oh God, help me be proactive and grow in the virtues that will help me attain my destiny, in Jesus' name, Amen.

Day 106 — Psalm 7, 27, 31, 34, 52

16th April

We Cannot Do Anything Apart from Christ

"Remain in me, and I will remain in you. No branch can bear fruit by itself; it must remain in the vine. Neither can you bear fruit unless you remain in me. I am the vine; you are the branches. If a man remains in me and I in him, he will bear much fruit; apart from me you can do nothing" **(John 15:4-5)**.

Success and attainment of one's dreams is sweet but require insight, effort and careful application of knowledge. Few people become successful or fruitful through luck. One needs to be connected to a particular source to become prosperous.

The Bible compares believers to branches of a vine. A branch by itself cannot accomplish much. If separated from the vine, it has no life of its own and withers within no time. We too cannot offer meaningful service on our own in the kingdom of God. With our limited human strength, evil forces can easily overwhelm us. Apostle Paul confirms this by testifying that the effective work He did was enabled by the grace of God (1 Corinthians 15:9-10). Understanding that the flesh is not strong enough to do anything of spiritual value is critical in walking with God. Bearing lasting spiritual fruit depends on our abiding in Christ.

Jesus instructs us to abide in Him at all times. Plugging ourselves into God's presence and power is an art we must learn and master. It requires determination, sacrifice and focus. To connect ourselves with God, we must acknowledge that we are nothing without Him.

Further Reading: 2 Timothy 3:1-5; Philippians 4:13

Prayer for the Day: *Father in the Name of Jesus, I ask You to help me abide and depend on You at all times so that I can bear lasting fruit, Amen*

Psalm 7, 27, 31, 34, 52

Day 107

17th April

Labour in the Kingdom with God's Power

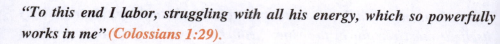

"To this end I labor, struggling with all his energy, which so powerfully works in me" (Colossians 1:29).

Walking with God and serving Him is intensive spiritual work. Since we are spiritual beings who have a soul and live in a body, we can connect with God's power and do His work.

Apostle Paul wrote to the saints in Colossae that he laboured to proclaim and teach the gospel to present his hearers perfect in Christ (Colossians 1:28). To labour with the energy God's Spirit provides means that, he yielded himself to God wholeheartedly. God puts immeasurable supplies of power at the disposal of those who fully surrender to His purposes. Believers who have not yielded to Him feel weak, weary and overwhelmed by challenges they encounter daily. We however do not have to succumb to weakness because the dynamic power of the Holy Spirit is readily available to as many as will ask for it.

Spiritual work such as prayer, reading the word of God, perfecting holiness in the fear of God and working out our faith requires spiritual energy. We risk succumbing to discouragement, weariness and hopelessness if we depend on flesh and blood to carry out the great spiritual work God intends us to do. Disciples in the early church were aware that they could not do God's work without His power. They prioritized fellowship, prayer and breaking of bread to receive spiritual strength to carry out their divine assignment.

Further Reading: 1 Corinthians 15:58; Acts 1:8
Prayer for the Day: Holy Spirit, today I pray that You may empower me to do God's work, Amen.

Day 108 — 1 Samuel 25-27

18th April

Brokenness is Key in Receiving God's Power

"The sacrifices of God are a broken spirit; a broken and contrite heart, O God, you will not despise" (Psalm 51:17).

The Holy Spirit possesses unlimited divine power as He is an integral part of the Godhead and co-equal with the Father and the Son. That notwithstanding, He abides in believers to empower them walk with God and attain their destinies. We need to know how to receive and maintain God's power because He can depart from us if we grieve Him.

To receive and walk in divine power, we need to activate spiritual keys taught in the word of God. One of them is repentance. Admitting our guilt and acknowledging our wrongdoing is an indication of brokenness. Some people are hard-hearted and unrepentant because they have been broken by the difficulties they have gone through in life, to the extent that they have lost their faith in God. Such cannot receive divine power.

The second key to brokenness is humility. God is attracted by the humble who readily acknowledge their dependence on Him. When we yield to God and walk in brokenness, He comes to our aid. Those whose hearts are broken before God can walk in the supernatural as His power is best manifested in our weakness. Apostle Paul admitted that he was aware that he could not do anything on his own but needed God daily to do the great work He had called him to do (1 Corinthians 15:9-10). We can emulate His example and have broken hearts and contrite spirits.

Further Reading: Hebrews 5:7-8; Ezekiel 36:26
Prayer for the Day: Oh God, a broken and contrite spirit thou shall not reject. May this be my portion in my daily walk with You, in Jesus' name, Amen.

Psalm 17, 35, 54, 63

19th April

Purity is Critical in Walking with God

"Blessed are the pure in heart, for they will see God" (Matthew 5:8).

The Lord our God is too pure to behold evil. He demands that we emulate His purity since His nature and character have no room for impurity, wickedness, and sin. With Him, there is no shadow of turning (James 1:17). Jesus taught that purity of heart is the password of seeing God. The pure witness the power of God at work in their lives and they shall dwell with Him in eternity. To successfully walk with God, we need to be sincere, truthful and pure. In addition, we ought to have a pure motive to be a vessel worthy of receiving and carrying God's power.

The process of becoming increasingly pure is referred to as sanctification. Through the blood of Jesus, we are purified and sanctified from all forms of unrighteousness as we apply it by faith. The word of God has a purifying effect on our lives (John 15:3). The more we tarry in the presence of God and soak in His word, the more He cleanses us from within so that we can be like Him in everything we do.

God desires truth in the innermost place (Psalm 101:6). As believers who sit under different servants of God for ministration, God requires us to do due diligence to ensure that only those who are committed to walking in purity minister to us. We must exercise discernment and not allow anyone claiming to be a servant of God to lay their hands on us because this transfers spiritual virtues from one person to another.

Further Reading: 1 Peter 1:15-16; Titus 1:15; 1 Thessalonians 4:3-7
Prayer for the Day: Father in the name of Jesus Christ, I pray that You may help me avoid all forms of physical, spiritual, and moral impurity, Amen.

Day 110 — 1 Samuel 28-31; Psalm 18

20th April

Submit to God to Overcome the Enemy

"Submit yourselves, then, to God. Resist the devil, and he will flee from you" (James 4:7).

God is able to elevate as many people as will pass the test of humility. However, many people – believers included – cannot enjoy the benefits of divine elevation because they have an exaggerated sense of themselves and are proud. They do not acknowledge God's power or ask for His help, even when it is the only means through which they can move from one level of growth to another.

The word of God teaches that pride comes before a fall (Proverbs 16:18). Many great people have missed the grace of God and forfeited their destinies because they were unwilling to humble themselves. On the other hand, many saints have manifested greatness and had a great impact in the body of Christ because they humbled themselves before the Lord. Our ability to wage warfare and defeat the enemy depends on how submitted we are to God. To resist the wicked schemes of the devil, we need to fully submit to God. As we obey God, His Spirit dwells in us. Our words become as a sword that the devil and his agents cannot withstand. In doing these, Satan will have no other option except to flee from those who are wholeheartedly yielded to God.

To cast out the devil and his demons, we must first check our degree of submission to God. Our authority, power and effectiveness depend on how much we have submitted to God.

Further Reading: **Luke 14:10-11; Daniel 4:37, 5:20; Numbers 12:3**
Prayer for the Day: **Oh Lord, help me submit myself fully to You, in Jesus' name I pray, Amen.**

21st April

Learn to Tarry in the Presence of God

Going a little farther, he fell with his face to the ground and prayed, "My Father, if it is possible, may this cup be taken from me. Yet not as I will, but as you will." Then he returned to his disciples and found them sleeping. "Could you men not keep watch with me for one hour?" he asked Peter (Matthew 26:39-40).

Prayer is the engine that propels genuine believers along the path ordained by God. When offered in faith and in line with the requirements of the word of God, it causes great things to happen (James 5:16b).

Although many believers know the significance of prayer in their walk with God, many go into the presence of God in haste. Technology, cares of life and pursuit of money among others have conspired to deny believers room to tarry in the presence of God. These things are part of a demonic conspiracy to weaken believers and render them spiritually ineffective and unproductive. Our Lord Jesus once prayed so intensely that He was transfigured. He instructed His disciples to pray at least an hour to overcome temptations.

As we continue seeking God for revival, we need to tithe our time faithfully every day. I firmly believe and teach the saints that every believer should spend at least two hours in prayer daily and half an hour studying the Scriptures. Those who do this with a sincere and genuine heart are guaranteed to experience a turnaround in their lives.

Further Reading: Luke 22:42-44; Acts 12:5; Acts 2:42-46
Prayer for the Day: Oh Lord, I desire to spend quality time in Your presence daily. Grant me the strength and ability to do this, Amen.

Day 112 — 2 Samuel 1-4

22nd April

Do Not Walk in Willful Sin

"Keep your servant also from willful sins; may they not rule over me. Then will I be blameless, innocent of great transgression. May the words of my mouth and the meditation of my heart be pleasing in your sight, O LORD, my Rock and my Redeemer" *(Psalm 19:13-14).*

The Lord our creator and redeemer is holy. He has no sin. He hates sin and judges it severely. He is especially firm on sin that is committed presumptuously because it shows dishonour to His holy name.

Although we are believers, we have come from the world where we considered sin frivolous. Lying, cheating, trickery, committing immorality and taking advantage of others sound harmless to the sinful but they are grave sins in the eyes of God. The Psalmist pleads with God to keep him from willful sins to avoid becoming a slave to these sins. Those who purposefully commit sin get to a point where it becomes a demonic bondage from which they cannot easily disentangle. The Psalmist seeks God's help in the words of his mouth and the meditation of his heart. The tongue is a small organ but with immense power. The heart on the other hand, is the wellspring of the issues of life. If it is corrupted by sin, the cause of that person's life heads towards destruction.

God's desire is for us to walk in purity of soul, body and spirit (1 Thessalonians 5:23). Aside from that, we should not take His word lightly but tremble at it (Isaiah 66:2).

Further Reading: 1 Samuel 15:22-23; Psalm 5:4-5
Prayer for the Day: Oh God, help me stay away from all deliberate sins, that Your Name may be honoured, in Jesus' name, Amen.

23rd April

Learn to Wait for God's Appointed Time

"Now the LORD was gracious to Sarah as he had said, and the LORD did for Sarah what he had promised. Sarah became pregnant and bore a son to Abraham in his old age, at the very time God had promised him" (Genesis 21:1-2).

Our lives are divided into times and seasons. Just as there are seasons of ploughing, planting, waiting for the crop to grow and harvest, so do we have seasons in the spiritual realm. We need to fill the cup of blessing God has set before us to receive the harvest He has promised.

Walking with God requires faith and patience. Even though God is almighty and can do as He pleases, He desires to see us grow in character before He can entrust us with spiritual power and divine elevation. Without godly character, we can easily cause disgrace in His kingdom by doing things against His will presumptuously.

The heroes of faith documented in the Scriptures left an impact in the world and waited for God's appointed time with great eagerness and patience. Sarah received the promised son at God's appointed time. The word of God also teaches us to wait on God through the example of Job. He was severely tested and lost his children and worldly possessions. Since he was a man of godly character, he endured to the end and God was glorified by his testimony (James 5:10-11).

Further Reading: Psalm 103:12; Ecclesiastes 3:1-8; Psalm 40:1-3
Prayer for the Day: My God and my Father, help me exercise patience until You fulfill all Your promises upon my life at Your appointed time, in Jesus' name, Amen.

Day 114 — 1 Chronicles 1-2

24th April

Engage in the Mystery of Spiritual Training

"Everyone who competes in the games goes into strict training. They do it to get a crown that will not last; but we do it to get a crown that will last forever" **(1 Corinthians 9:25).**

World-class sportsmen and athletes in different sports undergo focused training to perfect their art. Similarly, believers need to undergo spiritual training to become impactful. Spiritual training is different from physical training because it has eternal benefits while physical training only yields temporary benefits.

The word of God commands us to emulate sportspeople by subjecting our spirits to strict training. Apostle Paul admitted that he subjected his body to his spirit so that he could attain his destiny as a herald of the gospel. He was looking forward to a crown as a reward for his work in spreading the gospel. Training builds spiritual muscles. When we train ourselves to commune with God and tarry in His presence, we grow in faith and invoke the presence of God wherever we might be. Since training is not easy, we need to be psychologically prepared for the arduous work we have to do during training sessions.

Our spiritual gifts, natural talents and abilities become active and effective as we plug into God's power through spiritual exercises. These activate dynamic power to work in our lives in signs, miracles and wonders.

Further Reading: 1 Timothy 4:7-8; Matthew 5:44-48
Prayer for the Day: Oh Lord, today I pray that You will help me offer myself to be spiritually trained by You, in Jesus' name, Amen.

Psalm 43-45, 49, 84-85, 87

25th April

Discover the Benefits of Intimacy with God

"Because your love is better than life, my lips will glorify you" (Psalm 63:3).

God created man for intimacy. No other creature can relate with God as closely as man does. The Psalmist states that His love is better than life. Many people compare worldly possessions and achievements with matters of life and death. They only discover later that only the love of God can truly satisfy. Anything we treasure more than God becomes an idol. He detests idolatry and judges all things that attempt to take His place.

God gives true fulfilment to anyone who comes to Him with a sincere heart. His presence exudes peace, settlement and immeasurable joy. Man enjoyed intimacy with God before the fall. He would come to the Garden of Eden to fellowship with man in the cool of the day (Genesis 3:8). Whenever we approach God, our greatest desire should be to connect with Him and His love. His Spirit longs for us jealously and we should not grieve Him by being carried away by other things (James 4:4-5). The presence of God should be our permanent dwelling because in it we receive everything pertaining to life and godliness (John 15:7).

Many people in the church are not intimate with God. They do not respond appropriately to His immeasurable and unfailing love. Unlike them, we should be transformed into His likeness and not conform into the thinking patterns of the world that desire material possessions more than the creator.

Further Reading: *James 4:8; Matthew 22:36-38; Job 23:12*
Prayer for the Day: *Teach me how to walk intimately with You Oh Lord that I may partake of the benefits that go hand in hand with this, in Jesus' name, Amen.*

Day 116 — 1 Chronicles 3-5

26th April

Put God First in Everything You Do

"But seek first his kingdom and his righteousness, and all these things will be given to you as well" (Matthew 6:33).

The sovereign of the universe only accepts the first position in man's priorities because He deserves it. In His unsearchable wisdom, God created us in such a way that we are free to set our priorities. His will is that He may be preeminent in everything we do. The Lord Jesus Christ taught His disciples that they needed to lay aside every other person or thing for God. His kingdom and His righteousness should be the primary focus of every believer.

Scriptures teach that all things serve God (Psalm 119:91). When you have God in your life, all things will serve you as well. The three Hebrew men knew the secret of serving and walking with God. When they were thrown into the fiery furnace, He delivered them miraculously (Daniel 3:18-25). Apostle Paul was not harmed by a venomous serpent on the island of Malta because he was serving his divine mandate and put God first in everything he did (Acts 28:4-5).

When you give God the first place in everything you do, you fear nothing because God fights your battles and grants you victory. You exercise dominion over all creation in His name. As we put God first, He prompts us to ask Him for the nations and He will give them to us as our inheritance (Psalm 2:8).

Further Reading: Proverbs 16:3; Jeremiah 17:5-8
Prayer for the Day: Oh God, I pray that You may enable me to put You first in everything. Amen.

Psalm 73, 77-78

Day 117

27th April

God is Pleased By those Who Make and Honour Vows

In bitterness of soul Hannah wept much and prayed to the LORD. And she made a vow, saying, "O LORD Almighty, if you will only look upon your servant's misery and remember me, and not forget your servant but give her a son, then I will give him to the LORD for all the days of his life, and no razor will ever be used on his head" **(1 Samuel 1:10-11).**

Making vows was part of the traditions of the nation of Israel. To this day, many Israelites refer to making vows with God as "cutting deals." To them, God delights when His people make and fulfil vows.

Hannah was afflicted by barrenness for many years in her marriage. Her co-wife Peninnah who had children subjected her to mockery. Instead of becoming bitter with God, Hannah turned to God in prayer and promised to dedicate her son to His service. Pleased by this vow, God graciously gave her a son that she dedicated to God as soon as he was weaned.

A vow entails making a solemn commitment to do something in return, when God grants your request. As we make vows, we need to take caution so that we do not make thoughtless vows. To fulfill the promises we make requires that, we first think through what we are committing ourselves to beforehand. God has no pleasure in those who make vows to Him without an intention of honouring them.

Further Reading: Numbers 30:1-2; Ecclesiastes 5:4-6
Prayer for the Day: *Oh God today I pray that You may remind me of any unfulfilled vow and pledge so that I may honour it. Amen.*

Day 118 — 1 Chronicles 6

28th April

Align Your Thinking with the Will of God

"Do not conform any longer to the pattern of this world, but be transformed by the renewing of your mind. Then you will be able to test and approve what God's will is - his good, pleasing and perfect will" (Romans 12:2).

Our minds are an asset God has given to help us navigate through life. The mind is the nerve centre of our decision-making, which determines our success or failure. We cannot rise above our ability to reason. The godlier our minds are, the better our lives are going to be because God blesses those who comply with His word with success and prosperity.

The word of God encourages us to have the same mindset as Jesus Christ. Although He is God, He humbled Himself before the Father to the lowly state of a servant. He lay His life down for our redemption. As we cultivate a godly mindset, we lay down every claim to our rights. We die to self and live sacrificially to please God.

Scripture instructs us not to conform to the patterns of the world but let God transform the way we think by helping us view ourselves as He does. His will is the best for us. It is in levels and we walk in higher levels when we allow Him to transform us for His purposes. Therefore, we should never tire of asking God to transform us until we reflect the glory of Christ in every aspect.

Further Reading: Matthew 6:9-10; Philippians 2:5-9
Prayer for the Day: Heavenly Father in the Name of Jesus Christ, I ask You to help me align my mind with Your word as You continue transforming my life, in Jesus name, Amen.

Psalm 81, 88, 92-93

29th April

Guard against the Spirit of Pride

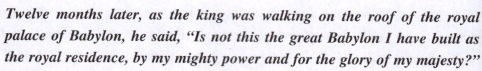

Twelve months later, as the king was walking on the roof of the royal palace of Babylon, he said, "Is not this the great Babylon I have built as the royal residence, by my mighty power and for the glory of my majesty?" (Daniel 4:29-30).

Pride is a lethal enemy of our destinies. It is probably the oldest sin in the universe. It was committed by Lucifer, who elevated himself against God's authority and attempted to overthrow it. Proud people are self-confident, self-reliant and self-indulgent. They leave no room for God in their lives and He sets Himself against them. They do not enjoy good and lasting success because He humbles and demotes them to manifest His power.

Nebuchadnezzar forgot that he became great with God's help. His heart was lifted up; he spoke blasphemously and angered God. Consequently, he was abased and became as a wild animal and dew fell on him for seven years. His pride cost him the throne of Babylon.

Like Nebuchadnezzar, many people become proud because of their achievements – education, financial or social. They choose to forget that they owe everything to God. To live successfully and attain our destinies, we must eschew the spirit of pride with all our might because it leads to destruction.

Further Reading: Proverbs 16:18; James 4:10
Prayer for the Day: Today in the name of Jesus', I renounce every spirit of pride that might be in my life, and purpose to walk in humility before God always, Amen.

30th April

Give Up Ownership

"You are not your own; you were bought at a price. Therefore honor God with your body" **(1 Corinthians 6:19b-20).**

We brought nothing into the world and we cannot take anything out of it. Ironically, many people spend their lives devising ways of how to accumulate as much as possible. They seek to increase their material possessions at the expense of doing the will of God to whom the earth and the fullness thereof belongs (Psalm 24:1).

We are not our own since the Lord has bought us at the price of His dear Son Jesus. As such, God entrusts our bodies and everything we have to us. We are stewards or managers of God's grace. We need to be faithful caretakers and recognize that we are workers in God's vineyard, not shareholders or owners.

God's will is that we become faithful stewards of everything God has entrusted us. Since we own nothing, we should use all the material and spiritual resources at our disposal for God's glory. We should be careful not to be unduly concerned of meeting our needs or living comfortable lives at the expense of doing the will of God and glorifying His name. The grace God has released into our lives by blessing us physically, socially, and financially should be utilized to advance His kingdom on earth because that is His will (Mathew 6:10).

Further Reading: *Romans 12:1-2; 2 Corinthians 6:2*
Prayer for the Day: *My God and my Father, help me surrender my every possession to You for Your glory, in Jesus' name I pray, Amen.*

Psalm 102-104

Day 121

1st May

Financial Impropriety Can Hinder the Supernatural

"So if you have not been trustworthy in handling worldly wealth, who will trust you with true riches? And if you have not been trustworthy with someone else's property, who will give you property of your own?" (Luke 16:11-12).

God uses different avenues such as our jobs, businesses, favour and influence to bless us financially. The manner in which we handle money is correlated to the degree of financial and spiritual blessings we receive from God. One of the principles that governs our financial increase is faithfulness. Scriptures teach that those who are faithful with little can also be faithful with much. The opposite is also true. Similarly, those who are untrustworthy with the property of other men will be unfaithful with their own and thus disqualify themselves from receiving blessings.

The Bible teaches that the way we handle money determines our ability to receive true riches, which include spiritual gifts, the anointing, our spiritual calling and the grace of God. We cannot attach any monetary value to these things because they come from God. He only gives them to those He chooses and we cannot purchase them because they are priceless. Gehazi was Elisha's servant and in keeping with Old Testament tradition, he was meant to receive Elisha's mantle as a servant of God (2 Kings 5:19-27). However, his love of money aborted his destiny and he ended up with leprosy. His experience should serve as a warning to us to be faithful with what is entrusted to us.

Further Reading: Luke 6:38; 1 Timothy 6:6; Ecclesiastes 11:1
Prayer for the Day: Oh God, grant me the grace to be faithful with the financial resources You have endowed me with, for Your Name's sake, Amen.

Day 122 — 2 Samuel 5:1-10; 1 Chronicles 11-12

2nd May

We Bear Lasting Fruit by Abiding in Christ

"You did not choose me, but I chose you and appointed you to go and bear fruit - fruit that will last. Then the Father will give you whatever you ask in my name" (John 15:16).

Farmers rejoice when their crops bear fruit. They spend much time and money to ensure that their crops have a conducive environment to bear fruit. God compares Himself to a gardener (John 15:1). He has done everything necessary for believers to bear fruit and advance His kingdom. He prunes our lives by removing everything that could hinder us from being optimally fruitful. He also supplies us with grace, power and anointing to propel us to our destinies.

A branch only bears fruit when it remains connected to the vine; we cannot bear spiritual fruit if we are disconnected from Christ. Our readiness and commitment to abide in Him determines our fruitfulness and the longevity of the fruit. Prayer is paramount in our lives since God uses this avenue to meet our needs. He is delighted to answer our requests, pleas and intercession as we abide in Him and bear fruit in His kingdom.

Some things we do as part of bearing fruit include serving God and setting a good example to others in speech, conduct, character, life and purity. When unbelievers look at us, they should see the glory of God by the spiritual fruit we produce (Galatians 5:22-23). Thus, we should strive to abide in Christ that we may bear lasting fruit.

Further Reading: Job 1:21-22; John 15:4-7
Prayer for the Day: Everlasting Father in the Name of Jesus', I ask for the enablement to bear lasting fruit in Your kingdom, for Your Name's sake, Amen.

Psalm 133

Day 123

3rd May

Learn from the Scriptures Every Day

"For everything that was written in the past was written to teach us, so that through endurance and the encouragement of the Scriptures we might have hope" (Romans 15:4).

The word of God is a sure guide to all who desire to walk with God. It contains lessons, examples, warnings, words of encouragement, wisdom and spiritual knowledge that is indispensable in walking fruitfully with God. Scriptures contain lessons that instruct us on walking in holiness.

In His wisdom, God chose the nation of Israel to reveal to the world His redemptive purpose and plan for the world. The Old Testament foreshadows the new and captures the history of Israel from their time in bondage in Egypt, their deliverance and journey to the Promised Land. It also documents their settlement in Canaan, their apostasy and exile in Babylon. The overriding theme of the word of God is His love for humanity and His desire to redeem man from the grip of sin and destruction.

The records provide us with information from which we learn and are able to develop endurance and be encouraged in our faith and hope in God. Hope works alongside faith to propel us to our divine destinies. This helps us find great pleasure in reading, studying and meditating on the word of God (Joshua 1:8).

Further Reading: 2 Timothy 3:16-17; 1 Corinthians 10:1-11
Prayer for the Day: Oh God I pray that my heart will be ready to learn from Your word daily, in Jesus' name, Amen.

Day 124 — Psalm 106-107

4th May

Be Generous Towards God's Work

"Now, our God, we give you thanks, and praise your glorious name. But who am I, and who are my people, that we should be able to give as generously as this? Everything comes from you, and we have given you only what comes from your hand" **(1 Chronicles 29:13-14).**

God owns everything and can do all things without involving man. However, since He is relational and loving, He has given man the awesome responsibility of exercising dominion over the earth (Psalm 115:16).

The kingdom of God advances through skills and financial resources. Usually, God partners with willing believers to meet the needs of His kingdom. He gives them ability to make wealth and the grace to share what they have for the sake of the kingdom. David understood the benefits of collaborating with God's people through giving. When he led the people in contributing resources for the building of the temple in Israel, he acknowledged that they were generous because they understood that what they had came from God.

To advance His interests on earth, God is looking for faithful givers. As such, we should respond to Him by giving generously every time he avails an opportunity. Generous people receive more from God. Understanding that we are products of God's grace that avails all things to us helps us respond generously to the needs in His kingdom.

Further Reading: *Job 41:11; 1 Corinthians 4:7; Psalm 50:7-13*
Prayer for the Day: *My God and my Father, I pray for enablement to overflow with generosity at all times, in Jesus' name, Amen.*

2 Samuel 5:11-25; 6:1-23; 1 Chronicles 13-16

5th May

Cultivate Intimacy with the Spirit of God

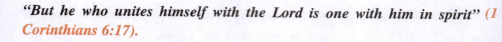

"But he who unites himself with the Lord is one with him in spirit" (1 Corinthians 6:17).

The church is the bride of Christ. Human beings long for each other when in love and likewise, Christ jealously longs for His people through His Spirit whom He sent to the earth as a helper when He ascended to heaven (James 4:4-5). The Lord desires singular devotion from His people the same way a Christian spouse is entitled to exclusive affection of a spouse.

The will of God for the church is intimacy. Every saint should have a strong, loving relationship with God that is maintained by regular fellowship, prayer and walking in holiness. The Holy Spirit is omnipresent and we should relate closely with Him. The early church knew the value of cultivating intimacy with the Spirit of God. This led them to spent hours in earnest prayer, eschew evil and desire God more than fame, wealth or a good name. Consequently, the Spirit of God regularly gave them guidance on how they could attain their destinies by walking in their specific callings (Acts 13:2).

Communing with the Holy Spirit is critical because He knows every detail of our lives. He is therefore the best Person to go to for comfort, direction and guidance. He is our helper and willingly reveals the things of God to us, enabling us to embrace them. Without His help, we cannot attain the fullness of the destinies God ordained for us.

Further Reading: *Esther 2:3-8; John 14:16*
Prayer for the Day: *Oh God, help me become intimate with You through Your Holy Spirit, in Jesus' name, Amen.*

Psalm 1-2, 15, 22-24, 47, 68

6th May

Walk in Purity to Preserve Your Destiny

"No one is greater in this house than I am. My master has withheld nothing from me except you, because you are his wife. How then could I do such a wicked thing and sin against God?" And though she spoke to Joseph day after day, he refused to go to bed with her or even be with her" (Genesis 39:9-10).

The destinies of many people have been compromised and aborted by impurity. Someone is considered impure if they have physical or moral blemish. Since God is holy and pure, He expects His people to emulate His character and stay away from all forms of impurity. His eyes are too pure to look on evil (Habakkuk 1:3). Since we all have divine destinies to attain, we should always strive to walk in purity. Our destinies are too important to be aborted by indulging in impurity.

Joseph stood out from his contemporaries because of walking in moral, spiritual and physical purity. Even though he was tempted severally to give up his high ideals, he stood steadfast because he feared God and believed in the seed of greatness God had deposited in him. He refused to compromise his faith in God by turning down the temptation to engage in fleeting sexual pleasure with Potiphar's wife. He also refused to be bitter when his brothers sold him as a slave to Ishmaelite traders. We too can secure our destinies by walking in purity.

Further Reading: Matthew 5:8; Psalm 18:26; 24:4
Prayer for the Day: My God in Jesus' name, help me walk in purity in every aspect of my life. Amen.

Psalm 89, 96, 100, 101, 105, 132

7th May

Strive to Become a Winning Believer

"This is love for God: to obey his commands. And his commands are not burdensome, for everyone born of God overcomes the world. This is the victory that has overcome the world, even our faith" (1 John 5:3-4).

God's desire is for His children to obey Him. His commands are profitable as they lead to blessings in those who willingly obey Him. Once we are born again, we receive inner strength to resist and overcome all the temptations and pleasures of the world.

Some believers are weak and thus keep losing spiritual battles. They succumb to some temptations and are unable to walk in dominion over the world even though they believe and serve the almighty God. This though, should not be the case for our walk with God is meant to progress from victory to victory. The worldly systems that negate faith in God should have no power over saints because they follow in the footsteps of Christ who triumphed over sin and the devil on the cross.

For our faith to overcome the world, it should be healthy and fruitful. If we feed on the word of God and apply Biblical doctrine, sin cannot have dominion over us. Although this is the case, the faith of some believers does not bear fruit because it is not accompanied by appropriate actions. The Scriptures teach that faith without actions is dead (James 2:17).

Further Reading: Job 1:1; Hebrews 12:2-4
Prayer for the Day: Dear Lord Jesus Christ, I pray that You may empower me to have faith that is accompanied by actions. Amen.

Day 128 — 2 Samuel 7; 1 Chronicles 17

8th May

Take Caution against the Enemy

"While people are saying, "Peace and safety," destruction will come on them suddenly, as labor pains on a pregnant woman, and they will not escape" (1 Thessalonians 5:3).

God has good plans for us to live an abundant life but the enemy intends to steal, kill and destroy. The devil uses sinister schemes and deception to direct God's people away from the path God has ordained. When the enemy fails to get hold of us in the present, he goes a few steps ahead of us and lays a trap. This is why we must always be alert and vigilant lest we fall into his trap (1 Peter 5:8).

When Jesus prayed and fasted at the beginning of His ministry, He was tempted but triumphed. When the enemy saw that He stood firm, he left and waited to strike at an opportune time (Luke 4:13). The enemy has not changed his tactics; when we resist and overcome him, he lies in wait to strike when we are weak and tired.

As we continue pursuing our destinies, we should have the wisdom to wage warfare against the plans of the devil. Destruction often comes upon people suddenly when they think that everything is secure and peaceful. We should therefore not be deceived by momentary peace because the kingdom of darkness can suddenly interfere with it.

Further Reading: 2 Timothy 4:7-8; Colossians 4:17, John 4:34, John 17: 4, Acts 13:25, Acts 13:36
Prayer for the Day: Father in the name of Jesus, I pray for the grace to fight a good fight and finish my assignment that I may receive my reward. Amen.

Psalm 25, 29, 33, 36, 39

Day 129

9th May

Prepare a Highway for Your Destiny

"Your people will rebuild the ancient ruins and will raise up the age-old foundations; you will be called Repairer of Broken Walls, Restorer of Streets with Dwellings" (Isaiah 58:12).

Although the attainment of our divine destinies depends on God, we have a role to play. On our own, we cannot and without our partnership, God will not. This thus needs that we understand and painstakingly apply the principles of the word of God on how to fulfill our destinies.

Prayer and fasting is one of the God-ordained means of priming us to move towards our destinies. They are acts of obedience and express our reliance on God for help to progress towards our destinies. It is however noteworthy that no matter how intensively we pray for our destinies in a certain season, God will not do some things instantaneously. Some aspects of our destinies require our growth in godly character as God moves to bring together the people, resources and spiritual gifts we need to walk in the fullness of His plan for us.

Biblical examples show that it is possible for God's people to fast for three, seven, twenty one or fourty days. Abstaining from food for spiritual purposes is a demonstration of our faith in God and dependence on Him. As we engage in these spiritual activities, we need to pray for both short-term and long-term issues. Praying for the future is preparing a highway to walk on as we move to our destinies.

Further Reading: Isaiah 40:3; Proverbs 15:19; Numbers 21:22
Prayer for the Day: Father, I ask for the grace and wisdom to build a spiritual highway for my destiny, in Jesus' name I pray, Amen.

Day 130 | 2 Samuel 8-9; 1 Chronicles 18

10th May

The Enemy Sows Tares While Men Sleep

Jesus told them another parable: "The kingdom of heaven is like a man who sowed good seed in his field. But while everyone was sleeping, his enemy came and sowed weeds among the wheat, and went away" (Matthew 13:24-25).

Human beings are spiritual entities. By virtue of our spiritual nature, we can interact with God and the angels. The devil and his demons are capable of interfering if given a chance. We should therefore be careful how we live because the enemy seeks to find loopholes through which he can sabotage, attack, destroy or even kill us.

Scripture teaches that the evil one capitalizes on the spiritual slumber of God's people to sow negativity. As believers, we must be watchful and alert so that the devil does not sow tares of wickedness in our lives. The enemy strikes when a person is asleep, weak and defenseless. Thus, we must make every effort to remain continually alert spiritually and sensitive to the Spirit of God who warns us of any impending danger.

Many believers let down their guard when times are good or they prosper. To avoid having tares planted in our lives and destinies, we need to be watchful and prayerful in spite of the successes and peace we enjoy. Waging spiritual warfare can help us abort the plans of the enemy before they take shape.

Further Reading: 1 Peter 5:8-10; Proverbs 14:12
Prayer for the Day: Father, I pray that I will not slumber spiritually so that the enemy does not sow tares in my life. In Jesus' name I pray, Amen.

Genesis 36, 37, 38; Matthew 21:1-22

11th May

Pray Continually

"pray continually" (1 Thessalonians 5:17).

Prayer is the oxygen that sustains believers and keeps them vibrant, without which we are weak, helpless and defenseless. This dictates that we make every effort to abide by the word of God which teaches that we pray without ceasing. Many people make the mistake of viewing prayer as an opportunity to ask God for what they lack. Their prayer times are like shopping sprees. They approach God with long lists of their needs without the interest of first cultivating an intimate relationship with Him. Such people end up discouraged and disappointed when God does not grant their requests.

The primary purpose of prayer is maintaining a relationship with God. The first phrase in the Lord's Prayer is, "Our Father in heaven…" (Matthew 6:9). Scriptures teach that God knows our needs before we ask (Matthew 6:8). They also teach that He is willing and able to meet all our needs according to His riches in glory in Christ Jesus (Philippians 4:19).

This knowledge is critical for believers so that they can be able to make meaningful and impactful prayers. We are encouraged to pray more when we receive answers to the prayers we have already made. We should also strive to know not just how to pray, but to do so in a manner that will attract answers. The will of God is that we should pray at all times without fail.

Further Reading: Luke 18:1-7; Acts 2:42-46; 1 Timothy 2:1-4
Prayer for the Day: *My Father and my God, today I pray that You may fill me with the spirit of prayer and intercession that I may be able to pray without ceasing, in Jesus' name, Amen.*

2 Sam 10; 1 Chronicles 19; Psalm 20

12th May

Do Not Give the Enemy a Foothold

"In your anger do not sin": Do not let the sun go down while you are still angry, and do not give the devil a foothold" (Ephesians 4:26-27).

Anger has destroyed the lives and destinies of many people. Believers should know that while anger is a legitimate and natural emotion that is experienced when they are disappointed, offended or go through loss, it can be abused by the evil one, and can lead to ruined destinies. It can degenerate into sins that include murder, suicide and cursing.

Some people come from families predisposed to anger. Moses was a descendant of Levi. Alongside his brother Simeon, Levi fell into a murderous rage that resulted in destruction when their sister Dinah was defiled in Shechem. Later when God called him to deliver Israel from the land of bondage, he sinned against God in a fit of rage by hitting a rock instead of speaking to it to discharge water for the people to drink (Numbers 20:7-12). This displeased God disqualifying him from entering the Promised Land.

Like Moses, many saints are denied the chance to attain their destinies by the things they did when they were angry. Scripture teaches that we can express anger. We are hitherto warned that we should not allow Satan to take advantage of our expression of it. We need to uproot the spirit of anger from our lives and have repentant hearts so that it does not keep us from fulfilling our destinies.

Further Reading: Revelation 12:10; John 10:10
Prayer for the Day: Today, in the Name of Jesus Christ, I renounce the spirit of anger, which may give the enemy an opportunity to gain a foothold in my life. Amen.

Psalm 65-67, 69-70

Day 133

13th May

Set Your Priorities Right

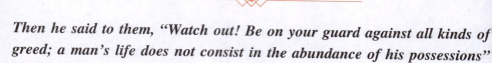

Then he said to them, "Watch out! Be on your guard against all kinds of greed; a man's life does not consist in the abundance of his possessions" (Luke 12:15).

Life is about priorities. Many people make the wrong assumptions that life is about accumulating as much money as one can. They ignore the truth that only God can truly satisfy. The world is full of unfulfilled, suicidal, hopeless and lost wealthy people. This happens because they focus greatly on the things that matter least, instead of eternal matters.

Setting our priorities right requires discipline, sacrifice and commitment because we only have twenty-four hours in a day. We eat, drink, travel, work and rest during those hours. A day is too short to finish doing everything and it is too much to be used in doing nothing. Therefore, we must govern the expenditure of our time.

Given the brevity of life and the many things that daily crave for our attention, we should not make the mistake of misplacing our priorities. This is expensive and doing so costs many people their destinies as they run for other things at the expense of their souls. A wise priority is to reach God who is our creator, redeemer, helper, sustainer and strength. We need to daily put Him at the driver's seat of our lives. With Him in charge, our lives are safe both in time and through eternity.

Further Reading: Matthew 6:33; Mark 8:36
Prayer for the Day: Father, today I pray that You may help me set my priorities right through the help of the Holy Spirit. Amen.

Day 134 | 2 Samuel 11-12; 1 Chronicles 20

14th May

Walk in Obedience to Fulfill Your Destiny

"If you fully obey the LORD your God and carefully follow all his commands I give you today, the LORD your God will set you high above all the nations on earth. All these blessings will come upon you and accompany you if you obey the LORD your God" *(Deuteronomy 28:1-2).*

God in His sovereignty delights in the obedience of His people. For this reason, He has tied man's ability to receive and maintain His blessings to obedience. Throughout Scriptures, the Lord demonstrates the superiority of obedience. He teaches that it is wise, profitable and worthwhile to obey His commands that are not after all burdensome (1 John 5:3). We move closer to our destinies as we obey God's voice. As wise children, we should have a strong desire to exhaust everything God has put in store for us through wholehearted obedience. God has set the boundaries He desires us to move to (see Exodus 23:30-31) and we advance towards them by obeying His commands.

Disobeying God is unwise and selfish. Since our destinies are intertwined with those of others, if we delay in obeying Him we delay our blessings and those of other people with whom our destinies are connected. We should be wise enough to walk in obedience for us to be a blessing to others. God desires to continue building, increasing and perfecting us as He accomplishes the good work He begun in each one of us (Philippians 1:6). When we obey Him, we experience growth and progress.

Further Reading: *Isaiah 1:18-19; Matthew 25:21*
Prayer for the Day: *Today in the Mighty Name of Jesus Christ, I ask for a willing and obedient heart, so that I may enjoy the blessings that follow this promise. In Jesus' name I pray, Amen.*

Psalm 32, 51, 86, 122

Day 135

15th May

Obey God Fully So that You Can Progress

The LORD had said to Abram, "Leave your country, your people and your father's household and go to the land I will show you…" So Abram left, as the LORD had told him; and Lot went with him. Abram was seventy-five years old when he set out from Haran" (Genesis 12:1,4).

Our destinies can be compared to a journey. To arrive at our desired destinations, we need to stay on course so that we can advance progressively, and enjoy the blessing of attaining the desires of our hearts. Our father of faith Abraham set a good example of obedience, when God called him to leave his country, his people and his father's household to go to a land He would show him. Naturally, the ties that bind people to their families are strong. It was therefore not easy for Abraham to leave his family and country for a land he had never been to before. It took personal surrender and a high degree of obedience for Abraham to do what God commanded him.

Abraham passed God's test because he fully trusted Him. His prompt obedience demonstrated his great faith in God's promise. Abraham did not procrastinate God's agenda for his life although he had to make the tough decision of leaving his ancestral land on short notice. Many believers fail to make progress in life because they are still in the process of deciding. They do not necessarily say no to God's command, but they do not take any action or make an effort to heed the command.

Further Reading: Exodus 34:11; Deuteronomy 6:24; Joshua 1:7

Prayer for the Day: My God in the Name of Jesus Christ, today I pray that You may grant me the grace to promptly obey You, in Jesus' name, Amen.

Day 136 | 2 Samuel 13-15

16th May

Allow God to Build Your Life

"For we are God's fellow workers; you are God's field, God's building" (1 Corinthians 3:9).

The Bible compares us to different things and in the quoted verse refers us as "God's building" among other things. This indicates that God is a builder. The progress of the building work God desires to do in our lives depends on how willing we are to cooperate with Him. He requires us to yield to making as He fashions us into His dwelling place.

In the natural realm, the completion of a house depends on the ability of its owner to pay the whole cost of building. In addition to that, one needs to avail materials to builders and pay workers. As God's building, we have to do the same thing. We need to be available and ready to pay the cost of being made into a spiritual dwelling. This includes leaving behind sinful lifestyles and desires and walking closely with God. It requires cultivating a close fellowship with God where he is the master planner. We also need to offer acceptable sacrifice for this building work to progress to completion. If we faithfully comply, God is faithful and will no doubt produce a finished product of us.

God is interested in our ability to host His presence in our lives. When the buildings of our hearts are complete and furnished, we shall carry divinity in us. When He is fully formed in us, signs, miracles and wonders will accompany us wherever we go proclaiming His Word.

Further Reading: *1 Corinthians 3:10-15; Philippians 1:6*
Prayer for the Day: *Dear Lord, I pray that You may build my life in Your wisdom and power, in Jesus' name, Amen.*

Psalm 3-4, 12-13, 28, 55

Day 137

17th May

The Lord Gives Us Power to Make Wealth

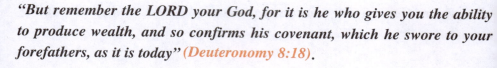

"But remember the LORD your God, for it is he who gives you the ability to produce wealth, and so confirms his covenant, which he swore to your forefathers, as it is today" **(Deuteronomy 8:18)**.

Many people try to build their lives and grow wealth through unscrupulous means. Some of them seek the help of the powers of darkness only for this wealth to destroy their lives. Since God knows that we need material resources to walk in the fullness of the destinies He designed us for, He generously gives us the power to make wealth. This is an integral part of the covenant He made with the patriarchs, which was meant to find its full expression in the church.

Wealth is spiritual. That is why Jesus was tempted by Satan to worship him so that He could be given the glory of the kingdoms of the world (Luke 4:5-8). True wealth is attached to worship. For this reason, we need to learn how we can use our wealth to worship the Lord as we express our gratitude to Him and He will open more doors for us. Our wealth should glorify God.

One lesson that is repeated throughout the Bible is that we must never let wealth master our hearts. Solomon states that if we focus our eyes on it, it will sprout wings and fly away from us (Proverbs 23:5). We need to be careful not to pursue wealth to the peril of our souls. True prosperous people are rich towards God and are materially well endowed because attaining destiny requires financial resources as well.

Further Reading: Genesis 26:10-12; Genesis 12:1-3
Prayer for the Day: Today I have learnt that God grants us wealth so that we may be able to fulfill our God ordained destinies. My God and my Father, I pray for the grace and wisdom to make wealth. Amen.

Day 138 — 2 Samuel 16-18

18th May

Access to the Best in the Land by Obeying God

"If you are willing and obedient, you will eat the best from the land; but if you resist and rebel, you will be devoured by the sword." For the mouth of the LORD has spoken" (Isaiah 1:19-20).

When God created man, He placed him in the Garden of Eden characterised by abundance, security, stability, holiness and fellowship. He charged man to extend that environment to the whole earth by being fruitful and subduing the earth (Genesis 1:28). The condition God set for man's enjoyment of these blessings was obeying His word.

Throughout the word of God, obedience stands out as a key theme for God's people in all generations. Those who obey are blessed and increased while those who rebel and disobey face judgement and punishment. God promises the willing and obedient the best of the land. The best of what the land can give is reserved for the righteous for their enjoyment. The key is willingness and obedience for God's economy knows no lack, recession or inflation.

Obeying God sends a strong message in the spiritual realm. When we obey Him, our inheritance in the spiritual realm is secured, with a guarantee of a manifestation in the physical. God has released great grace for the church to enjoy abundance in all things so that the saints can partner with Him in advancing His kingdom to the uttermost parts of the earth.

Further Reading: Deuteronomy 28:1-14; Isaiah 3:10
Prayer for the Day: My God and my Father, I pray that I will eat the good of the land as I obey Your word in Jesus' name, Amen.

Psalm 26, 40, 58, 61-62, 64

Day 139

19th May

Become One with Christ

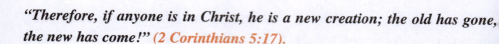

"Therefore, if anyone is in Christ, he is a new creation; the old has gone, the new has come!" (2 Corinthians 5:17).

One of the possibilities we have through Christ's redemptive work is that we can partake the divine nature through God's great and glorious promises (2 Peter 1:4). We can become one with Christ and live in the same way Jesus lived on earth. United thus with Christ, we will readily walk in signs, miracles and wonders as divine power accompanies us wherever we go and in everything we do. Once His fullness dwells in us, we are empowered to proclaim the gospel to the ends of the earth and have His kingdom established.

To become one with Christ, there are principles that need to be followed. The first step is repenting and confessing Jesus as Lord and Saviour. Secondly, we need to walk in line with the word of God, allowing it to fully transform us into His glory, and to attain the stature of our Lord Jesus Christ.

The ultimate aim of God in saving us is that we might become one with Him. This unity begins when we are redeemed and continues as we yield to the Holy Spirit, to a point when we shall share in the glory of our Saviour Jesus Christ.

Further Reading: John 17:20-21; John 10:30
Prayer for the Day: Oh God, help me to be truly one with Christ in my daily walk with Him, in Jesus' name, Amen.

Day 140 | 2 Samuel 19-21

20th May

Appreciate the Gift of Spiritual Hunger

"Blessed are those who hunger and thirst for righteousness, for they will be filled" (Matthew 5:6).

Deprivation of food and pure drinking water causes desperation to many people. Famine has claimed the lives of many as they were unable to receive adequate nutrition to live healthy lives. The same is true of our spiritual lives. Many people are in a spiritual wilderness where they are likely to get destroyed if they do not receive divine help. In the kingdom of God, we only receive what we hunger and thirst for. Jesus taught that those who long for the spiritual things are to be envied because of the blessing of God that rests upon them. As we seek God, He responds to us in proportion to our spiritual appetites. It is therefore critical we learn how we can maintain a healthy appetite for spiritual things.

In His wisdom and grace, God fills the hungry with good things as He honours their hunger and thirst for Him. An indicator of being safely on the road to one's destiny is having an appetite. Lack of spiritual appetite is an indicator of spiritual ill-health. Those who desire God passionately receive spiritual rewards that have tangible results. The word of God commands us to crave for the pure milk of the word of God, which can make us grow in Christ (1 Peter 2:2). Since growth is progressive, we should endeavour to maintain our appetite for God as He moves us closer to our destinies each day.

Further Reading: *Amos 8:11; Luke 1:53; 1 Peter 2:2-3*
Prayer for the Day: *Dear Lord, I pray for hunger and thirst for righteousness in my daily walk with You, in Jesus name, Amen.*

Psalm 5, 38, 41-42

Day 141

21st May

Do Not Be Deceived by Worldly Success

"You say, 'I am rich; I have acquired wealth and do not need a thing.' But you do not realize that you are wretched, pitiful, poor, blind and naked. I counsel you to buy from me gold refined in the fire, so you can become rich; and white clothes to wear, so you can cover your shameful nakedness; and salve to put on your eyes, so you can see" (Revelation 3:17-18).

God's plan to prosper man is beyond question. However, many people including some believers, are deceived by worldly success which lead them to losing touch with spiritual realities. The anchor Scripture documents the state in which the Laodicean church was. Their material success led the saints into feeling self-sufficient and in need of nothing. However, the Lord described them as wretched, pitiful, poor, blind and naked. Their spiritual health was in a sorry state and they could not effectively represent the Lord who called them from the world.

Like the saints in Laodicea, many believers today are in spiritual misery because their devotion to God was stolen by worldly wealth. Wealth can deceive us into thinking that we are doing well when we are lost in sin. To be safe, we need to increase our reliance on God as He blesses us. Material prosperity is temporal and finances are only a small segment of the great destiny God has ordained for us.

Further Reading: Matthew 5:3-4; 1 Timothy 6:6-10
Prayer for the Day: My God and my Father, help me have a right perspective of material and spiritual wealth as I trust You to prosper in both. Amen.

Day 142 — 2 Samuel 22-23; Psalm 57

22nd May

Glorify God and You Will be Satisfied

"Because your love is better than life, my lips will glorify you. I will praise you as long as I live, and in your name I will lift up my hands. My soul will be satisfied as with the richest of foods; with singing lips my mouth will praise you" (Psalm 63:3-5).

The love of God is immeasurably great. It made Him give His only begotten Son to redeem us from sin and destruction. He lavishes us with all good things out of love and desires that we spread it to others for His glory.

The Psalmist understood this truth and was committed to ascribing all glory to God. He often broke out in songs of praise, glorifying God for who He is and for His mighty works. Consequently, his soul was continually satisfied with good things. Those blessings encouraged him to extol God the more.

God redeemed us in order to glorify Himself through us. When we serve the purpose for which He created us, He gives divine rest and fulfillment which gives great satisfaction. We are work in progress and should be aware that God desires to accomplish great work in and through us. We therefore need to seek more of the glory of God so that we can increase and become like Christ. We cannot afford to rest until we manifest the fullness of God's glory to our generation.

Further Reading: 2 Corinthians 3:18; Philippians 3:7-10; Colossians 3:17, Psalm 76: 21(a)

Prayer for the Day: My God, help me glorify You as I manifest the fullness of Your glory while serving my purpose in my generation, in Jesus' name, Amen.

Psalm 95, 97-99

23rd May

Guard against Bitterness to Attain Your Destiny

"See to it that no one misses the grace of God and that no bitter root grows up to cause trouble and defile many" **(Hebrews 12:15).**

Many species of marine-life are destroyed or killed by plastic pollutants thrown into water bodies. After consuming them, the toxic substances get into their systems causing dysfunctions that bring death. The same is true of the destinies of many people; they have been corrupted, aborted or killed by spiritual pollutants, which entered their lives with or without their knowledge.

One of the greatest enemies of destiny is bitterness. It grows a bitter root that makes the heart of the person who harbours it uninhabitable to the grace of God. Bitterness also dries up the anointing of the Holy Spirit upon a person, making it impossible for them to attain their destiny.

Bitterness corrupts the heart, soul and flesh of the one who harbours it. It can also make one fight unnecessary battles out of fear and insecurity. A good example is the case of King Saul who engaged in a bitter war between Israel and the Philistines. To sustain it, he recruited into the army any brave or mighty man he came across (1 Samuel 14:52). Many were maimed and lost their lives in the process.

Bitterness acts as an avenue of demonic oppression. Bitter people have relationship problems and are prone to depression. Bitterness works closely with the spirit of unforgiveness, anger, regret, suicide and eventually leads to eternal destruction.

Further Reading: Deuteronomy 29:18; Matthew 18:21-35
Prayer for the Day: I renounce every form of bitterness in my heart in Jesus' name, Amen.

2 Samuel 24; 1 Chronicles 21-22; Psalm 30

24th May

Be Careful When Making Decisions

"This day I call heaven and earth as witnesses against you that I have set before you life and death, blessings and curses. Now choose life, so that you and your children may live" **(Deuteronomy 30:19).**

Bad decisions play a key role in destroying life. Divine wisdom is quite important as far as making good decisions is concerned. Our lives are a sum total of the decisions we make daily. Even small decisions have great impact in our lives; other major and miscalculated decisions may have dire long-term consequences that may cause the suffering of many. Those who make wrong decisions – especially significant ones – hurt not only themselves but also those around them. The nation of Israel suffered greatly when King David made the wrong decision to conduct a census against the will of God (see 1 Chronicles 21:1). Consequently, the land was afflicted by a plague that claimed the lives of seventy thousand men (1 Chronicles 21:14).

As we make decisions, we need to ask God for guidance so that we do not take the wrong steps. We also need to consider the pros and cons of the choices we make bearing in mind the effects on us and others. To do this successfully, we need divine insight and reliance on the word of God which is meant to light up our path and be the lamp of our feet until we attain our destinies (Psalm 119:105).

Further Reading: *Joshua 24:15; Proverbs 3:31; 8:10*
Prayer for the Day: *Father, I ask You to always help me be in line with Your will in my decision making on issues concerning my life, Amen.*

Psalm 108-110

Day 145

25th May

Train Yourself to Wait Patiently on the Lord

"I waited patiently for the LORD; he turned to me and heard my cry" (Psalm 40:1).

We live at a time when almost everything has become instant. Access to meals, drinks, critical documents and many government services have been fast-tracked because of the rapid growth of technology. This phenomenon can have potentially harmful consequences if we approach God with the mentality that He should do what we pray instantly. He is too loving to answer every whim because many of the desires of the unregenerate man contravene His purposes.

God's perspective of time is different from ours (2 Peter 3:8). Since He is sovereign, He demands that we conform to the way He views time. Destinies of many well-meaning people have been destroyed by inability to exercise patience when God required them to do so. The only sin that has made many people casualties of destiny is inability to wait patiently on God. Saul sinned against God when he offered a sacrifice instead of waiting for Samuel the priest to dispense his priestly duty (1 Samuel 13:8-13). Consequently, he was rejected from becoming king in Israel even though God would have wanted him to be the shepherd of His people.

God decides how long we should wait before He fulfills the promises He has made. Since patience is a fruit of the Spirit (Galatians 5:22-23), we should desire to bear it as we march towards the peak of our destinies.

Further Reading: Proverbs 14:29; James 5:7; Ephesians 4:2
Prayer for the Day: Patience is a fruit of the Holy Spirit that must be exercised by every child of God. Dear Father, grant me the ability to exercise patience that I may hear You, Amen.

Day 146 — 1 Chronicles 23-25

26th May

Emulate Christ's Character

"Take my yoke upon you and learn from me, for I am gentle and humble in heart, and you will find rest for your souls. For my yoke is easy and my burden is light" (Matthew 11:29-30).

We bear the name Christians because we identify ourselves with the teachings and lifestyle of Jesus Christ our Saviour. This term was first used on followers of Christ by Gentiles in Antioch who observed that believers behaved like Christ in everything they did (Acts 11:26).

Christ lived and died to set an example for us. He taught many lessons on His Person, mission and relationship with God. Through His teachings and personal example, He modelled a path for us to follow. Scripture encourages us to take His yoke and learn from Him because He is gentle and humble at heart. He stands out as the best example, the greatest teacher and the most devoted redeemer.

We follow Christ by having faith in Him. As we trust Him and follow His footsteps, we can do what pleases God our creator. Christ walked in the Spirit and pleased God in everything. He set the example of prayer, devotion to the word, obedience and self-sacrificial love. When He was just about to be crucified for our redemption, He prayed for the will of God to be done (Luke 22:42-44). As His followers, we need to learn, internalise and emulate these traits with total dedication.

Further Reading: Romans 13:13-14; 1 Corinthians 11:1; John 13:15
Prayer for the Day: Oh Lord, help me to emulate Your character in my daily walk with You, in Jesus' name, Amen.

Psalm 131, 138-139, 143-145

Day 147

27th May

The Easiest Person to Become is Yourself

Then Saul dressed David in his own tunic. He put a coat of armor on him and a bronze helmet on his head. David fastened on his sword over the tunic and tried walking around, because he was not used to them. "I cannot go in these," he said to Saul, "because I am not used to them." So he took them off (1 Samuel 17:38-39).

God is a designer and He created each of us uniquely. He has a unique path He desires each of us to follow to attain our destinies. The wisest decision we can make as disciples of Christ is to pursue our original purpose with God's help. This is because God has already prepared a path for us to follow until we become what He preordained for us. Sadly, many people do not attain their destinies because they follow a path that is different from what God had in mind. They spend much time and effort trying to become what God never intended ignoring the fact that the easiest person to become is oneself.

David refused to follow that destructive path when the opportunity arose for him to execute Goliath, a Philistine fighter who had taunted and humiliated Israel for many days. Scriptures document that he refused King Saul's military attire in favour of a sling and five stones. Every tree bears after its own kind without struggling. The same is true for us; we can attain the destinies God intended for us if we exercise fidelity to His calling.

Further Reading: Jeremiah 29:11; Joshua 1:8
Prayer for the Day: My God and my Father, today I pray that You may enable me attain the fullness You have in store for me, in Jesus' name, Amen.

Day 148 | 1 Chronicles 26-29; Psalm 127

28th May

Allow God to Send You into the World

"Then I heard the voice of the Lord saying, "Whom shall I send? And who will go for us?" And I said, "Here am I. Send me!" (Isaiah 6:8).

The spirit realm controls everything that happens in the physical. However, they are both governed by principles that were set by God before creation. One such principle is that to operate on the earth, one needs to have a body. This is why Jesus became man His work could only be effectual if He was legally on the earth. The Bible teaches that God is Spirit (John 4:24) which means that He can only operate on earth through human agents. We need to internalize this truth as we continue serving Him by fulfilling the Great Commission.

God's greatest agenda on earth is the salvation of mankind and execution of His Government on earth through man (Genesis 1: 26 -28, Isaiah 9:7, Mathew 6:10, Revelation 5:9-10, Revelation 11:15). It informs everything He does for and through man. When Jesus died and rose again for our justification, He instructed His disciples to propagate the good news to the uttermost ends of the earth and promised that His abiding presence would be with them always (Matthew 28:18-20). Out of His great love, God is looking for people He can send into the world to represent Him. He constantly searches among the sons of men for vessels He can work through to reconcile mankind to Himself. He chooses these vessels as He wishes.

Further Reading: *Matthew 9:35-38; 2 Corinthians 5:20*
Prayer for the Day: *Oh God, today I avail myself to You, that You may send me to transform and impact lives, Amen.*

Psalm 111-118

Day 149

29th May

Bear Fruit Lest You are Judged

So he said to the man who took care of the vineyard, 'For three years now I've been coming to look for fruit on this fig tree and haven't found any. Cut it down! Why should it use up the soil?' "'Sir,' the man replied, 'leave it alone for one more year, and I'll dig around it and fertilize it. If it bears fruit next year, fine! If not, then cut it down'" **(Luke 13:7-9).**

Farmers cultivate land and invest in technology, machinery, inputs and seeds with a view to reaping a harvest. They also exercise patience as they wait for the former and latter rain to water their crop for a good harvest. God has invested His love, grace, power, mercy and patience upon us. In return, He expects us to bear fruit.

We bear fruit as we allow the word of God to work on our hearts and transform us. It equips and empowers us to represent the Lord to a lost and dying world with love, zeal and patience. We do this in partnership with the Holy Spirit who convicts the world of righteousness, sin and judgment (Joh 16:8).

Bearing fruit attract rewards while those who are unfruitful will be cut down and banished to eternal damnation. As long as we have the breath of life, we owe God the duty of producing spiritual fruit so that His kingdom can extend to the uttermost ends of the earth.

Further Reading: *John 15:8, 16; Galatians 5:22-23*
Prayer for the Day: *My God in Jesus' name, help me bear spiritual fruit and escape the judgment that will befall the unfruitful, Amen.*

Day 150 — 1 Kings 1-2; Psalm 37, 71, 94

30th May

Do not be Overconfident

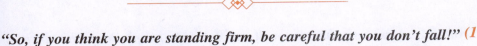

"So, if you think you are standing firm, be careful that you don't fall!" (1 Corinthians 10:12).

The life of a Christian requires focus, diligence and commitment. A believer faces many distractions and opposing forces and cannot therefore depend on his or her strength, intelligence or ability. The enemy is always moving about like a roaring lion looking for someone to devour (1 Peter 5:8). We therefore need to be careful when God blesses and prospers us, lest we succumb to temptations and suffer downfall.

Scriptures repeatedly admonish us to put our confidence in God alone. It is a folly to trust in our own strength because in the face of an onslaught from the kingdom of darkness, it cannot sustain us. When an individual prospers in faith and does exploits in the name of the Lord, there is a risk of attributing it to meticulous planning, effective intercession or a diligent spiritual walk. Everything a believer does is enabled by the grace of God. Man has no power to cause anything to happen; he solely depends on God's power that is availed through the Holy Spirit. Walking in the Spirit enables us to be vigilant against demonic forces that always plot to bring us down with an aim to disgrace the redemptive work of Christ.

Further Reading: Proverbs 16:18; Philippians 2:5-9; Proverbs 3:5-6

Prayer for the Day: Father, I ask You to help me depend on You always, in Jesus' name, Amen.

Psalm 119:1-88

Day 151

31st May

Watch and Pray to Escape Temptations

"Watch and pray so that you will not fall into temptation. The spirit is willing, but the body is weak" (Mark 14:38).

Every day, believers face seductive situations that promise more than they can offer. The devil uses deception and outright lies to lure people to sin against God's revealed will. In His great wisdom, God designed a way through which believers can grow their relationship with Him and overcome all the temptations. Prayer is an indispensable part of a believer's lifestyle. It gives access to divine power by which we overcome temptations and live a life that pleases God.

Our Lord Jesus modeled a life of prayer that all His disciples ought to emulate. He prayed with dedication, zeal and commendable consistency. He instructed them to make prayer an integral part of their lives irrespective of their situations and circumstances. The early church followed His example and God gave them numerous victories in all the battles they faced.

Prayer for divine empowerment to overcome temptations and the power of sin is also demonstrated in the lives of Old Testament saints. Moses, David, Daniel, Joseph and Job were men of prayer. By their constant and unfailing prayers, they demonstrated that they had faith that saw them overcome every challenge and circumstance in their lives. They could not have been as successful and impactful had they not spent quality time communing with God.

Further Reading: Luke 18:1-8; Luke 11:1; Zechariah 12:10
Prayer for the Day: Oh God, I ask You to anoint me with the spirit of grace whenever I spend time with You, I pray in Jesus' name, Amen.

Day 152 — 1 Kings 3-4; 2 Chronicles 1; Psalm 72

1st June

Watch Out Against Spiritual Poverty

"A little sleep, a little slumber, a little folding of the hands to rest - and poverty will come on you like a bandit and scarcity like an armed man" (Proverbs 24:33-34).

The Lord Jesus used parables to expound valuable spiritual truths. He used natural phenomena to teach about the kingdom of God. He understood that people could easily grasp lessons He taught using natural things they could identify with. Like Jesus, Solomon used many natural examples from which we learn spiritual truths that help us walk with God. Similarly, Job 12:7-10 and Psalm 111:2 instructs us to consider natural phenomena.

Spiritual poverty affects people who have a laidback attitude towards seeking spiritual wealth. As they take a break from spiritual disciplines, walking in holiness or compromise their spiritual integrity, the enemy pounces, stealing their spiritual virtues. This leaves them poor, wretched and pitiful. The devil is a thief and his mission is to steal, kill and destroy (John 10:10). We must stay alert lest he steals from us our highly priced spiritual wealth.

Attaining our divine destiny is a battle. To emerge victorious, we need to be continually alert so that we can maintain the territories we have conquered, and gain entry into new ones that are in His will for us. This requires alertness and commitment to watch over one's soul through prayer, obeying the word, relying on God and pursuing holiness with all our strength.

Further Reading: 1 Peter 5:8-9; Revelation 3:17
Prayer for the Day: My God in the name of Jesus Christ, help me to guard against spiritual slumber that leads to spiritual poverty, in Jesus' name, Amen.

Psalm 119:89-176

2nd June

Discover and Guard the Secret of Your Strength

So Delilah said to Samson, "Tell me the secret of your great strength and how you can be tied up and subdued..." Then she said to him, "How can you say, 'I love you,' when you won't confide in me? This is the third time you have made a fool of me and haven't told me the secret of your great strength" (Judges 16:6, 15).

Attaining destiny requires spiritual and physical strength. While we gain and maintain physical strength by taking care of our bodies, we can only gain spiritual strength from our relationship with God. We need to discover and guard the secret of our strength to fulfill God's plan for our lives.

God chose and anointed Samson to begin the deliverance of Israel from the oppression of the Philistines. He set the boundaries within which Samson was to live, for him to succeed in his mission. Samson had no morals and violated God's instructions. He was seduced by Delilah to whom he revealed the secret of his strength which was in his hair, which God had commanded that it should never be shaved. When Delilah got the truth, she betrayed him by revealing this fact to the Philistines who shaved him, leading to the loss of his strength.

The secret of your strength as a believer could be in prayer and fasting, reading and meditating on the word of God, and walking in holiness. When you forsake these things, you jeopardise your spiritual life. The secret of our strength must therefore be guarded so that we escape the downfall the enemy so much desires for us.

Further Reading: Proverbs 4:23; Psalm 46:1

Prayer for the Day: Father in the name of Jesus Christ, help me guard the source of my strength, that I may remain steadfast at all times, in Jesus' name, Amen.

Day 154 — Song of Solomon 1-8

3rd June

Guard against Backsliding

"Therefore a lion from the forest will attack them, a wolf from the desert will ravage them, a leopard will lie in wait near their towns to tear to pieces any who venture out, for their rebellion is great and their backslidings many" (Jeremiah 5:6).

God desires that we consistently walk with Him from the day we confess Jesus as Lord to the day He calls us to be with Him. However, we face opposition from the kingdom of darkness, the flesh and the world, which can slow us down, derail or cause us to abandon our walk of faith. Ancient Israel was not different from us. After God delivered them from slavery by His mighty hand, they often turned away from His ways or forsook Him in favour of idols. To draw them back, the Lord sent prophets or chastised them as a loving father with the hope that they would return.

Scripture documents the hardships God allowed Israel to go through when they forsook Him including attacks by fierce wild animals. This should serve as a warning to us not to backslide or forsake the Lord.

Some causes of backsliding include spiritual and material success, which can distract one's attention from God and focus on worldly things that have no eternal value. Unfortunately, some believers are in a backslidden state. They no longer follow Christ with zeal. They have forsaken their first love, which should never be the case.

Further Reading: Jeremiah 2:13; Revelation 2:4
Prayer for the Day: Oh God, help me guard against every form of backsliding by helping me stand steadfast in the faith, in Jesus' name, Amen.

4th June

The Word of God is a Mirror

"Anyone who listens to the word but does not do what it says is like a man who looks at his face in a mirror and, after looking at himself, goes away and immediately forgets what he looks like" **(James 1:23-24).**

Grooming is an integral part of most people. They use mirrors to ascertain that they look good as they venture out of their homes to their engagements. God's word teaches us to apply the same diligence when taking care of our inner man. We should be certain that he reflects Christ.

James aptly compares the word of God to a mirror. He says that whenever we listen to God's word, we should hold our lives against it to see whether we mirror it. By so doing, we identify areas of our lives that need rectification. To have a fruitful walk with God, we must treasure His word and allow it to teach, correct, rebuke and train us in righteousness (2 Timothy 3:16-17).

The word of God makes us aware of the things we need to pursue. All those who have successfully walked with God attach a high premium to His word. We too can be sure that God will enable us serve His purpose and attain our destinies if we let His word mirror our lives and reveal what is in our hearts. The Holy Spirit will help us respond accordingly.

Further Reading: *Psalm 119:9, 11; Job 23:12*
Prayer for the Day: *My God, help me allow Your word shed light on every area of my life, Amen.*

5th June

Transformation is Progressive

"And we, who with unveiled faces all reflect the Lord's glory, are being transformed into his likeness with ever-increasing glory, which comes from the Lord, who is the Spirit" (2 Corinthians 3:18).

The greatest need of every believer is transformation. Everyone has areas that need to be upgraded to the full stature of Christ. Only after being transformed to the version God desires, can we then attain the fullness of our destinies. The Holy Spirit abides in every believer to enable him or her discern the will of God and do it.

Since we are born sinners and separated from God, our thinking patterns, character and attitudes are naturally skewed away from Him. Thus, when we get born again, we need to submit to the Holy Spirit to teach us to go back to God. As we become more intimate with Him through His Spirit, our countenance increasingly reflects His holy image (Genesis 1: 26-27). Our appetites, speech and disposition resemble Him as we learn from Him. God's desire is for us to partake in His nature. Towards this, He has given us everything we need for life and godliness including access to this transformative power (2 Peter 1:3-4). Through His promises, we are able to walk in the fullness of His purpose and reflect His image in every aspect. Our success in manifesting His glory can encourage other believers to surrender to His transforming grace in order to attain the fullness of His plan for them and hence their destinies.

Further Reading: 1 Corinthians 13:12; Ephesians 4:11-13
Prayer for the Day: Lord, I ask for grace to yield to Your transformative touch, in Jesus' name, Amen.

Proverbs 7-9

6th June

Sinning Deliberately Can Destroy Your Life

"If they have escaped the corruption of the world by knowing our Lord and Savior Jesus Christ and are again entangled in it and overcome, they are worse off at the end than they were at the beginning. It would have been better for them not to have known the way of righteousness, than to have known it and then to turn their backs on the sacred command that was passed on to them" (2 Peter 2:20-21).

The Bible defines sin as transgression of the law (1 John 3:4). It also cautions that anyone who knows the good they ought to do but fails to do it commits sin (James 4:17). Sin has debilitating consequences both in time and eternity, as it leads to separation from the life-giving presence of God. Some people commit sin without intending to do so. However, others plan and scheme on how to violate God's holy word, and deliberately do what He has prohibited in His word. These are sins of commission. Scripture warn such people of judgment and destruction. Those who sin intentionally are compared to a dog that returns to its vomit and to a sow that wallows in the mud after it has been cleaned.

Sinning deliberately indicates an open defiance to God's commands. Scripture cautions that those who know God's holy command, but willfully and consciously break it are worse than those who have never known the way of righteousness. We must eschew deliberate sin because it destroys destinies.

Further Reading: Hebrews 6:4-6; Hebrews 10:26; Luke 11:24-26
Prayer for the Day: Oh God, today I ask You to help me abstain from all deliberate sins, in the name of Jesus, Amen.

7th June

Know and Pursue Your Original Version

Then I said, "Here I am, I have come - it is written about me in the scroll" (Psalm 40:7).

The purposes of God are forever settled in heaven and cannot be changed. Since God is all-knowing, He knows all the plans He has concerning the destinies of each of us. His word says that His plans for us are good and are intended to make us get a great future (Jeremiah 29:11). God can reveal to us what He intended us to do and become if we ask Him. He delights in partnering with His people to accomplish what He designed them to do.

God is a detailed planner and record keeper. He has a book for each of us detailing His plans and purposes for us. In His foreknowledge, He had an original version of each of us. God desires that we discover and pursue it. Our anchor Scripture is a Messianic psalm that documents that God had a book concerning His Son and everything He would do to reconcile sinful mankind to Himself. Since Jesus was fully surrendered to doing the will of God, He walked in line with the will of the Father and accomplished His mission on earth.

As followers of Christ, we need to emulate Him so that we can attain our destinies. We should align ourselves with His will because that is the only way we can walk in the fullness of our destinies.

Further Reading: Hebrews 10:7; Jeremiah 1:5
Prayer for the Day: My God and my Father in the name of Jesus Christ, I ask You to enable me discover and pursue my original blueprint, in Jesus' name, Amen.

Proverbs 13-15

8th June

Yield to the Potter's Touch

"So I went down to the potter's house, and I saw him working at the wheel. But the pot he was shaping from the clay was marred in his hands; so the potter formed it into another pot, shaping it as seemed best to him" (Jeremiah 18:3-4).

The word of God describes the Lord as a potter. He carefully, lovingly and faithfully works through the circumstances of His people to make them useful in His kingdom. The nobler the vessel a potter desires to make, the more time and effort he puts into fashioning his clay. The same is true of God.

The basic raw materials potters use are clay and water. They also need a wheel and a kiln in which to dry and harden the vessels they make. To perfect their work, they take quality time working on clay to ensure that it is of good quality before shaping it into his or her vessel of choice. Similarly, God takes each of His children through a meticulous process of making until they become worthy vessels.

Scripture records Jeremiah's encounter with the Lord in a potter's house. Many are unable to yield themselves to God's hands to be shaped as the pot Jeremiah saw in the potter's hands. In such cases, God shapes them into other vessels. We should be careful to become what God originally intended. The greatest service we can render to God is submitting to Him and allowing Him to make us into vessels He can use to glorify Himself.

Further Reading: Isaiah 45:9; Isaiah 64:8
Prayer for the Day: Oh Lord, today I pray that You may enable me yield to You as You mould me into the vessel You desire, Amen.

9th June

Keep Yourself Pure from Worldly Corruption

"For the grace of God that brings salvation has appeared to all men. It teaches us to say "No" to ungodliness and worldly passions, and to live self-controlled, upright and godly lives in this present age, while we wait for the blessed hope - the glorious appearing of our great God and Savior, Jesus Christ" (Titus 2:11-13).

As we draw closer to the second coming, wickedness and corruption is bound to increase in the world. Bible prophecy indicates that the love of many will grow cold as a result (Matthew 24:12). Satan is the god of this world (2 Corinthians 4:4) and has bound many in sin, addictions, impurity, moral corruption, separating them from God. However, believers have been regenerated and can live godly, holy lives despite the corruption that pervades most of the world. Scriptures command us to keep ourselves pure from the rot in the world. To achieve this, we need to depend on the grace of God and exercise self-control under the leadership of the Holy Spirit.

The best way of denying ungodliness and impurity is to surrender ourselves to the sanctifying work of the Holy Spirit. Sanctification is the process by which believers become holy through believing and obedience of the word of God. The closer we draw to God, the more strength we receive in our inner man to crucify all the desires of the flesh. It helps us abstain from all forms of evil and creates within us a zeal to do the will of God.

Further Reading: **2 Peter 1:3-4; 1 Thessalonians 5:22-23; 1 John 3:3; Ephesians 5:3**
Prayer for the Day: **Father in Jesus' name, help me be pure in spirit, soul and body, that I may be able to accomplish Your will, Amen.**

Proverbs 19-21

10th June

What You See Determines What You Get

"The LORD said to Abram after Lot had parted from him, "Lift up your eyes from where you are and look north and south, east and west. All the land that you see I will give to you and your offspring forever" (Genesis 13:14-15).

We have physical and spiritual eyes. Our ability to perceive in the spiritual realm is critical because it determines what we receive from God. We cannot attain our earthly and eternal destinies if we are spiritually blind because spiritual realities can only be perceived spiritually.

Vision is paramount in possessing the inheritance God has in store for us. When God called Abraham, He intended to bless mankind through him. He expected him to have a clear vision of the great blessings, which included the descendants He would give him. He made it clear that he would possess as much land as his eyes could see. Since we are Abraham's descendants through Christ, having a good vision is necessary in helping us see the destinies and inheritance God has for us. He is ready to bless, increase and help us as long as we can see what He intends to do, and agree with Him.

Poor spiritual vision has cost many their destinies and inheritance because God only walks with us to the extent we are ready to perceive and believe. This is why we need to pray for our inner eyes to be healthy.

Further Reading: Ephesians 1:17-18; Isaiah 33:17; Joel 3:10
Prayer for the Day: Oh Lord, I pray for my inner eyes to clearly perceive God's plan for my life, in Jesus' name, Amen.

Day 162 | Proverbs 22-24

11th June

Fix Your Eyes on God

"Though an army besiege me, my heart will not fear; though war break out against me, even then will I be confident. One thing I ask of the LORD, this is what I seek: that I may dwell in the house of the LORD all the days of my life, to gaze upon the beauty of the LORD and to seek him in his temple" *(Psalm 27:3-4).*

We live in a fallen and corrupt world. As a result, our faith in God can be shaken by the disasters, misfortunes, calamities and the prevalence of sin bound to happen in the end-times. However, God's desire is for us to be overcomers. He has given us the privilege of trusting Him for help and grace to overcome any opposition against us.

The key to living a truly successful life is fixing our eyes on the Lord. When our attention is fully focused on God, none of the storms of life will shake us. Our growth and increase are also guaranteed once our attention is firmly on God. The Psalmist was confident that he could fight and overcome an army singlehandedly as long as the Lord was with Him. He prayed that God would help him to dwell in His house all the days of his life just to gaze upon His beauty. This should be our prayer so that we can overcome the challenges we face.

Further Reading: Hebrews 12:2-3; Proverbs 18:10
Prayer for the Day: *Oh Lord, grant me the ability to dwell in Your house as I gaze upon Your beauty, and seek You in Your temple, Amen.*

1 Kings 5-6; 2 Chronicles 2-3

12th June

See Yourself as God Sees You

"Ah, Sovereign LORD," I said, "I do not know how to speak; I am only a child." But the LORD said to me, "Do not say, 'I am only a child.' You must go to everyone I send you to and say whatever I command you" (Jeremiah 1:6-7).

To enable us serve His purposes and fulfill our destinies, God has deposited in us gifts, talents, potential and abilities. He has given us diverse gifts of His grace (Romans 12:6-8). Even the rebellious have gifts given by God, which they can exploit to touch lives and propagate the kingdom of God (see Psalm 68:18).

When the Lord called Jeremiah to become a prophet to the nations, Jeremiah despised himself. He said that he did not know how to speak since he was only a child. However, God instructed him to boldly proclaim his message to everyone He would send him to. He had to change the way he viewed himself. Saul too saw himself as weak and incapable of fulfilling the assignment of shepherding God's people. He was a descendant of Benjamin which was the least clan in Israel (1 Samuel 9:21).

Like Jeremiah and Saul, many believers today feel weak and incapable of fulfilling their destinies. Some have a low self-esteem. Others have been humiliated, wounded and adversely affected by the challenges they have experienced in life. We can best fulfill our divine assignments if we align ourselves with God's perspective about us.

Further Reading: Psalm 139:14; Exodus 4:10-17
Prayer for the Day: My God and my Father, today I pray that You may enable me see myself as You see me, even as I strive to fulfill my divine assignment, in Jesus' name, Amen.

Day 164 — 1 Kings 7; 2 Chronicles 4

13th June

God Can Bring Victory to Your Level

"But Jael, Heber's wife, picked up a tent peg and a hammer and went quietly to him while he lay fast asleep, exhausted. She drove the peg through his temple into the ground, and he died" (Judges 4:21).

One of the greatest blessings we can receive from God is gaining victory in what He has called us to do. His perfect will is that we be fruitful in our careers, businesses, ministries and in every aspect of our lives. He delights in doing this because He created and redeemed us for dominion. Our success and prosperity glorifies Him and contributes to the advancement of His kingdom.

God brought victory through a weak person whom no one could expect. He delivered Sisera the commander of Jabin's army to Jael, a woman, causing her to drive a peg into his head killing him instantly. There was no way Jael could have fought or overcome an experienced army man other than by divine help. Like Jael, we can trust God to grant us victory notwithstanding how lowly we are. David had a similar experience. To end the reproach that Goliath had caused to Israel, God empowered David to use a sling and a stone to kill him (1 Samuel 17:40).

Irrespective of the opposition we face, God can grant us victory at our levels. We can walk confidently by faith as God faithfully ensures our success when we trust Him.

Further Reading: Isaiah 41:10-11; Hebrews 13:5-6
Prayer for the Day: *Dear Lord, help me exercise faith and trust that You can bring victory to me regardless of my level, in Jesus' name, Amen.*

1 Kings 8; 2 Chronicles 5

14th June

Entrust Your Future to God

After this, the word of the LORD came to Abram in a vision: "Do not be afraid, Abram. I am your shield, your very great reward." But Abram said, "O Sovereign LORD, what can you give me since I remain childless and the one who will inherit my estate is Eliezer of Damascus?" (Genesis 15:1-2).

Many people live in fear because they are not certain of the direction their lives may take. Some have what may appear to be genuine logical reasons for fear such as suffering from terminal illnesses, while others have the fear of the unknown.

Our father of faith Abraham was fearful about his future because he was advanced in age and had no biological child. He feared that Eliezer would be his heir although God had promised to give him a son of his own. However, by His grace and love, God fulfilled His promise and Isaac was born. His birth brought joy and fulfillment to Abraham and his wife Sarah.

Fear has caused many to suffer depression, others feel hopeless because they have no hope for the future. How we live today is influenced by the way we perceive our future. We invest in prayer, walk in righteousness and pursue holiness because we have the conviction that we shall bear fruit. All believers need to replace fear with faith because without faith we cannot please God. Our past failures should not hinder us from straining forward to attain the destinies God preordained for us.

Further Reading: Matthew 6:25-34; James 4:14-16
Prayer for the Day: *Today, I dispel fear in my life and embrace faith in the name of Jesus Christ, Amen.*

15th June

Desire the Manifest Presence of God

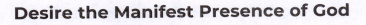

The LORD replied, "My Presence will go with you, and I will give you rest." Then Moses said to him, "If your Presence does not go with us, do not send us up from here" (Exodus 33:14-15).

God is omnipresent, but His power is only manifested in specific places and to specific people. He is the God of the whole universe but His presence only manifests tangibly in the lives of those who fear and please Him. When God created man, He placed him in the Garden of Eden where he was divinely empowered to bear fruit for God's glory. He commanded him to subdue the earth and have dominion over it (Genesis 1:28).

Our anchor verse records Moses' prayer that the presence of God would go with him as he led Israel to the Promised Land. He was not ready to proceed with the journey until the manifest presence of God was with them. When the presence of God goes with you, you can prosper anywhere and in everything. Joseph succeeded in everything he did because God was with him. He granted him favour when he was in Potiphar's house and when he was imprisoned after Potiphar's wife bore false witness against him (Genesis 39:3,21).

The presence of God can shield you from the enemies who hotly pursue you. Saul was afraid of David (1 Samuel 18:12) and pursued him with an aim to destroy him. Despite of this, David flourished in the City because God was with him (2 Samuel 5:9-10).

Further Reading: 1 Kings 8:10-13; Matthew 28:20; Isaiah 7:14
Prayer for the Day: *Oh Lord, may Your presence always go with me and give me rest in my daily walk with You, in Jesus' name, Amen.*

Psalm 134, 146-150

16th June

Be Strong and Courageous

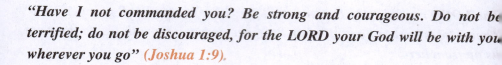

"Have I not commanded you? Be strong and courageous. Do not be terrified; do not be discouraged, for the LORD your God will be with you wherever you go" (Joshua 1:9).

To succeed in life, we need inner strength and courage to confront physical and spiritual enemies. Out of fear or ignorance, many people are weak and timid. They recoil at the sight of battles yet we live in a world that is populated by men and demonic powers determined to deny us breakthroughs to our destinies.

The devil and his demons are at work every day to make sure they steal, kill and destroy our lives. We must not play victim or allow the devil to abort the good plans God has for us. God commanded Joshua to stand firm and be courageous to carry out the assignment that was handed down to him by Moses. To possess the Promised Land that was inhabited by several enemy nations, Israel needed a bold and unwavering leader. Joshua was equal to the task as he had walked intimately with God and learned how to shepherd God's people under the mentorship of Moses.

As New Testament saints, we have to be bold, steadfast and immovable in our faith. God requires us to be strong in the Lord and in the power of His might (Ephesians 6:10-12). We can overcome every enemy and possess our inheritance in Christ when we firmly refuse to fear or be discouraged, but stand firmly on God's word.

Further Reading: *2 Timothy 1:7; Matthew 16:18*
Prayer for the Day: *My God and my Father, may You empower me to be strong and courageous so as I can possess my inheritance, in Jesus' name, Amen.*

Day 168 — 1 Kings 9; 2 Chronicles 8

17th June

Refuse to Give Up Easily

"And he said unto him, What is thy name? And he said, Jacob. And he said, Thy name shall be called no more Jacob, but Israel: for as a prince hast thou power with God and with men, and hast prevailed" *(Genesis 32:27-28 KJV).*

Attaining our destinies can be likened to running a long race. A long-distance runner needs dedication, grit and tenacity. A believer requires endurance to fight spiritual battles, wait on the Lord without faltering and gain the victories that are critical in moving from one level to another.

The word of God describes God as a man of war (Exodus 15:3). Like a wrestler, He engages His people and enemies alike in battle – always with the predictable outcome of winning every battle. God desires to transform our character into the version that walks in the fullness of his power. He wrestled with Jacob through the night and when the latter prevailed, his name was changed to Israel. The change of name was accompanied by a change of fortunes. The name Jacob means "supplanter" or "deceiver" while Israel means "wrestled with God."

To win, Jacob had a militant spirit. He refused to give up. As we walk with God, we need this trait because spiritual success only comes to those who are determined to pursue it without giving up.

Further Reading: Matthew 11:12; 2 Samuel 2:23; 2 Chronicles 15:5-7
Prayer for the Day: My God, I pray that You may empower and help me never to give up in my walk with You, in Jesus' name, Amen.

Proverbs 25-26

Day 169

18th June

Unbelief Can Ruin Your Destiny

"And with whom was he angry for forty years? Was it not with those who sinned, whose bodies fell in the desert? And to whom did God swear that they would never enter his rest if not to those who disobeyed? So we see that they were not able to enter, because of their unbelief" (Hebrews 3:17-19).

The word of God teaches that we cannot please God if we do not walk by faith (Hebrews 11:6). Our good intentions, high hopes and attempts to please God without faith are vain. This is why we should allow Scriptures to instruct us on how to walk by faith in God. Unbelief refers to lack of faith in God. A person who walks in unbelief refuses to believe in God and His word no matter the amount of evidence provided. Unbelief - which can only be called distrust - contradicts God's word and casts aspersions on His name and character.

Our father of faith Abraham set the example of faith we should emulate. He believed God's promise against all odds until he fulfilled His promise of giving him a son (Romans 4:17-20). Unbelief is disastrous and leads to judgment and destruction. The officer at the gate when Elisha prophesied plenty in Samaria refused to believe God's word that He would supply adequate food to the people by the following day. As a result of his unbelief, he died in the stampede as the people scrambled to access food the next day (2 Kings 7:2, 17).

Further Reading: 1 Corinthians 10:1-5; Matthew 21:21; Matthew 14:31
Prayer for the Day: Thou wicked spirit of unbelief, I cast you out of my life, "go" in the name of Jesus Christ, Amen.

19th June

Exercise Authority in Your Mountain of Influence

"Now give me this hill country that the LORD promised me that day. You yourself heard then that the Anakites were there and their cities were large and fortified, but, the LORD helping me, I will drive them out just as he said" (Joshua 14:12).

God created and redeemed man to rule the universe on His behalf. In His benevolence, God has given each of us a gift and provided grace to discover and manifest our potential in different areas.

Scholars have classified the main spheres in which man can have dominion into seven categories. These are widely referred to as the seven mountains of influence: family, business, media, sports, education, religion and governance. Each of us has at least one major area of influence to shine and prosper. Some people have divine grace and can make outstanding impact in more than one mountain of influence. No matter the number of mountains God has called us to thrive in, we can succeed with divine empowerment.

All the people who attained greatness in Scriptures and history were focused and determined to do what God called them for. World class scholars, athletes, politicians, artists, ministers of the gospel and teachers believed God's plan for their lives and pursued them relentlessly. They refused to quit and relied on His power to impact lives and transform destinies.

Further Reading: Luke 19:13; 1 Corinthians 4:1; Matthew 6:10
Prayer for the Day: Oh God help me exercise authority in the areas You have called and graced me in, I pray this in Jesus' name, Amen.

Ecclesiastes 1-6

20th June

Enthrone God in Your Life

"For the LORD is our judge, the LORD is our lawgiver, the LORD is our king; it is he who will save us" (Isaiah 33:22).

The Lord our God is a great king. He is enthroned in heaven as King forever (Psalm 29:10). His rulership is absolute and His sovereignty unquestionable. The above Scripture highlights the three major dimensions of His authority: judge, lawgiver and king. These three areas represent the judiciary, legislature and executive, which individually and/or collectively are in charge of in governments worldwide. God rules over every creation and desires to put it under His rulership so that it can serve His holy purposes. He desires to manifest His glory as Lord and Savior by reconciling all things to Himself by redeeming them through His Son's blood (Colossians 1:23).

God requires us to set our priorities right so that He is the main agenda. Every aspect of our lives, families, ministries and nations should be under the lordship of Jesus Christ. He is the undisputable King of kings and Lord of lords. To fulfill His redemptive purposes, God desires to partner with us to put the earth under the dominion of His perfect will.

Some ways in which we can enthrone God in our lives include walking in holiness, maintaining a thankful attitude that is full of praise, trembling at His holy word, and pursuing holiness and peace in every aspect of our lives. When God gets the supremacy, everything else falls into place.

Further Reading: Revelation 17:14; Psalm 47:2; Matthew 5:34-35
Prayer for the Day: Father in the Name of Jesus Christ, I enthrone You in every area of my life. Oh Lord, take all the preeminence, in Jesus' name, Amen.

Day 172 | Ecclesiastes 7-12

21st June

Desire to Know God

"I want to know Christ and the power of his resurrection and the fellowship of sharing in his sufferings, becoming like him in his death" (Philippians 3:10).

Our spiritual lives are an integral part of our destinies. This is because we are spirit beings with souls that are harboured in physical bodies. Many people abort their destinies because they only put effort in their physical engagements, forsaking their spiritual lives. This misnomer should be avoided. No matter how spiritually mature and gifted we are, none of us can claim to know God enough. This is why we need to invest time, effort and energy into knowing God. Apostle Paul often prayed for the recipients of his epistles to seek the knowledge of God. He was also determined to know Christ and witness firsthand the power of the Holy Spirit that resurrected Christ from the dead. He also was committed to fellowship with Christ in His sufferings so that he could emulate Him, dying to the self in order to save mankind.

As we draw closer to the end-times, we are bound to witness a barrage of doctrinal attacks from the kingdom of darkness. False Christs, prophets and teachers are spreading false knowledge about God and misleading those who are ignorant and untaught in the Scriptures. As believers, the Holy Spirit is our teacher. He helps us to know God through the teaching of the word of God and by divine revelation of spiritual truths, so that we can discern and walk in the perfect will of God.

Further Reading: Ephesians 1:17-18; Deuteronomy 7:9
Prayer for the Day: Oh God, today my prayer is that I may know You more, in Jesus' name, Amen.

1 Kings 10-11; 2 Chronicles 9 — Day 173

22nd June

Do Not Grieve the Holy Spirit

"And do not grieve the Holy Spirit of God, with whom you were sealed for the day of redemption" (Ephesians 4:30).

The Holy Spirit is the third Person of the Godhead. He is co-equal with the Father and the Son. However, they have different functions: the Father created, the Son redeemed and the Holy Spirit regenerates. These three roles are critical in the salvation of humanity. The ascension of the Lord Jesus opened the way for the Holy Spirit to dwell in believers. Before ascending, Jesus commanded them to wait in Jerusalem for the gift of the Father (Acts 1:4). This promise was fulfilled on the Day of Pentecost when all the disciples were filled with the Holy Spirit and divinely empowered to fulfill the Great Commission (Mathew 28:19-20).

Grieving the Holy Spirit refers to doing things that offend Him and desecrate His Person and contradict His holy nature. This could be in our thoughts and speech as well as in our actions. The ambition of every believer should be to cultivate fellowship with God through His Spirit who abides in us. Grieving and resisting the Holy Spirit exposes one to danger. When Israel rebelled against God's voice, the Spirit of God became their enemy and fought against them (Isaiah 63:10). Instead of moving away from God, we should draw closer to Him every day. We can do this by learning how to become friends with God. Genuine friends take care of each other's feelings.

Further Reading: Ephesians 1:13-15; John 14:16; 1 Thessalonians 5:19
Prayer for the Day: Holy Spirit, I repent of the many times I have grieved You and pray that I may always seek to have fellowship with You as You guide and lead me into all truth, in Jesus' name, Amen.

Proverbs 30-31

23rd June

Our Faith in Christ Transcends this Life

"If only for this life we have hope in Christ, we are to be pitied more than all men" (1 Corinthians 15:19).

God's redemptive purposes are eternal. They predate our creation and outlive our life on earth. The will of God is that we should live with a perspective of eternity. We shall live beyond the grave because our inner man is indestructible. We should have confidence and enjoy abundant life both in this life and in eternity because this is God's plan for us. In this life, God promises to provide everything we need for life and godliness. We can partake of the divine nature and walk as Christ did through His enabling power (2 Peter 1:4). In the life to come, we shall share in the glory of Christ our Lord the same way He shared in our humanity (1 Corinthians 15:49).

Having a right perspective of our earthly lives and heavenly destiny is critical because it can help us prepare for eternity. Our earthly lives are like a poor reflection of the glory we shall share with Christ in the coming age (1 Corinthians 13:12). It is unwise to live for material benefits which are temporal, while God's intention is for us to pursue eternal life and all the benefits it confers on believers. We brought nothing into the world and we cannot take anything out of it (1 Timothy 6:7-10). Our lives on earth are an opportunity to prepare to live in the presence of God forever and ever.

Further Reading: *John 3:16; John 11:25; 1 John 5:3-4*
Prayer for the Day: *My Father in the name of Jesus Christ, I pray that my faith will bear fruit both in this life and in eternity, Amen.*

1 Kings 12-14

24th June

Beware of the Powerless Cross

"For Christ did not send me to baptize, but to preach the gospel - not with words of human wisdom, lest the cross of Christ be emptied of its power" (1 Corinthians 1:17).

Jesus was crucified and shed His blood on Calvary for the redemption of mankind. The place where He shed His sinless blood is the highest and most powerful altar on earth. The cross of Christ is at the centre of God's redemptive purpose because forgiveness of sin is only possible through the shedding of blood (Hebrews 9:22). The finished work of the cross granted us access to the presence of God (Matthew 27:51).

Removing the Holy Spirit from the equation of the redemptive work of Christ renders the cross powerless and ineffective. Salvation, healing, blessings and eternal life are impossible without the power of the Holy Spirit. When Apostle Paul went to the church in Corinth, his resolution was to preach the good news with God's power. He ensured that he did not use persuasive words of human wisdom but demonstrated the power of the Holy Spirit so that the saints there could have authentic faith (1 Corinthians 2:1-5). The cross of Christ is God's avenue of releasing His power. We need to hold it with the honour it deserves and allow its power to permeate every area of our lives, until we are fully conformed to the image of Christ and have a stature like His (Colossians 1:28).

Further Reading: John 19:30; Luke 24:49; John 16:7
Prayer for the Day: Oh Lord, help me partake the power of the cross of Christ, and the redemptive power in it through Jesus Christ, Amen.

Day 176 — 2 Chronicles 10-12

25th June

Invest in the Kingdom of God

"Do not store up for yourselves treasures on earth, where moth and rust destroy, and where thieves break in and steal. But store up for yourselves treasures in heaven, where moth and rust do not destroy, and where thieves do not break in and steal" (Matthew 6:19-20).

The parable of the talents (Matthew 25:14-31) depicts God as an investor. It shows that He gives each of His children talents so that they can put them into profitable use for the advancement of His kingdom. The will of God is that we should emulate His character and invest in His kingdom. The time, money or effort we expend in the kingdom of God is an investment that has temporal and eternal rewards.

As we walk with God, we need to ensure that every investment we make in His kingdom is done with the right motive. We must not do kingdom business with selfish interests because everything we do must aim at glorifying God. He does not make any investments in His kingdom geared towards advancing personal interests and selfish ambitions.

Giving is one of the principles of the kingdom of God. Naturally, when seeds are sown, they yield a crop. The same is true of the kingdom of God. God sees the things we do in secret for His glory and in response to His word and rewards us openly. Investing in the kingdom of God is storing incorruptible eternal treasures.

Further Reading: Luke 6:38; 2 Corinthians 8:7; 2 Corinthians 9:6
Prayer for the Day: My God and my Father, today I pray that You may help me invest in Your kingdom, where moth and rust do not destroy, Amen.

1 Kings 15:1-24; 2 Chronicles 13-16

26th June

You Reap What You Sow

"Do not be deceived: God cannot be mocked. A man reaps what he sows" (Galatians 6:7).

The kingdom of God is governed by tested and tried principles. It is like silver refined seven times in a furnace (Psalm 12:6) and its truth is eternal. The Scriptures are the firm foundation upon which everything believers do stands.

One of the unbreakable truths of the word of God is that we always reap what we sow. When God created animals and plants, He gave them the ability to bear after their own kind. Plants have seeds that when nurtured, grow into fruit-bearing trees. God has programmed the earth to have seedtime and harvest time as long as it endures (Genesis 8:22). All the natural and spiritual seeds we sow bear a crop – some thirtyfold, others sixtyfold while others a hundredfold.

Our actions are also seeds. If we sow good and walk in righteousness, we reap a bountiful harvest of good. On the other hand if we make the unwise decision of sowing evil, we reap a proportional amount of evil and corruption. This is why we need to ask God to help us make the right choice of seeds because it is bound to bear fruit in the fullness of time. Since the word of God abides forever, it is a wise and profitable decision to live as it commands because it shall yield eternal life when Christ is revealed.

Further Reading: 2 Timothy 4:14; Revelation 2:23; 22:12; Hosea 8:7
Prayer for the Day: A man reaps what they sow. I pray for power to say no to evil and with the help of the Holy Spirit, strive to always sow good, in the name of Jesus Christ, Amen.

Day 178   1 Kings 15:25-34; 1 Kings 16:1-34; 2 Chronicles 17

27th June

God Keeps Records of Our Lives

"And I saw the dead, great and small, standing before the throne, and books were opened. Another book was opened, which is the book of life. The dead were judged according to what they had done as recorded in the books" *(Revelation 20:12).*

One of the attributes of the divine nature is record keeping. In His great and unsearchable wisdom, God keeps accurate records of everything we do. On the Day of Judgment, He shall use the records of our works to reward those who have done what pleased Him. This should stir us to make every effort to do the right thing always right.

Since God is a faithful and just judge, He takes notice of our tears, prayers, missionary work and the discipleship we do and records them. As a result, we ought to allow Him guide us in everything. The only works that will qualify rewards on that decisive day are those aligned to His holy will.

Many believers fail to serve God with commitment because they make the wrong assumption that He is distant and does not notice the service they offer Him. We should not be blind as to the truth that God takes notice and records everything done by the saints in His name. This should encourage us to serve Him diligently as we know that our labour in Him is not in vain (1 Corinthians 15:58).

Further Reading: Psalm 56:8; Hosea 13:12
Prayer for the Day: Dear God, I ask for ability to do right so that when You hold me to account, I will not be ashamed of my work, in Jesus' name, Amen.

1 Kings 17-19

28th June

Seek Prosperity for the Sake of God's Work

"For the sake of the house of the LORD our God, I will seek your prosperity" (Psalm 122:9).

The Lord our God is holy and owns the heavens, the earth and everything therein (Psalm 24:1). Scriptures describe the glory of the heavenly city where God lives in words that display majesty and great affluence. In short, God has a taste for good things. Since we are His children, we should emulate His excellence.

David was a man after God's own heart. He was devoted to doing God's will and set aside great wealth with a view to putting up a temple for God. His kind gesture impressed God. Although God did not allow him to build the temple because he had shed so much blood, He allowed his son Solomon to build a magnificent temple (1 Chronicles 22:1-17). He wrote that he would continually seek divine prosperity for the sake of God's house.

In His great wisdom, God meets the needs of His kingdom through the work of the hands of His people. He gives them the power to make wealth (Deuteronomy 8:18) and in return, they support His work. God desires we prosper financially so that we can meet the growing needs of the church. He has His kingdom at heart when He blesses us since it is His priority. As we seek His Kingdom first, He ensures divine increase.

Further Reading: *Psalm 25:27; 2 Corinthians 8:1-9*
Prayer for the Day: *My God, all wealth and riches belong to You. Grant me the ability to make wealth that I may partner with You, in Jesus name, Amen.*

1 Kings 20-21

29th June

Wisdom and Revelation are Critical for Dominion

"I keep asking that the God of our Lord Jesus Christ, the glorious Father, may give you the Spirit of wisdom and revelation, so that you may know him better. I pray also that the eyes of your heart may be enlightened in order that you may know the hope to which he has called you, the riches of his glorious inheritance in the saints" *(Ephesians 1:17-18).*

A believer's life should glorify God. It should impact the lives of other believers and unbelievers alike, and should demonstrate the power of God. It should be marked by growth from one level of glory to another, as one increases in divine wisdom and the revelation of God.

Apostle Paul often prayed for the recipients of his letters that they would have a deeper knowledge of God. Spiritual matters are perceived spiritually (1 Corinthians 2:13-14). Paul was praying that the spiritual senses of saints be strengthened by their knowledge and understanding of God's nature, power and purposes, within the context of their destinies. With this understanding, they could possess divine inheritance reserved for them by God.

The will of God is for all believers to walk in dominion over all creation (Genesis 1:26-27). He redeemed all mankind from destruction by the death of His Son and desires that we preach the gospel to the ends of the earth, guided by divine wisdom and revelation.

Further Reading: 2 Chronicles 1:11; Psalm 119:16; Proverbs 2:10
Prayer for the Day: Father, I pray that You may enable me walk in divine wisdom and revelation, in Jesus' name, Amen.

1 Kings 22; 2 Chronicles 18

30th June

Seek Divine Exemption

"If you do not let my people go, I will send swarms of flies on you and your officials, on your people and into your houses. The houses of the Egyptians will be full of flies, and even the ground where they are. But on that day I will deal differently with the land of Goshen, where my people live; no swarms of flies will be there, so that you will know that I, the LORD, am in this land" (Exodus 8:21-22).

We live in a fallen world characterised by diverse calamities that include epidemics, motor and aviation accidents, fire outbreaks, famine and floods. When Israel cried to God for deliverance, He sent Moses. God exempted His chosen people from the ten plagues that befell the land as God demonstrated His mighty power to those who opposed His plan to deliver Israel. As the ten plagues were wreaking havoc on the Egyptians, the Israelites enjoyed unprecedented calm in the territory God had set aside for them.

When we walk with God by faith, we enjoy exemption from the financial, social and spiritual challenges that afflict many. We thrive while others struggle. Our impact grows and our effectiveness is multiplied even as situatins in the world move from bad to worse. We are able to sail through the circumstances of life confidently having the awareness that with God's help and guidance, no challenge will be too big for us to overcome.

Further Reading: *Psalm 91:7-13; Isaiah 43:2*
Prayer for the Day: *My God, I have learnt that as I walk with You by faith, I can enjoy divine exemption from challenges and calamities in life. Lord Jesus, grant me this divine exemption, In Your name, Amen.*

Day 182 — 2 Chronicles 19-23

1st July

Our Security is in Faith in God

"who through faith are shielded by God's power until the coming of the salvation that is ready to be revealed in the last time. In this you greatly rejoice, though now for a little while you may have had to suffer grief in all kinds of trials" **(1 Peter 1:5-6).**

The life of a believer is a journey through an unfriendly territory that is occupied by those who oppose God's plans (Deuteronomy 7:1-26). As believers, we face enemies that would want us to backslide, compromise or abandon the faith we profess in Christ. However, we need not fear because God assures us of His abiding presence and unlimited access to His securing power through faith.

Apostle Peter states that we can walk in joy notwithstanding the diverse trials faced in life. He says that before we receive complete salvation when Jesus Christ returns, we are shielded by faith in God's power. This makes it necessary for us to have active faith in God. Faith refers to confidence or trust in God.

To enjoy divine security, we need to agree with the word of God, speak faith-filled words and make confessions that agree with the teachings of God's word. Nothing is impossible for the man who has faith (Mark 9:23). We should therefore trust God to enable us navigate all the threats we face because of our faith in Him.

Further Reading: Romans 10:17; Proverbs 18:10
Prayer for the Day: *Oh Lord in Jesus' name, do help me walk by faith and partake the benefit of divine protection, Amen.*

Obadiah; Psalm 82-83

2nd July

Serve God's Purpose for Your Life

"For when David had served God's purpose in his own generation, he fell asleep; he was buried with his fathers and his body decayed" *(Acts 13:36).*

God created every one of us with a specific purpose. He is committed to helping us prosper in doing what He has designed us for as long as we depend and align ourselves with His plan. To fulfill our divine purpose, we must first discover it by asking God to reveal to us the sole reason of our existence. We can also discover our purpose by identifying the things that move us to action and acting on them with the spiritual power and strength God provides.

David discovered that God had called him to become a shepherd of his people. He devoted himself to seeking God's blueprint for his kingship and did everything God commanded. He was a man after God's own heart as he steadfastly pursued God's purpose for his life until it was fulfilled (1 Samuel 13:14). He governed God's people with righteousness and justice. He also promoted true worship in the land by pointing people to God. His commitment to God was exemplary.

Many people are unhappy and unfulfilled in life because they have never discovered their divine purpose. They live outside God's plan and thus cannot receive all the spiritual and material resources He intended for them. Discover your purpose and pursue it with all your might.

Further Reading: John 18:37; Job 36:5; Ephesians 1:11, 1 Chronicles 14:2
Prayer for the Day: Oh God, help me fulfil my divine assignment, in Jesus' name, Amen.

3rd July

Do Not Take God's Glory

"On the appointed day Herod, wearing his royal robes, sat on his throne and delivered a public address to the people. They shouted, "This is the voice of a god, not of a man." Immediately, because Herod did not give praise to God, an angel of the Lord struck him down, and he was eaten by worms and died" (Acts 12:21-23).

God is sovereign and greater than all he has created. He is not comparable to anything. He is full of power, glory and majesty. He is a jealous God who protects the integrity of His name from people and forces that oppose, resist or undermine His power and authority. King Herod set himself against God's plan for the proclamation of the gospel by the early church. He opposed and threatened the saints with the intention of discouraging them from doing the work God had called them to do. God judged him for taking His glory. Instead of acknowledging God and praising Him, he became proud and felt as if he was a god. An angel struck and worms begun eating him until he died.

God does not allow anyone to share His glory. He judges those who rebel against Him through self-exaltation. Nebuchadnezzar ran into trouble with God when he became proud. He declared that he had built Babylon as the royal residence by his mighty power and for the glory of his majesty (Daniel 4:30). For such utterances, God humbled him and his kingdom was restored after he acknowledged that only God deserves praise and glory.

Further Reading: *James 4:10; 1 Peter 5:5; Luke 14:11*
Prayer for the Day: *Almighty God, thou art worthy; there is no other like You, receive all the glory and honour forever and ever, Amen.*

2 Kings 5-8

Day 185

4th July

Your Words Reveal What is in Your Heart

"The good man brings good things out of the good stored up in his heart, and the evil man brings evil things out of the evil stored up in his heart. For out of the overflow of his heart his mouth speaks" **(Luke 6:45).**

Speech is a medium of communication. Words are an outflow of the good or bad stored up in our hearts. What we say reveals who and what we are. The word of God teaches that we should be careful with what we speak because they reveal what is hidden in our hearts.

The heart is deceitful above all things (Jeremiah 17:9) and it has potential to harbour all forms of evil and wickedness. Some of the forms of impurity that find expression through the tongue include gossip, slander, lies, deception and curses. These oppose God's plan for man's destiny and He judges those who unrepentantly harbour them.

The righteous speak what is right and honourable. However, the words of the wicked are like crude weapons that injure and demean God's people. To attain our destinies, we must learn to refute all negative words spoken against us because if unaddressed, they can create roadblocks to our blessings and hinder us from fulfilling God's purpose. We also need to be careful about the words we speak lest they become a snare to others.

Further Reading: James 3:1-12; Matthew 12:36-37; Isaiah 54:17
Prayer for the Day: Everlasting Father in Jesus' name, may my heart always be pure that my speech may be wholesome, for out of the abundance of the heart the mouth speaks. Amen.

2 Kings 9-11

5th July

Thanksgiving is a Product of Humility

"Sacrifice thank offerings to God, fulfill your vows to the Most High, and call upon me in the day of trouble; I will deliver you, and you will honor me" (Psalm 50:14-15).

It takes humility to cultivate and maintain a heart of gratitude towards God and people. Man is naturally proud and self-confident. Many people have a sense of entitlement and do not see the need to express gratitude when good is done to them. However, the will of God is that we should be humble and appreciative of everything He does for and through us.

Expressing gratitude shows that one does not take for granted what is done to them by either God or man. Whenever God helps us, or works through others to come to our aid, we should be careful to express our heartfelt gratitude. Israel was in distress and Samuel offered a suckling lamb as a sacrifice to the Lord. By this act, the people acknowledged that they had come that far with God's help. Consequently, the Philistines never attacked Israel again during the days of Samuel. God granted Israel permanent victory over their enemies (1 Samuel 7:9-12).

The Lord lifts those who humble themselves before Him and acknowledge His deeds. As believers, we must cultivate grateful hearts. As we commune with God daily, we should bear in mind that our prayers are incomplete without thanksgiving. This is the key that opens doors to the supernatural.

Further Reading: 1 Thessalonians 5:18; 2 Corinthians 4:15; Philippians 4:6-7

Prayer for the Day: Dear lord, today I offer You my sacrifice of thanksgiving for whom You are and what you've been to me, 'receive it Lord,' Amen

2 Kings 12-13; 2 Chronicles 24

6th July

Beware of the Sin of Ingratitude

"But mark this: There will be terrible times in the last days. People will be lovers of themselves, lovers of money, boastful, proud, abusive, disobedient to their parents, ungrateful, unholy" **(2 Timothy 3:1-2).**

Today, the sin of ingratitude is rampant. Biblical prophecy indicates that it is bound to get worse as we draw closer to Christ's second coming. In the eyes of God, thanklessness is a grave sin that has short-term and long-term consequences. It closes the doors of increase and favour besides hindering God's people from realising their full potential.

As disciples of Christ, we should not take anything for granted. Having a sense of entitlement makes it hard or impossible to express gratitude. However, when we understand God's plan for our lives and His willingness to provide everything we need for life and godliness, we cannot withhold our gratitude to Him. We should find a way of expressing our gratefulness because unspoken gratitude amounts to ingratitude.

Expressing gratitude may include speaking words of praise, giving thanksgiving offerings, singing and making prayers of thanksgiving. Jesus cleansed the ten lepers but only one Samaritan returned to thank Jesus for cleansing him. He praised the Lord in a loud voice and he was made whole (Luke 17:15-19). The realms of increase and the miraculous are only accessible to those who express gratitude to God. We should always have a reason to thank God not withstanding what we go through, or the challenges we face, because He deserves all our praises.

Further Reading: *John 6:11, 23; Romans 1:20-21*
Prayer for the Day: *Today, I repent of every form of ingratitude in my life, oh Lord, forgive me, in Jesus' name, Amen.*

Day 188 — 2 Kings 14; 2 Chronicles 25

7th July

Stay Away from Every Idol

"I am the LORD; that is my name! I will not give my glory to another or my praise to idols" (Isaiah 42:8).

An idol is an image or a representation of a god used as an object of worship. Any person or thing that consumes one's thoughts, words, time, energy or money other than God is an idol. We should be careful not to entertain any idol in our lives because God judges all those who worship them because this is His reserve. Some modern-day idols include technology, money, romantic relationships, betting and comfort.

God's majesty cannot be compared to anything. His glory and power are beyond human comprehension. He created man to worship Him and does not permit any of us to pay allegiance to any other god. He detests idolatry and warned Israel not to have any other god before Him (Exodus 20:2-3).

To avoid being deceived into worshipping idols, we should learn to acknowledge God and credit Him for all our undertakings and victories all the time. Worshipping Him in a worthy manner requires that we acknowledge what He has done. Unlike idols, which cannot do anything because they have no power, our God is majestic in holiness, awesome in glory and works wonders. He performs miracles, signs and wonders for and through those who believe Him. He moves mountains and provides rest from oppression and unfruitful labour.

Further Reading: Exodus 15:11; 34:14; Psalm 115:16; 1 Samuel 15:29
Prayer for the Day: Everlasting Father in Jesus' name, help me ascribe all glory to You every day, Amen.

Jonah 1-4

Day 189

8th July

Put Your Focus on God, Not on Your Troubles

"For our light and momentary troubles are achieving for us an eternal glory that far outweighs them all" **(2 Corinthians 4:17).**

Before we share in Christ's glory when He is revealed, we have to live in this fallen world. We are bound to face different forms of trials, tests and temptations as God permits. We however need not fear because God's word assures us that He will not allow us to be tempted beyond our ability to endure (1 Corinthians 10:13).

The word of God promises that our blessings are always more than all the sufferings, troubles and trials we are bound to face. It describes our sufferings as light and temporary. This should encourage and comfort us because our troubles aim at revealing the glory of God to us both in time and in eternity. Afterwards, we shall receive eternal rewards that are incomparable to the short-term pains we have to endure as we press on towards our heavenly home.

It is unfortunate that many people suffer from depression and others commit suicide because they ignore the goodness of God. To have a successful walk with God, we need to be careful not to give too much attention to our troubles but see beyond them as opportunities for God to manifest Himself. When we triumph, He receives the glory. Have faith in God and He will help you become an overcomer because those who trust in Him will never be put to shame.

Further Reading: John 16:33; Psalm 34:19-20; Romans 8:18
Prayer for the Day: Oh God, help me to put my focus on You and not on the troubles and challenges I encounter, for You will never put me to shame, in Jesus' name, Amen.

Day 190 — 2 Kings 15; 2 Chronicles 26

9th July

Do Not Compare Yourself with Others

"Each one should test his own actions. Then he can take pride in himself, without comparing himself to somebody else" (Galatians 6:4).

We are all unique and God has a peculiar purpose and destiny for each of us. God has endowed us with different talents, calling, and gifts that are meant to minister to the needs of the body of Christ. He has called us to complement and not compete with each other. Instead of appreciating what God has freely given, some people compare themselves with others. They end up ungrateful instead of appreciating what God has done.

Comparing oneself with others triggers ingratitude. Celebrating what you have creates a conducive environment to manifest the glory of God in you, thus receiving more from Him.

Each one of us should run our own race. When we understand this, it helps us avoid comparing ourselves with others who are endowed differently and whom God has marked different paths for. Focusing faithfully on what God has called us to do guarantees success. Cain became jealous and killed his brother Abel who offered an acceptable sacrifice to God. Had he done the right thing, God would have accepted his sacrifice. The Lord had warned him that if he failed, sin would devour him (Genesis 4:7). Envy, anger, bitterness, and destruction follow those who compare themselves with others because they fail to follow the path God ordained for them.

Further Reading: *2 Corinthians 10:12; 2 Corinthians 8:8*
Prayer for the Day: *Oh Lord my God, the maker of the heaven and the earth, I am forever grateful for whom I am. Dear Lord, help never compare myself to others for I am uniquely made for a purpose, Amen.*

10th July

Worship is Incomplete without Sacrifice

Isaac spoke up and said to his father Abraham, "Father?" "Yes, my son?" Abraham replied. "The fire and wood are here," Isaac said, "but where is the lamb for the burnt offering?" **(Genesis 22:7).**

All major religions have an element of worship deeply embedded in them. Some ungodly forms of worship demand human sacrifices. Although the Bible records many instances where worshippers offered sacrifices to God, many believers today do not understand that true worship must be accompanied by sacrifice. To sacrifice is to surrender something precious for another more valuable one. Since worshipping God is ultimately valuable, we have to lay aside the things we used to enjoy when we were sinners. We must put an end to worldly music, ungodly attitudes, indecent speech and dressing.

Sacrifice enhances the power of worship. Failure to include sacrifice by believers paints their faith in bad light because they lose spiritual battles they could have won easily, had they worshipped the Lord in the way He has prescribed in His word. True worshippers of God offered worthwhile sacrifices because this is integral. God seeks worshippers who worship Him in spirit and in tuth (John 4:24). They are open to God with no ulterior motives or hypocritical behavior, because they know that He examines the intentions of the heart. True worship expressed to God attracts a great reward and only exalts God for who He is. It signifies a life totally surrendered to Him.

Further Reading: 2 Samuel 24:24; Malachi 1:6-10; Luke 14:26-28
Prayer for the Day: Heavenly Father in the name of Jesus, help me complete my acts of worship by offering acceptable sacrifices in Your Name, Amen.

11th July

Trust God in Your Storms

A furious squall came up, and the waves broke over the boat, so that it was nearly swamped. Jesus was in the stern, sleeping on a cushion. The disciples woke him and said to him, "Teacher, don't you care if we drown?" (Mark 4:37-38).

God allows us to face storms so that He can glorify Himself. Trouble, pain, sicknesses, lack and oppression may occur in the lives of believers so that He can manifest His power as He receives the glory. When we believed in the Lord, we began a new life of faith. Trusting God in this life of faith means that we should believe Him to offer guidance and protection from all the storms that might buffet us as we move towards our destinies.

Scriptures record that Jesus was in a boat with His disciples when they encountered a storm. Tired after a long day in ministry, the Lord was asleep and was woken up by panicked disciples who asked Him if He did not care that they were about to perish. They had little faith and doubted His ability to calm the storm. However, He calmed it down by only a word (Mark 4:39).

God allows storms into our lives to test our faith. People whose faith has been tested and proven can believe God for great things. Most of those who have healing ministries are able to exercise their faith because God helped them receive healing for their sicknesses. Trust God in your storms.

Further Reading: *Psalm 46:1; Psalm 34:19; Isaiah 43:2*
Prayer for the Day: *My God and my Father, help me trust You in every storm of my life, in Jesus' name, Amen.*

Amos 1-5

Day 193

12th July

Agree with God So that You Can Walk with Him

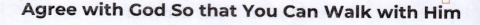

"Do two walk together unless they have agreed to do so?" (Amos 3:3).

We can only walk with God if we agree with Him. He requires every form of disputation and disagreement laid aside, so that we can have a fruitful walk with Him. Since He is faithful to all His promises (2 Corinthians 1:20), we can trust Him to keep His part of the deal if we commit ourselves to walking faithfully with Him.

Scriptures contain different examples of people who enjoyed abundant lives through walking in agreement with God. Jacob made a covenant that he would give a tithe of everything God gave if He would keep him safe, increase him and provide all his needs when he fled from his brother Esau who was determined to kill him (Genesis 28:20-22). Hannah, a God-fearing and prayerful woman, was barren but vowed to the Lord that she would give back the very son He would bless her with. She requested specifically for a male child (1 Samuel 1:11-12). The Lord honoured her plea and gave her Samuel whoserved God with distinction in Israel.

The Lord our God is a covenant-keeping God. When we faithfully commit ourselves to walking in agreement with Him, we can trust Him to do great and extraordinary things. With this understanding, when we enter into a covenant with God, we can trust Him to keep His part because He never fails to accomplish what He promises.

Further Reading: Psalm 89:34-37; Numbers 23:19
***Prayer for the Day:** Oh God, I am grateful that I have a relationship with You, 'the covenant-keeping God,' help me trust You and have a covenant relationship with You, Amen.*

13th July

Trials Test Our Love for God

"Does Job fear God for nothing?" Satan replied. "Have you not put a hedge around him and his household and everything he has? You have blessed the work of his hands, so that his flocks and herds are spread throughout the land. But stretch out your hand and strike everything he has, and he will surely curse you to your face" *(Job 1:9-11).*

A trial is the act of undergoing testing. When our faith is tried as believers, it ascertains authenticity. The Scriptures say that this is necessary because our faith has more worth than silver or gold (1 Peter 1:7), it must be proved whether it is genuine, so that it can bring glory, praise and honour to His name.

Even though Job was blameless, upright, feared God and shunned evil (Job 1:1), the enemy sought God's authority to attack him. He challenged Job's sincerity in worshipping God, attributing his firm commitment to worship as being a response to the divine protection and increase he enjoyed. He expected Job to deny God once his possessions were attacked.

Job maintained his integrity by standing firm in faith despite great suffering and massive losses. His wife, unable to bear all the troubles her husband faced, told him to curse God and die. Job firmly declined (Job 2:9-10), promising to remain steadfast in God. This is the example we should emulate when our faith is tested.

Further Reading: *Deuteronomy 7:19; 2 Thessalonians 1:4; 1 Thessalonians 3:2-3*

Prayer for the Day: *Oh God, I ask for ability to remain steadfast in my love for You even when it is greatly tested, Amen.*

2 Chronicles 27; Isaiah 9-12 — Day 195

14th July

Tests Humble Us So that We Don't Become Proud

"Be careful to follow every command I am giving you today, so that you may live and increase and may enter and possess the land that the LORD promised on oath to your forefathers. Remember how the LORD your God led you all the way in the desert these forty years, to humble you and to test you in order to know what was in your heart, whether or not you would keep his commands" **(Deuteronomy 8:1-2).**

God requires every saint who walks with Him to be humble. His word instructs us to humble ourselves before His mighty hand. Humbling oneself is a deliberate act of the will. It is a decision we must consciously make to subject our will to God's will.

God chose Israel to be His vessels of manifesting His power, love and majesty to the world. He blessed, increased and prospered them greatly despite stiff opposition from people and spiritual forces. He gave them grace and power to overcome all their enemies to the glory of His name.

As happened to the Israelites, God can allow us go through painful and trying experiences to inculcate in us a godly character. Instead of becoming bitter and resentful towards Him when this happens, we should willingly yield to His holy will and walk in humility. That way, we will enjoy His blessings.

Further Reading: Deuteronomy 28:47; 2 Samuel 2:22; Isaiah 29:19; 1 Peter 5:6

Prayer for the Day: Father, today I have learnt the importance of walking in humility. Help me always walk in humility that I may share in Your blessings, Amen.

Day 196 | Micah 1-7

15th July

God's Work is Progressive, Not Instant

"being confident of this, that he who began a good work in you will carry it on to completion until the day of Christ Jesus" (Philippians 1:6).

We live at a time when technology has infiltrated almost every aspect of our lives. Many things happen instantly as automation takes over many activities that were previously done manually consuming lots of time. We should watch against any form of deception implying that we can have instant spiritual growth because God's work is progressive, not instant.

God's word states that we are the temple of the Holy Spirit and living stones that God is building into spiritual house (1 Peter 2:5). God has set apart a specific role He desires each of us to play in His kingdom. We therefore need to allow Him build and equip us through His Spirit so that we can fit into our calling. Our ability to occupy the place God intends depends on our ability to surrender to the builder's touch.

Jesus is in the business of building the church against which the gates of hell cannot prevail (Matthew 16:18). Unfortunately, many believers are unable to resist the machinations of the enemy because they have failed to allow the Lord to build them. Our availability and ability to yield to God and pay the price determines the completion speed of the spiritual houses God is building. Therefore, allow God to do His work in you.

Further Reading: 2 Corinthians 3:18; 1 Kings 6:7
Prayer for the Day: My God and my Father, today I surrender totally to You, as You build me for Your glory, Amen.

2 Chronicles 28; 2 Kings 16-17

16th July

Commitment Leads to Success

"Don't let anyone look down on you because you are young, but set an example for the believers in speech, in life, in love, in faith and in purity" **(1 Timothy 4:12).**

An old adage says that success is sweet but its roots are bitter. This is true because nothing good comes cheap. All the people who have made a great impact in scholarship, technological innovations and in the body of Christ were diligently committed to the cause they chose. They invested time, energy, effort and faith in what they did, yielding in great results.

The word of God teaches that commitment leads to success. Those who remain focused to what they do enjoy breakthroughs. Apostle Paul instructed his spiritual son Timothy to be fully committed to the faith he professed despite his young age. He also instructed him to diligently set an example for other believers in speech, life, love, faith and purity.

Attaining our destinies is part of the success we should desire to achieve. We need to be fully committed to what we believe God has called us to do, pursuing it with all our might until we become all that God meant us to be. Half-hearted commitment, compromise and slothfulness only lead to failure and regrets. We can depend on the Holy Spirit to strengthen us in our commitment to pursue our destinies.

Further Reading: 1 Timothy 4:15; Proverbs 12:24; Isaiah 38:3; Ephesians 6:7

Prayer for the Day: My God, grant me the ability to be diligently committed to You so that I may enjoy divine success, in Jesus' name, Amen.

Isaiah 13-17

17th July

You Can Move from Strength to Strength

"They go from strength to strength, till each appears before God in Zion" (Psalm 84:7).

Walking with God can be compared to running a marathon. It is a long-term commitment meant to last a lifetime. It demands an unfailing source of strength. We are able to overcome our fears, weaknesses, doubts and limitations through depending on God's supernatural power, availed to those who believe in the Lord through the Holy Spirit. We can serve our purpose and finish strong when God's dynamic power abides in us.

The word of God says that those who trust in the Lord shall renew their strength and mount up with wings as eagles (Isaiah 40:31). This is why faith is critical in the life of every believer. When we trust God with all our hearts, He connects us with divine supplies of grace, love and power, which propel us toward the destinies for which God ordained us.

The kingdom of God suffers violence and the forceful lay hold of it by force (Matthew 11:12). Christ has called us to be militant so that we can possess the blessings and inheritance He has kept in store for us. By the grace of God, we can increase progressively until we resemble Christ through the power of the gospel (Colossians 1:28). We increase from faith to faith, grace to grace and strength to strength as we walk intimately with God.

Further Reading: *1 Chronicles 29:12; Jeremiah 16:19; 1 Samuel 2:10*
Prayer for the Day: *Holy Lord, renew my strength by Your Holy Spirit day by day as I walk closely with You, in Jesus' name, Amen.*

Isaiah 18-22

Day 199

18th July

Spiritual Capital Can Make a Difference in Your Life

That same night the LORD said to him, "Take the second bull from your father's herd, the one seven years old. Tear down your father's altar to Baal and cut down the Asherah pole beside it" (Judges 6:25).

Every entrepreneur requires capital to start an enterprise. As believers, we need spiritual capital to pursue and fulfill our destinies. This is because life is spiritual and we must have spiritual backing to live successfully.

Many people face challenges as they attempt to make progress towards their destinies. This could be a result of lack of spiritual capital. Scripture documents the instructions God gave Gideon so that he could separate himself from his background that was full of evil, and position himself in God's will. His father was an idol worshipper who had raised an altar for Baal. When the Lord appeared to Gideon, He instructed him to tear down the altar his father had raised and build a new one for the living God. The idolatrous background Gideon came from hindered him from manifesting the seed of greatness God had deposited in him. By obeying God's command, he could become the mighty man of valour he was predestined to be (Judges 6:12).

Spiritual capital is more valuable than material possessions. We can increase our spiritual capital through prayer and fasting, giving sacrifices and offerings, giving to the needy as well as to the elderly. Offering your body as a living sacrifice, prophetic ministration and having spiritual covering helps us build our spiritual capital.

Further Reading: 2 Kings 3:26-27; Ephesians 1:3; Revelation 3:7
Prayer for the Day: Dear Lord, give me wisdom that I may understand how to build spiritual capital for my destiny, to the glory of Your Holy name, Amen.

Day 200 | Isaiah 23-27

19th July

Trusting God Makes Us Immovable

"Those who trust in the LORD are like Mount Zion, which cannot be shaken but endures forever. As the mountains surround Jerusalem, so the LORD surrounds his people both now and forevermore" (Psalm 125:1-2).

Scriptures predict rough and tumultuous times on earth at the end of age. All things that can be shaken will be shaken so that only the permanent will remain (Hebrews 12:27). However, those who believe in the Lord have nothing to fear since He is on their side, upholding them with His righteous right hand. Even when the foundations of the earth are shaken, those whose faith is firmly grounded in God are safe both in time and eternity.

The Psalmist states that trusting God makes us as unshakeable as Mount Zion. God's power and presence surrounds His people forever and no power of the enemy can reach them in their stronghold. Solomon also stated that the name of the Lord is a strong tower to whom the righteous run and are safe (Proverbs 18:10). We build our lives upon this foundation, which is forever strong.

As we walk with God, He surrounds us and secures us ensuring that our divine destinies are safe. Our faith in Him helps us overcome all the forces of darkness and ushers us into the realms of abundance, security and well-being both in time and eternity.

Further Reading: *Colossians 3:16; Hebrews 4:16; Romans 1:17*
Prayer for the Day: *Thank you Lord for those who trust upon You shall never be shaken. May my faith withstand the storms of the enemy, in Jesus' name, Amen.*

2 Kings 18:1-8; 2 Chronicles 29-31; Psalm 48

20th July

Desire to Receive the True Anointing

"As for you, the anointing you received from him remains in you, and you do not need anyone to teach you. But as his anointing teaches you about all things and as that anointing is real, not counterfeit - just as it has taught you, remain in him" (1 John 2:27).

We live in times when counterfeits abound in almost every sector. Motor vehicle parts, clothes, electronic devices and furniture among others, have counterfeits that resemble the original. In the spiritual realm, the devil has perverted the faith of many by releasing counterfeit spirits that have power to perform miracles and wonders, but only lead to destruction, not peace as the Holy Spirit does.

Apostle John cautions believers that as long as the anointing they have received from the Lord abides in them, they are safe. They do not need anyone else to teach them because the Holy Spirit teaches them all things. Since He is omniscient and authentic, He gives us access to true knowledge and wisdom which leads to eternal life.

We need to ask God to give us discerning hearts to differentiate between the true anointing from the counterfeit. As believers, we also must be ready to walk in the Holy Spirit by continually being filled by Him. When we receive the true anointing and walk in it, we enjoy divine protection and cannot be misled by the evil power that is at work.

Further Reading: John 4:24; 1 John 2:20
Prayer for the Day: My God and my Father, grant me the true anointing that I may withstand the evil powers and forces at work in this age, Amen.

Day 202 | Hosea 1-7

21st July

Pray for All Leaders without Discrimination

"I urge, then, first of all, that requests, prayers, intercession and thanksgiving be made for everyone - for kings and all those in authority, that we may live peaceful and quiet lives in all godliness and holiness"(1 Timothy 2:1-2).

As believers, we are dual citizens; we belong to the nations God has placed us in but we also have a heavenly citizenship where we will spend eternity with the Lord (Philippians 3:20). However, before then, God requires us to be patriotic citizens of our earthly nations. One of the greatest patriotic obligations we owe our nations is to pray for our leaders.

Scriptures point out the need for believers to pray for all leaders because they determine the peace of the nation, which leads citizens into enjoying peace, quietness and godliness. If the political decisions made by those in authority are ungodly, God can intervene and redirect their hearts when believers take their place and seek Him diligently. Without prayer, the enemy can cause divisions along tribal, ethnic and ideological lines. He is likely to devour the souls of many nations through the misleading S leaders, some of who engage in demonic activities.

Nations follow the path leaders take. If leaders propagate hatred and division, citizens are denied peace. If leaders advocate for peace and stability, citizens enjoy growth and godliness. Be patriotic, diligently pray for and offer support to the leaders God ordained for your nation.

Further Reading: Proverbs 21:1; Proverbs 14:34

Prayer for the Day: *Heavenly Father, grant me a patriotic spirit that I may lovingly pray for all leaders without biases according to Your word, Amen.*

Hosea 8-14

22nd July

Guard Your Heart Diligently

"Above all else, guard your heart, for it is the wellspring of life" **(Proverbs 4:23).**

The heart is the nerve centre of our lives. It determines the path our lives take and thus we need to guard it lest our lives take an undesirable trajectory that leads to destruction. Many people follow a certain path that seems right to them but end in destruction (Proverbs 14:12). We must guard our hearts diligently lest we are misled to destruction by corrupt influences.

Our hearts determine our choices. The purity of our hearts is key. If our hearts are pure, all things become pure. Walking in righteousness and enjoying the grace of God is a decision and determination of the heart. On the other hand, the corrupt have their minds and conscience corrupted hindering them from living and walking in holiness (Titus 1:15). Guarding our hearts is a divine duty we cannot delegate to anyone, since we are responsible for the outcomes of our lives.

The main reason we must guard our hearts is that spiritual corruption begins in the heart. The enemy sows bitterness, hatred, murmuring, greed and all manner of impurity into the heart. To curb this, we ought to pray relentlessly. God increases His grace upon the pure enabling them to make a lasting impact through godly lives.

Further Reading: Jeremiah 17:9-10; 2 Peter 1:4; Isaiah 1:4; Matthew 15:19-20
Prayer for the Day: My heart is the wellspring of life. My God, fill me with Your Holy Spirit who is my help, that I may always guard my heart with all diligence, Amen.

Isaiah 28-30

23rd July

Learn to Seek the Kingdom of God first

"But seek first his kingdom and his righteousness, and all these things will be given to you as well. Therefore do not worry about tomorrow, for tomorrow will worry about itself. Each day has enough trouble of its own" **(Matthew 6:33-34).**

God desires to raise a generation that seeks Him first. He is eager to find a holy remnant devoted to Him and through whom He manifests His power and glory. Unfortunately, even though many believers are aware of this, they are unable to be the remnant God seeks.

Christ taught His followers to set their priorities right. This meant seeking the kingdom of God and His righteousness as a matter of priority. Seeking God diligently is an expression of strong faith in His word. God takes care of all the needs of those who comply with this command. When we walk by faith and do what God commands, He enables us defeat the spirit of worry that keeps many in continual suspense because of uncertainty of what the future holds.

Unbelievers have their focus on material well-being and they pursue possessions at the expense of the more valuable spiritual wealth. To seek God in a worthy manner requires divine wisdom to attach the right value to God. He promises to reveal Himself and manifest His power and glory to those who call on Him. Seeking God is not in vain, as He keeps His promise by answering those who call on Him.

Further Reading: Matthew 13:44-45; Jeremiah 29:13
Prayer for the Day: *My Lord in Jesus' name, may my main priority in this life be about seeking Your Kingdom and Your righteousness first, Amen.*

Isaiah 31-34 — Day 205

24th July

Worry is an Enemy of Destiny

"Therefore I tell you, do not worry about your life, what you will eat or drink; or about your body, what you will wear. Is not life more important than food, and the body more important than clothes? Look at the birds of the air; they do not sow or reap or store away in barns, and yet your heavenly Father feeds them. Are you not much more valuable than they? 27 Who of you by worrying can add a single hour to his life?" *(Matthew 6:25)*

Some people are unduly concerned about their daily needs. They have restless hearts because they worry that many things will go wrong. Others have sleepless nights as they think about food, clothing and shelter. They live in panic and anxiety. Their worrisome and fearful thoughts expose them to emotional health problems such as stress and anxiety. Some of them know God's promises of provision and care for His creation, but are unable to believe and possess it.

Jesus taught His disciples that life is more precious than any need we might have. God loves us so much to live us without food and clothing. He faithfully cares for and provides nourishment to the birds of the air to which He attaches much less value as compared to us.

Worry is an expression of unbelief. It is an indicator of lack of faith in God, which displeases Him. We cannot maximize our potential and fulfill our destinies if our focus is on our needs and not on God.

Further Reading: Philippians 4:6-7; Luke 12:26; Proverbs 18:24, Hebrews 13:5

Prayer for the Day: Today in the name of Jesus Christ, I renounce every form of fear and worry in my life, 'come out' in Jesus' name, Amen.

Day 206

Isaiah 35-36

25th July

We are Ordained for Abundant Life

"…I have come that they may have life, and have it to the full" ***(John 10:10b).***

Everything belongs to God. He is sovereign and all creation owes its existence to Him. By His grace, He has provided all we need for life and godliness (2 Peter 1:3-4) and we can live in abundance as God originally intended.

The Lord our God provides superabundant supplies in all things. He is rich in mercy (Ephesians 2:4), full of grace (Ephesians 1:7) and is love (1 John 4:8). He gives us anything we ask by faith and in accordance with His will. We are His creation and it is His business to sustain us as He provides us with what we need in life.

Jesus came to earth to reconcile us back to God. He shed His blood sacrificially for our sake. By faith, we can live abundant lives as we continually receive His grace, power and divine enablement to do the will of God. His word promises that He will meet all our needs according to His riches in glory. Our redeemer breaks all limitations and barriers the kingdom of the enemy may place on our path. The Bible states that the Breaker (the Messiah) will go up before the saints leveling every mountain and breaking every resistance until the saints climb to the peak of their destinies (Micah 2:13 AMP).

Further Reading: Romans 8:32; Deuteronomy 28:11; Proverbs 12:11

Prayer for the Day: My God, You ordained a life of abundance for me and I pray that I may enjoy the abundance to the full, in Jesus' name, Amen.

Isaiah 37-39; Psalm 76

Day 207

26th July

God's Power is Magnetic

"Very early in the morning, while it was still dark, Jesus got up, left the house and went off to a solitary place, where he prayed. Simon and his companions went to look for him, and when they found him, they exclaimed: "Everyone is looking for you!" (Mark 1:35-37).

The Great Commission charges believers with the great responsibility of spreading the good news of God's love and salvation accompanied by obedience to the teachings of Jesus in all the earth (Matthew 28:18-20). It is an enormous responsibility, which requires divine power to fulfill, because only God can draw sinful men to a loving relationship with Himself.

Through the Holy Spirit, God has provided dynamic power to win the world over to Himself (Acts 1:8). Jesus demonstrated this to His disciples by going through many towns and cities proclaiming the good news. He did good and great things wherever He went. All men sought Jesus after He had communed with God. They knew that He had power to heal the sick and deliver the oppressed. Scriptures reveal the secret of His power; He spent quality time with God in prayer, which released magnetic power to draw men to Himself.

To reach out to the lost, we must seek divine power. It is only through divine enablement that we can reach the whole world with the gospel of Christ. Spiritual power is critical in attracting and causing impact in peoples' lives including our own.

Further Reading: Mark 1:33; Acts 10:38; Matthew 4:25; 7:28; Acts 5:16
Prayer for the Day: My God, fill me with Your power that I may influence many people by its magnetic pull, to the gory of Your name, Amen.

Day 208 | Isaiah 40-43

27th July

Don't Despise Humble Beginnings

"Your beginnings will seem humble, so prosperous will your future be" (Job 8:7).

Naturally, all things begin small. Large trees grow out of tiny seeds and world-class companies and institutions have humble origins. In His great wisdom, God has designed all things to progress gradually from small beginnings to greatness.

The above verse emphasises this. It encourages us that even though our spiritual and material abilities might initially be weak and unimpressive, we can cultivate them to a level where they become great and impactful. Jesus used the parable of the mustard seed to teach His disciples how the kingdom of God grows and increases in impact. Although the mustard seed is the smallest among all seeds, it grows into a large tree that offers shelter to flocks of birds (Matthew 13:31-32).

Our beginnings might be small, but God helps us to have a great ending. By faith, we can advance from our place of weakness and increasingly become stronger. The grace of God is readily available to all who seek it. His power is perfected in weakness and He is able to make them strong. Believers should avoid comparisons, competitions, strife, envy, bitterness and discouragement if they wish to be great. They should resist these steadfastly for they have a bright future in Jesus' name.

Further Reading: **Zechariah 4:9-10; 1 Samuel 15:17**
Prayer for the Day: **Irrespective of my humble beginning, I pray for enablement to work towards a great future, Amen.**

Isaiah 44-48

28th July

Grow in the Grace of God

"But grow in the grace and knowledge of our Lord and Savior Jesus Christ. To him be glory both now and forever! Amen" (2 Peter 3:18).

Wrong doctrine on the grace of God is one of the greatest dangers of the end-times. Many are deceived that the grace of God is a license to living an ungodly life. The Bible warns of severe judgment because by abusing the grace of God, they deny the Lordship of Jesus Christ (Jude 1:4). The word of God commands us not to take the grace of God for granted (2 Corinthians 6:1).

The grace of God was fully revealed to mankind through Jesus (John 1:17) whose death on the cross reconciled us with God. When we receive the grace of God, He expects us to grow in it as well as in the knowledge of the Lord Jesus. This glorifies God and pleases Him.

The amount of grace a person carries determines the impact. Two people can have the same calling, occupy the same fivefold ministry office, but have differing impact depending on the grace in their lives. For maximum impact, we should increase our knowledge of the grace of God and diligently seek to grow in it. We have unlimited access to the throne of grace where we can receive mercy and grace to help us in our times of need (Hebrews 4:16).

Further Reading: 2 Peter 1:2; Titus 2:11-14
Prayer for the Day: My God and my Father, grant me the ability to grow in Your grace, in Jesus' name, Amen.

29th July

Run Your Race with Perseverance

"Therefore, since we are surrounded by such a great cloud of witnesses, let us throw off everything that hinders and the sin that so easily entangles, and let us run with perseverance the race marked out for us" **(Hebrews 12:1).**

The life of a believer can be compared to an athlete. We are in a race to the destiny God ordained for us. He desires that we get to the finishing line. If an athlete does not run according to the rules, he gets disqualified. A believer too may be disqualified from the spiritual race if he or she fails to live according to the principles of the word of God thus rendering the race vain.

Scriptures encourage us that many other saints ran the spiritual race before us, and finished it. They are now cheering us as they await our victory. We are commanded to put aside every hindrance that stands in our way and also the sin that can derail us. We are also admonished to run with perseverance the race set before us.

To emerge victorious in our walk with God, we must check our doctrine to ensure that it agrees with His word. One of the major tests we must pass is that of love. God is love and He requires us to emulate His character. Many people are watching to see how much we reflect God in our love for others.

Further Reading: *Galatians 5:6-7; 2 Timothy 4:7-8*
Prayer for the Day: *My God and my Father, grant me the ability to run with perseverance the race of faith set before me, in Jesus' name, Amen.*

Isaiah 49-53

30th July

Strive for Spiritual Maturity

"In fact, though by this time you ought to be teachers, you need someone to teach you the elementary truths of God's word all over again. You need milk, not solid food! Anyone who lives on milk, being still an infant, is not acquainted with the teaching about righteousness. But solid food is for the mature, who by constant use have trained themselves to distinguish good from evil" (Hebrews 5:12-14).

A parent's greatest joy is to see his or her child grow from infancy to maturity. Social, intellectual and financial development are indicators of growth which make an individual live a life independent of other people. Our heavenly Father being better than our parents withholds nothing from us. He helps us grow in His knowledge so that we can partner with Him in advancing His kingdom.

It is unfortunate that many believers live recklessly and neglect spiritual growth and maturity. Scriptures record that the recipients of the epistle to the Hebrews should have become spiritually mature but remained infants. They failed to learn critical lessons on walking in righteousness and thus failed to have the impact God desired. God has made available all the spiritual and material resources we need to walk in spiritual maturity (2 Peter 1:3). As wise children, we should strive to know His perfect will concerning our maturity so that we can relentlessly pursue it.

Spiritually mature believers normally partner with God to spread the influence of His kingdom (Ephesians 3:10). They motivate other believers to pursue and with divine enablement attain their destinies.

Further Reading: 1 Corinthians 13:11; Colossians 1:28; Ephesians 4:11-13

Prayer for the Day: Oh Lord, my prayer today is that I may be able to strive for spiritual maturity, in Jesus' name, Amen.

Day 212 — Isaiah 54-58

31st July

Develop Giving and Receiving by Faith

"Cast your bread upon the waters, for after many days you will find it again" (Ecclesiastes 11:1).

The kingdom of God operates on established principles in His word, which is forever settled in heaven. Giving and receiving is one of them. Believers function in natural and spiritual realms. What we do in the spiritual realm determines what happens in the physical. Giving determines receiving both in quality and quantity.

Scriptures teach that every believer should develop a discipline of giving. Failure to do this can be interpreted to mean spiritual immaturity and disobedience to God's purpose. This is because as much as we need material resources to rise to the peak of our destinies, we also need spiritual resources. Giving is similar to casting our bread in many waters. It is impossible to retrieve a piece of bread thrown into an ocean. However, God promises that He will make a way for us to find it after many days. Whenever we see a need that requires giving, we should not hesitate to address it. Whatever we give leaves our hands but because God is just, He ensures that we receive much more.

God rewards generosity by releasing different kinds of blessings to those who practice it. We need to give by faith and we shall certainly receive because the word of God which is exalted above His name (Psalm 138:2) cannot fail to accomplish what it is sent out for (Isaiah 55: 11).

Further Reading: **2 Corinthians 8:7; Luke 6:38; 2 Corinthians 9:7**
Prayer for the Day: **Oh God, give a heart that gives generously at all times for all the silver and gold belongs to You, Amen.**

Isaiah 59-63

1st August

Read the Bible for Yourself and Take Action

"Now the Bereans were of more noble character than the Thessalonians, for they received the message with great eagerness and examined the Scriptures every day to see if what Paul said was true"

(Acts 17:11).

The word of God is the greatest gift God has given us. It contains teachings, counsel, encouragement and warnings that are meant to help us attain our destinies. God has given us the ability to read and meditate on His word so that we can understand His plan and live by it. We should meditate, study, understand and obey His word.

Scripture commends the Bereans for being of noble character. They not only eagerly received the message, but also verified the authenticity of what they heard. Not so with many believers today. Instead of being studious in the word of God, they passively listen to sermons without verifying it.

The secret of growing in faith and walking with God is hearing His word, understanding and obeying it. God watches over His word to perform it and blesses all those who live by it. Our growth and maturity in His kingdom depend on our ability to obey what He commands (Deuteronomy 28:1). Genuine faith in God is tested through obedience. Therefore, we must act on what we hear from God to bear lasting fruit.

Further Reading: James 1:22-25; Joshua 1:8-9; Deuteronomy 6:5-7

Prayer for the Day: Father, embolden me so that I can obey Your word at all times, Amen.

Day 214 — Isaiah 64-66

2nd August

Be Careful about Your Relationships

Do not be misled: "Bad company corrupts good character" *(1 Corinthians 5:33).*

Man is a social being who regularly interacts with others. Lonely people may suffer mental breakdowns. Our relationships have a great effect on us whether we are conscious of it or not. If the people we relate with closely are ungodly, it is most likely that we will follow their evil ways. On the other hand, if we relate closely with godly people, we are likely to be encouraged to get close to God. Friendships that are godly have many benefits as they help the saints in advancing the interests of the kingdom of heaven.

When God called Abraham the father of faith, He instructed him to leave his country, his people and his father's household and go to the land He would show him (Genesis 12:1, Acts 7: 2-4). Abraham disengaged from them but was unable to leave Lot his nephew behind (Genesis 12:5). Lot later became a thorn in his flesh because his shepherds quarreled with those of Abraham over grazing fields (Genesis 13:5-7).

God may require that we separate ourselves totally from others when He wants to bless us. Some of the people around us may appear harmless and friendly, but could later become a source of pain and grief. They could also hinder us from attaining our destinies. Scriptures encourage us to have godly people as close associates and discourage us from spending time among scoffers, mockers and the ungodly (Psalm 1:1).

Further Reading: *1 Corinthians 5:1-11; Proverbs 22:24-25; Ecclesiastes 4:9-10.*

Prayer for the Day: *My God and my Saviour, I ask for the grace to dissociate from all potential corrupting influences and the wisdom to establish and sustain godly relationships, Amen.*

2 Kings 20-21

3rd August

Decisively Deal with Worthless Words

Therefore this is what the LORD says: "If you repent, I will restore you that you may serve me; if you utter worthy, not worthless, words, you will be my spokesman. Let this people turn to you, but you must not turn to them" (Jeremiah 15:19).

The tongue is a small organ. However, it is potentially the most destructive because it carries the power of life and death (Proverbs 18:21). God expects His children to restrain its power within the bounds of His holy word.

Serving God involves using the tongue to proclaim the good news and to sustain the weary (Isaiah 50:4). The tongue needs to be aligned with the will of God. Jeremiah was called and anointed by God to deliver His word to Israel but warned him against entertaining worthless words so that he could be His spokesperson. When our tongues are subjected to the governance of God, we only speak what is in line with His will. We bless and not curse, and do not utter words that could harm others. We convey the love of God and declare His power, mercy and goodness as well as His dislike of sin. When we do this, our hearers pay attention and depart from their wicked ways.

When we walk in the fear of God, we do not do things that dishonor Him. This includes the words of our mouth and the meditation of our hearts that must be clean so that they are acceptable before the Lord.

Further Reading: Matthew 12:36-37; Romans 14:12; Colossians 3:17
Prayer for the Day: May my speech be seasoned with grace always that You may be honoured Oh Lord, Amen.

4th August

Eradicate Iniquity in Your Life

"Have mercy on me, O God, according to your unfailing love; according to your great compassion blot out my transgressions. Wash away all my iniquity and cleanse me from my sin. For I know my transgressions, and my sin is always before me" (Psalm 51:1-3).

God is holy and demands we be holy too. His word says that He hates wickedness and desires purity from all who confess His name. Scriptures make a distinction between sin and iniquity. It refers to sin as missing the mark. It could be accidental or an isolated premeditated action of breaking God's law. However, iniquity is more insidious; it is a problem in someone's character. A person bound by iniquity is deformed in thought and character.

David acknowledged his iniquity before God and asked Him to cleanse him from his sin. This happened after he committed adultery with Bathsheba (2 Samuel 11:4-5). When God sent Nathan to point out his sin, he readily confessed and sought forgiveness.

Many believers are bound by iniquity because they are not humble to repent and forsake it. It enslaves and masters them denying freedom and peace of mind. God desires truth in the innermost place (Psalm 51:6). We need to embrace His law and walk in holiness. Cleansing ourselves is one of the indicators that we are preparing for the Lord's imminent return (1 John 3:3).

Further Reading: *Psalm 19:13-14; Hebrews 10:26-29; 2 Peter 2:20-22*
Prayer for the Day: *My God and Saviour, help me identify and get rid of every iniquity in my life, in Jesus' name, Amen.*

Nahum 1-3

Day 217

5th August

Consider Your Ways

This is what the LORD Almighty says: "Give careful thought to your ways" (Haggai 1:7).

God has given us the privilege of reasoning with Him, with others and with ourselves. We can observe, assess and make informed decisions and choices. Unfortunately, the lives of many are pale shadows of what they should be because they do not take time to meditate and act on God's word.

In ancient Israel, God reasoned with His people through prophets. He often sent them with messages. In the times of Haggai, they had neglected the temple as they built magnificent houses for themselves. Inevitably, they suffered misfortunes. The Lord punished and frustrated their efforts in order to win them back. God chastens His children out of love with a desire that they amend their sinful ways.

As we walk with God, we should pay close attention to the voice of reason. We should do regular audits of our lives to see if we are sticking to the path God set for us. We should carefully consider our thoughts, actions, character and the impact of our walk of faith. God promises to lavish us with His goodness if our ways please Him. He is a shield to those who trust Him and no one ever trusted Him and was put to shame.

Further Reading: Isaiah 1:18; Psalm 119:6; Proverbs 20:25

Prayer for the Day: *My Lord and Saviour Jesus Christ, help me to carefully consider my ways and amend areas where I have missed the mark, Amen.*

Day 218

2 Kings 22-23; 2 Chronicles 34-35

6th August

You Were Created for Dominion

Then God said, "Let Us make man in Our image, according to Our likeness; let them have dominion over the fish of the sea, over the birds of the air, and over the cattle, over all the earth and over every creeping thing that creeps on the earth" (Genesis 1:26 NKJV).

God works in the lives of men by grace. He saves, gives the gifts of the Holy Spirit, fulfills His promises by grace and empowers us to take dominion in all spheres of influence. God created man to have dominion over all creation as indicated by today's scripture.

Dominion is the ability to take charge, rule, or be in control. The first thing we must do to take dominion is discover our uniqueness and the gifts He has given us. Secondly, we need to discover the way God configures us because He calls us in line with the way He created us. Thirdly, we should find the specific area God desires us to shine because we can only have dominion in one area. Our prosperity in the kingdom of God is aimed at making us manifest the glory of God to the world.

God has provided us with all the resources we need to become what He ordained. As obedient children of God, we should strive to subject all creation to God's power as this glorifies and honours His name.

Further reading: Genesis 1:28; Luke 19:11-13
Prayer for today: Lord, I pray that you help me understand my area of dominion and take charge by your grace in Jesus' name, Amen.

Zephaniah 1-3

7th August

Sin Renders Prayer Ineffective

Surely the arm of the Lord is not too short to save, nor his ear too dull to hear. But your iniquities have separated you from your God; your sins have hidden his face from you, so that he will not hear (Isaiah 59:1-2).

Ignoring prayer is a great mistake. Those who neglect this discipline land in trouble as the evil one pursues them to destroy them. To pray effectively, we should have faith that God lives and act on communing with Him daily. The Bible commands us to pray without ceasing and not to grow faint in prayer (1 Thessalonians 5:17 and Luke 18:1). God is near and He cares about us. He is accessible to all who call on Him.

Some believers do not receive answers to their prayers because they are bound by sin. Sin is destructive as it weakens people spiritually rendering them ineffective and unproductive. Prayer and sin cannot coexist in the same heart; prayer will consume sin or sin will choke prayer. If not adequately addressed by repentance, sin paralyses the spiritual life of the one who commits it.

The prayers of the sinful and rebellious are abominable in the eyes of God. We therefore need to cultivate repentant hearts and turn away from every sin. We also need to ask the Holy Spirit to search our hearts and point out any sin that is not repented, so that we can act on it.

Further Reading: I John 1:8-9; Psalm 139:23-24
Prayer for the Day: Oh God, search my heart today, and forgive any hidden sins in my life, in Jesus' name, Amen.

Day 220 — Jeremiah 1-3

8th August

We Must Pray in the Will of God to Receive Answers

"This is the confidence we have in approaching God: that if we ask anything according to his will, he hears us. And if we know that he hears us - whatever we ask - we know that we have what we asked of him" (1 John 5:14-15).

God answers prayer that is offered according to His will. Our intercessions and petitions must be aligned with the word of God to receive answers from God. We need to take time to understand the will of God in everything we desire to do.

God turns down prayers that negate His will and purpose. Unfortunately, many people who fail to receive answers to prayer engage in fights and wrangles that further corrupt their hearts. Others are covetous and have murderous hearts, and their prayers emanate from wrong motives. For such, God does not honour their requests or pay attention to their pleas. James exhorts believers to be careful about the motives of their prayers.

The need for believers to make prayers in the will of God is critical especially in the end-times. Wickedness has increased greatly and the love of many toward God has grown cold (Matthew 24:12). We should however examine our hearts so that we can make prayers that bring delight to God. Those whose hearts are not fully committed to God often offer casual prayers which do not avail much. The Holy Spirit is only committed to those whose hearts are stayed on God not on selfish desires.

Further Reading: *James 4:1-4; Ephesians 5:17*
Prayer for the Day: *Lord, search my heart and examine the motive of my prayers, so that I may not pray a miss, Amen.*

Jeremiah 4-6

9th August

Faith Triumphs Over Opposition

Shadrach, Meshach and Abednego replied to the king, "O Nebuchadnezzar, we do not need to defend ourselves before you in this matter. If we are thrown into the blazing furnace, the God we serve is able to save us from it, and he will rescue us from your hand, O king. But even if he does not, we want you to know, O king, that we will not serve your gods or worship the image of gold you have set up" (Daniel 3:16-18).

To have faith that triumphs in the face of opposition demands that we work out our faith so that it becomes unshakeable. Shadrach, Meshach and Abednego had unrelenting faith, as they did not doubt that God existed. Their faith was in who God is, not in what He was able to do. They believed Him irrespective of whether or not He could rescue them from the fiery furnace. Their faith was immovable and life or death had no effect on it. They were ready to face the consequences of trusting God even if it cost them their lives.

To walk in the supernatural, we need to have unconditional faith in God. Whether He answers prayer or fails to, He remains the sovereign of the universe. Many Christians have lost their faith because of attaching it to what God can do, not on who He is. We should avoid this at all costs. Faith that is not founded on God is weak and cannot overcome evil powers. Our faith needs to be anchored in God not on His works because nothing is impossible with Him.

Further Reading: 1 John 5:4; Hebrews 11:32-39
Prayer for the Day: Father God I pray that you strengthen my faith in you, regardless of the opposition I may face, Amen.

Day 222 — Jeremiah 7-9

10th August

The Just Shall Live by Faith

"For therein is the righteousness of God revealed from faith to faith: as it is written, the just shall live by faith" (Romans 1:17, KJV)

The just shall live by faith is a timeless principle in the Scriptures. Quoting the words in Habakkuk 2:4, Paul reiterates the value of faith in the foundation and establishment of the lives of the saints.

Evil, wickedness, and tough times will not decrease but intensify. However, by faith in the word of God and in His mighty power, believers can enjoy divine immunity from the turbulence that will befall the world. The Bible says, "…When the enemy shall come in like a flood, the Spirit of the LORD shall lift up a standard against him" (Isaiah 59:19, KJV). It is crucial to note that God does not remove the flood. Rather, He raises the standard of His people through the power of the Holy Spirit so that they are above the storms that the enemy instigates. This makes them overcome demonic attacks of insecurity, diseases, hunger, spirits of death and all the evils in the world.

Believers are distinguished from unbelievers through their ability to thrive in the midst of crises by virtue of their faith. Their faith in God helps them overcome the wiles of the enemy. They hold on to God even during their most trying moments. They fully understand that without faith it is impossible to please God (Hebrews 11:6). In due time, they receive their full reward from Him.

Further Reading: Hebrews 11:1; Ephesians 6:10-11; 16
Prayer for the Day: Oh Lord, may my faith remain steadfast forever, in Jesus' name, Amen.

Jeremiah 10-13

11th August

The Shield of Faith is Powerful

"In addition to all this, take up the shield of faith, with which you can extinguish all the flaming arrows of the evil one" **(Ephesians 6:16).**

Every believer should guard his faith jealously because it is the shield that guarantees security from the flaming arrows of the enemy. Faith refers to confidence in God, who promises to richly reward all who trust in Him. The Book of Hebrews gives an example of people who were imprisoned, persecuted, insulted and deprived of property but overcame all this adversity by faith in God (Hebrews 10:33-35).

Faith is a sure shield. It offers protection from powers of darkness that abound in the world. It is listed among God's armour which believers should put on to stand in the spiritual battlefield. Demonic attacks are like arrows reinforced with fire to make them more lethal. Have confidence in God because it is impossible to please Him without it (Hebrews 11:6). The Bible is a book of possibilities but we cannot walk in them without faith.

Without faith, we cannot access our miracles and the supernatural. Having little or no faith limits the things God can do in and through someone. We need to pray for our faith because if it fails, it limits our ability to receive from God. We should not pray out of despair but out of a conviction that faith works.

Further Reading: Hebrews 11:1; 2 Corinthians 10:3-5
Prayer for the Day: Oh God, help me take up the shield of faith always, that I may extinguish the flaming arrows of the enemy.

Day 224 — Jeremiah 14-17

12th August

Power in the Blood of Jesus

"The blood will be a sign for you on the houses where you are; and when I see the blood, I will pass over you. No destructive plague will touch you when I strike Egypt" *(Exodus 12:13).*

The blood of Jesus is central in God's redemptive plan for mankind. It offers atonement for sin because in God's standards, sin cannot be forgiven without the shedding of blood (Hebrews 9:22). Even though the Bible talks about many types of blood, only the blood of Jesus offers salvation, healing and deliverance.

Both the Old and the New Testaments were sealed with blood. The former used the blood of bulls and goats (Hebrews 10:4) while the blood of Jesus (Matthew 26:28) sealed the latter. When the time came for the Lord to deliver His people from Egypt, He required them to slaughter a lamb and smear its blood on the doorposts. When the angel of death came, he passed over every house that had the mark of the blood. The occupants were exempted from destruction.

The word of God teaches that the blood of the Lamb and the words of the testimonies of God's people are vital tools in overcoming the enemy. Every believer needs to know how to apply the blood of Jesus in their lives because it is a very powerful weapon in defeating the power of the enemy in our lives.

Further Reading: Exodus 12:1-13; Hebrews 12:24; Revelation 12:11
Prayer for the Day: Thank You God for the blood of Jesus. Help me apply it in my life in Jesus' name, Amen

Jeremiah 18-22

13th August

Divine Exemption through Godly Company

"She went away and did as Elijah had told her. So there was food every day for Elijah and for the woman and her family. For the jar of flour was not used up and the jug of oil did not run dry, in keeping with the word of the LORD spoken by Elijah" (1 Kings 17:15-16).

The company a person keeps can determine whether he or she will receive a divine exemption. The wrong company can expose one to misfortune and judgment as God resists people whose ways are not upright.

An example of a person who enjoyed divine exemption is the widow who fed Elijah when there was a famine in Israel. The Lord miraculously provided her with food for Elijah, herself and her family, exempting them from famine and possible death. The Bible records the outcome of her obedience to the instruction of the man of God as we can see in our anchor Scripture. Before her encounter with Elijah, she only had enough flour and oil for one meal for her and her son. She was certain that provision would not come any time soon and she was ready to die together with her son, out of starvation (1 Kings 17:12). However, meeting Elijah changed her fate and a divine exchange took place. She received a divine exemption and was fully supplied throughout the famine.

Your company can determine your prosperity. Be mindful of the company you keep because it can help you get out of trouble. The presence of the man of God made all the difference in her life.

Further Reading: Psalm 1:1-3; 1 Corinthians 15:33
Prayer for the Day: Oh God, may my association with the godly people bring divine exemption in my daily endeavors, in Jesus' name, Amen.

Day 226 — Jeremiah 23-25

14th August

Bad Company Can Hinder Your Purpose in God

"Woe to me!" I cried. "I am ruined! For I am a man of unclean lips, and I live among a people of unclean lips, and my eyes have seen the King, the LORD Almighty." Then one of the seraphs flew to me with a live coal in his hand, which he had taken with tongs from the altar **(Isaiah 6:5-6).**

Encountering God helps us realise who we are and set ourselves apart for the Lord. When prophet Isaiah saw the glory and holiness of God, he realized his unworthiness because he was living among people of unclean lips. He learned that he could not act as God's spokesman among the people because of his unworthy conversations. It took confession and cleansing with a live coal by an angel, to be God's spokesman.

Isaiah's example teaches us to dissociate with bad company because it hinders the attainment of our God-given purpose. The same way bad company leads people to destruction, associating with the right company connects us to our destiny and purpose in God. Every saint who loves his or her destiny should abandon all forms of bad company.

Both spiritual and material prosperity depends on the company you keep. God makes a clear distinction between people who truly love Him and those who do not. It is important to renounce bad company because it corrupts good character and attracts God's wrath. This warning needs to be taken seriously because Scriptures say that those who relate closely with fools cannot escape destruction.

Further Reading: *1 Corinthians 15:33; Proverbs 13:20*
Prayer for the Day: *My God and my Father, grant me the grace to dissociate myself from bad company that could hinder my divine purpose.*

Jeremiah 26-29

Day 227

15th August

The Church is a City of Refuge

Then the LORD said to Joshua: "Tell the Israelites to designate the cities of refuge, as I instructed you through Moses, so that anyone who kills a person accidentally and unintentionally may flee there and find protection from the avenger of blood" (*Joshua 20:1*).

The Lord offered the children of Israel designated cities of refuge to which they could run and find refuge if they unintentionally killed their brethren. These cities offered security to people who had sinned inadvertently because the law did not afford them the chance to live.

Cities of refuge are symbolic of the church which is a place of divine protection and spiritual covering. When you join a church congregation, you should do due diligence to check whether it has a divinely sanctioned authority or spiritual covering. This is because the church is an umbrella to protect members from the attacks of the evil one. A believer can experience divine protection by virtue of the authority they submit to.

No one can bestow upon himself the honour of serving as a priest, because it is only God who chooses the people to serve Him as priests. He is the ultimate spiritual cover and He delegates it only to those He has chosen. Every believer should therefore walk in discernment and willingly submit to the spiritual covering that God has approved of. We are living in perilous times where there are many wolves in sheep's clothing. A believer should seriously seek God's direction on where to fellowship.

Further Reading: Hebrews 5:4; Hebrews 10:25; Genesis 22:2b
Prayer: My God in Jesus' name, help me willingly submit to the spiritual authority You have put me under, Amen.

Day 228 — Jeremiah 30-31

16th August

The Anointing Preserves God's people

"Do not touch my anointed ones; do my prophets no harm" *(Psalm 105:15).*

The anointing of the Holy Spirit is God's way of preserving His beloved. The Psalmist records that the Lord instructs the enemies of His people not to hurt them. The Holy Spirit is God's seal of ownership upon His people and offers approval and security. The fact that God has given an integral part of Himself to believers can be compared to a customer who makes a down payment on a commodity he intends to purchase.

The main reason the devil desires to tempt believers to grieve the Holy Spirit is because He is the only warranty they have for their lives. The Bible commands believers not to grieve Him because of the great role He plays in God's redemption plan. Every believer should be filled with the Holy Spirit because the word of God teaches that those who do not have the Spirit do not belong to Christ (Romans 8:9).

The Holy Spirit is the Comforter, Advocate, Helper, Intercessor, Standby and Counselor (John 16:7, AMP). He is also a teacher who guides them into all the truth (John 16:13). Apostle John says that the lessons the anointing offers believers are enough to sustain them in all things. He helps God's people to continually abide in the Father and enjoy the many benefits He has in store for His children. Our present and future are safe and secure, as long as we walk in the Spirit.

Further Reading: *2 Corinthians 1:21-22; Ephesians 4:30*
Prayer for the Day: *Holy Spirit, I pray that You may remain in me and help me not to grieve You in my daily walk with God Almighty, Amen.*

Jeremiah 32-34

Day 229

17th August

Sowing Righteousness

"At Caesarea there was a man named Cornelius, a centurion in what was known as the Italian Regiment. He and all his family were devout and God-fearing; he gave generously to those in need and prayed to God regularly" (Acts 10:1-2).

Cornelius, a Gentile centurion, sowed in mercy by giving alms to the poor alongside devotion and regular prayers (Acts 10:2-4). God was pleased because his righteous deeds had gone up before Him as a memorial. He and his household were marked for salvation because they lived in a godly life and showed acts of mercy (Acts 10:6, 22). They were not only saved but became pioneers of salvation and baptism of the Holy Spirit among the Gentiles (Acts 10:44). We can likewise reap the love of God through sowing seeds of righteousness by doing the work the Lord has commanded (Matthew 6:1-4).

The Lord can also exempt us from lack if we take His command to give seriously. He promises that those who give will be given, multiplied and increased to a degree commensurate with their generosity (Luke 6:38).

The implication of this message is that one can be exempted from lack and enjoy abundance by virtue of being generous. Giving is a key principle if you want to receive. Believers who do not enjoy the maximum benefits of what they sow should search their hearts and find out what hinders their harvest. The Holy Spirit will reveal the reason for lack of productivity if we ask Him.

Further Reading: Hosea 10:12; 2 Corinthians 9:6
Prayer for the Day: Oh God, help me sow generously in righteous acts so that when the time is ripe, I may reap abundantly, Amen.

Day 230 — Jeremiah 35-37

18th August

Seedtime and Harvest

"As long as the earth endures, seedtime and harvest, cold and heat, summer and winter, day and night will never cease" **(Genesis 8:22).**

The earth is controlled by the principle of sowing and reaping. God is just and ensures that all men harvest whatever they plant (Galatians 6:7). God has pronounced that as the earth exists, there will always be a time of scattering seed and a time of harvest. Those who sow good seeds can confidently look forward to receiving a harvest. Every good or bad deed a man engages in is a seed and it will certainly bear fruit. Therefore, each person needs to use the ability God has given him to do good. This includes helping the needy, the weak, and the poor.

The Lord commands us not to withhold good from those who deserve it. The power of life and death is in the tongue (Proverbs 18:21). When the people whose pain or suffering you alleviate by attending to them tell you, "God bless you," their words activate God's blessings. The Lord promises to rescue those who are concerned with the weak and the poor. He promises them protection and security from death. When they fall ill, the Lord sustains them on their sickbed (Psalm 41:1-3).

Since God blesses those who sow the right seeds, we should be diligent in our places of work. Those in authority should not mistreat those under them while employers should treat their employees with fairness, compassion and dignity.

Further Reading: **Psalms 41:1-3; Galatians 6:7**
Prayer for the Day: **Lord, I repent of the many times I sowed bad seeds and grieved Your Holy Spirit. Grant me the ability to sow seeds that befit repentance, in Jesus's name, Amen.**

Jeremiah 38-40; Psalm 74, 79

19th August

Promotion Comes from the Lord

"No one from the east or the west or from the desert can exalt a man. But it is God who judges: He brings one down, he exalts another" **(Psalm 75:6-7).**

In the secular world, people are elevated on the basis of merit. However, God sovereignly decides whom to promote in His kingdom. Many people who do not know ths secret work very hard to get promotions at their workplace without knowing that their human effort cannot sustain them. Understanding the key to seeking the kingdom of God as a first priority is crucial because all good and perfect gifts originate from Him(James 1:17).

God makes a way for us when we seek Him. He grants us the smoothness to do things with ease while other people struggle. He exempts His beloved from hard and fruitless labour because they seek His interests as the primary concern. His provision in every area of need comes as a bonus because He is just and owns everything (Psalm 24:1). His additions will always be sufficient to meet all the needs of His people.

Knowing and believing that God is a rewarder of all who diligently seek Him (Hebrews 11:6) is critical in activating the promise of receiving divine promotion. When He chooses to reward someone, He does it in His capacity as God; His rewards are sufficient to keep a person adequately supplied alongside generations after him.

Further Reading: Psalm 127:1-2; Matthew 6:33
Prayer for the Day: Lord, I thank you for it is You that grants promotion. I am grateful for when my time comes it shall be so, in Jesus' name, Amen.

Day 232 — 2 Kings 24-25; 2 Chronicles 36

20th August

Seek the Kingdom of God

"But seek first his kingdom and his righteousness, and all these things will be given to you as well" (Matthew 6:33).

Seeking the kingdom of God is the greatest privilege and responsibility accorded to us. It is an opportunity to invest in the eternal riches of the kingdom of heaven. The Lord is committed to availing the things unbelievers toil for to those who prioritise His Kingdom and His righteousness.

As disciples of Jesus invest all their time and energy in seeking the establishment of God's kingdom, He takes care of their needs. Scriptures teach that seeking His kingdom above all else is key to receiving rest from all the hassles unbelievers subject themselves to as they labour for their basic needs. He is aware that they need these things and has enough ways of providing if they have faith in Him. He also says that this spirit has taken root in many people because they have little faith and are full of worry. God can freely give them what many people labour to get over a lifetime if they fully devote themselves to seeking His kingdom.

When we walk in the ways of the Lord and meet conditions in His Word, God will bless us so abundantly that we will not have enough room to keep the blessings. A moment of favour with God is more valuable than a lifetime of human effort.

Further Reading: *Matthew 6:26-32; 1 Corinthians 4:20*
Prayer for the Day: *Heavenly Father, above all else, may I always seek Your kingdom first, Amen.*

Habakkuk 1-3

Day 233

21st August

Don't Peg Your Faith on Miracles Only

Then Joseph said to his brothers, "I am about to die. But God will surely come to your aid and take you up out of this land to the land he promised on oath to Abraham, Isaac and Jacob." And Joseph made the sons of Israel swear an oath and said, "God will surely come to your aid, and then you must carry my bones up from this place" **(Genesis 50:24-25).**

Joseph demonstrated faith in God and enjoyed its fruits. When he was about to die, he was full of faith and told his brothers that the God of their fathers would come to help them. The words of faith Joseph spoke bore fruit. Faith in God and His purposes made Joseph flee from Potiphar's wife when she approached him with the intention of engaging in immorality (Genesis 39:9-12). Walking with God requires that we believe He existed before the need we have. He is the everlasting God and does not change with circumstances. Our faith should not be pegged on miracles but enveloped by His existence. Faith holds the confidence that God rewards all those who seek Him diligently (Hebrews 11:6).

For our faith to bear lasting fruit, we must guard against backsliding, which is becoming increasingly common in the last few days. We must commit ourselves to walking in holiness and purity. The devil is on a mission to attack and discredit the faith of believers and we should be steadfast and alert to resist and overcome him.

Further reading: Hebrews 11:1; Hebrews 10:35; 1 John 5:4
Prayer for the Day: Father in heaven, may my faith rest on who You are and not just on what You do, Amen.

Day 234 — Jeremiah 41-45

22nd August

Use the Weapon of Prayer

'Pray without ceasing" (1 Thessalonians 5:17).

Each child of God should have the revelation that God answers prayer. Many people fail to pray diligently because they do not understand the power in this discipline. No believer is greater than his prayer life. Consequently, we should invest time in prayer especially in these end-times when so many unexpected things are bound to happen. The spirit world is continuously getting more vicious because forces of darkness are aware that their doom is near and are more furious now than ever.

Prayer is one of the greatest weapons God gave us. From the time one gets saved, they should be taught how to pray daily and purposefully in order to benefit in their walk with God. Our lives are spiritual and the things that happen to us originate from the spiritual realm. Since we are spiritual beings, the warfare we engage in is not of flesh and blood (Ephesians 6:12). We should therefore be alert so that we can confront and triumph over spiritual enemies that stand on our way (2 Corinthians 2:14).

So many people live in uncertainty and are not sure of the directions their lives may take. To live with confidence, we should tap the power of prayer that many people have neglected to their own peril. Praying consistently and in faith will give us the confidence we need to face every situation in life.

Further Reading: Ephesians 6:18; 2 Corinthians 10:3-5; James 5:17-18
Prayer for the Day: My God, grant me the tenacity to pray, as it is a vital spiritual weapon, Amen.

Jeremiah 46-48

23rd August

Depend on God with All Your Heart

As the king of Israel was passing by on the wall, a woman cried to him, "Help me, my lord the king!" The king replied, "If the LORD does not help you, where can I get help for you? From the threshing floor? From the winepress?" (2 Kings 6:26-27).

In ancient Israel, cities were fortified with large walls to keep away enemies. During attacks, enemies would build embankments around cities to hinder people from getting in or out. The city of Samaria was once thus besieged and its inhabitants were unable to access supplies. A woman cried out to the king for help. The king replied that the only sure source of help was the Lord, as the threshing floor had no grains and the winepress had no drink. Only God could help in this situation. This applies to us. We cannot escape occurrences such as wars, natural disasters and pestilences without God's help. Believers who desire to see the goodness of God must make Him their source and helper.

Although the Samaritan woman had access to the king, he had no solution for her problem. We too might have access to highly positioned people including the president, government officials and politicians. Unfortunately, they may not have the solutions you need because your case may be beyond human intervention. Instead of looking for connections and godfathers, seek God as the first priority; have Him as your Father. He is committed to hearing and answering the prayers of those who seek Him wholeheartedly (Jeremiah 29:13).

Further Reading: Jeremiah 33:3; Matthew 7:7
Prayer for the Day: Oh God, may I always put all my trust in You, for You alone never fails.

Day 236 — Jeremiah 49-50

24th August

God Changes Times and Seasons

"See, I am doing a new thing! Now it springs up; do you not perceive it? I am making a way in the desert and streams in the wasteland" **(Isaiah 43:19).**

God is in charge of seasons (Ecclesiastes 3:1). He changes times and seasons because He is sovereign. We should at all times strive to align ourselves with what He is doing. Scriptures assure us that God always does something new, but cautions us to be alert in order to perceive it.

We are living in times when we need spiritual eyesight to behold the things the Lord is doing. Two words are crucial in the above Scripture: the first is "see" which refers to the ability to comprehend with the spiritual eyes. It is about discerning with the eyes of the heart. The second is "perceive" which means to become aware, realize, understand, or interpret in a particular way. Whenever God ushers in a new season, He desires that we may perceive what He is doing and take Him at His word. We do this by walking by faith and obeying His commands.

We should be careful to open our spiritual eyes so that we do not miss the new season God has released in our careers, ministries, callings, homes, cities and nations. He has given us this new season to serve His purposes and prepare the world for His imminent return.

Further Reading: **Luke 12:56; 1 Chronicles 12:32**
Prayer for the Day: **Oh God, help me discern the seasons that come my way, and the grace to do what is required in each season.**

Jeremiah 51-52

25th August

Co-work with God in Prayer

"Ask and it will be given to you; seek and you will find; knock and the door will be opened to you" (Matthew 7:7).

All believers need to co-work with God by downloading what He has done in the spirit realm into the physical through prayer. The Bible describes believers as God's fellow workers (1 Corinthians 3:9). The Lord has placed us on earth to represent Him. As His emissaries, He is always waiting for us to ask, seek and knock at His door so that He can offer us what we need.

Our prayers should be continuous and unfailing. Those who prepare their lives by praying ahead of time receive answers unlike those who wait for trouble to come then start praying out of desperation. It is critical for those who desire to receive the manifestation of God's promises in their lives to pray because only those who ask receive, those who seek find, and those who knock have doors opened. This requires combining prayer with sacrifices, obedience and any other thing as the Holy Spirit guides. The guidance of the Holy Spirit on how and what to pray for is crucial as He is the master intercessor (Romans 8:26).

What has God spoken to you about? What door has He promised to open? Partner with Him in prayer and see His plans unfold.

Further Reading: Daniel 9:1-4; 1 Kings 18:1, 41-45
Prayer for the Day: My God, I ask for understanding of what You have released in the spirit realm and help me pursue its manifestation through prayer, Amen.

26th August

Take Dominion through the Key of Knowledge

"Woe to you experts in the law, because you have taken away the key to knowledge. You yourselves have not entered, and you have hindered those who were entering" (Luke 11:52).

When we understand the plan of God for our lives, it is easy to pursue it and eventually take dominion in our spheres of influence. The knowledge of God's plan for our lives is critical in taking dominion. From the days of John the Baptist, the kingdom of God suffers violence and the violent take it by force (Matthew 11:12). The greatest battle we face is that the enemy has taken away the key of knowledge that was meant to enable people to enter the kingdom of God.

The above scripture makes it clear that the devil used the experts of the law to hinder people from entering into the kingdom of God. They had been entrusted with the ability to interpret the law to people and enlighten them on how to receive the kingdom of God. However, they were distracted by the enemy to serve his purposes. They not only failed to enter the kingdom of God but also hindered those who were trying to do so.

As a believer, it is vital to seek to know God's will for our lives lest we are deceived. The key of knowledge can empower us to have dominion as God intended from the beginning. Invest your time in God's presence to know Him more and discern His will for your life.

Further Reading: **Ephesians 1:17-19; Ephesians 5:17; Philippians 3:10**
Prayer for the Day: **Oh God, I pray that You may reveal Yourself to me and help me understand Your will, Amen.**

27th August

Commitment is the Secret to Success

"Be diligent in these matters; give yourself wholly to them, so that everyone may see your progress" (1 Timothy 4:15).

Not all successful people are necessarily the most intelligent or educated. A good number could be categorized as average. However, one thing that is common with all of them is their commitment towards the cause they believe in. Commitment does not see obstacles; it only sees growth and countless possibilities. A committed person sees challenges as opportunities and overcomes them by grit and determination. Such people please God, as they spare no effort in their quest to do His will.

Commitment makes life move forward. Life is full of hurdles and we are bound to face many things which could hinder our progress and neutralize our attempts to advance. However, through commitment, we can forge ahead and attain greatness and fulfillment. Commitment helps us live successfully despite being surrounded by circumstances that could lead to failure. Many people think that they can have a great life without effort, discipline or hard work. This is impossible because greatness is costly.

We cannot move forward without wholehearted commitment. In giving Timothy the keys to progress in his calling and ministry, Paul admonished him to be willing to suffer or subject himself into strict discipline. An old adage says, "no pain, no gain," meaning that good things do not just happen. Someone has to be willing to make them happen. Make things happen in your life through the key of commitment.

Further Reading: Proverbs 12:24; John 18:37; Acts 20:24
Prayer for the Day: My God and my Father, my greatest desire is to be committed to your divine assignment always, in Jesus' name, Amen.

Day 240 — Ezekiel 1-4

28th August

Be Wholeheartedly Committed to God

"Trust in the LORD with all your heart and lean not on your own understanding; in all your ways acknowledge him, and he will make your paths straight" (Proverbs 3:5-6).

Your commitment to God should be a priority because it determines how far you go in all areas of life. If God closes a door, money, credentials, family and social networks cannot open it. We should therefore humble ourselves before God and seek His will for our lives. The enemy cannot close a door God has opened for you no matter how hard he tries. Conversely, even if you toil with all your strength but God has closed a door, your efforts will be in vain. I believe and teach that a moment of favor with God is better that a lifetime of human effort.

If God is not on your side, you will face frustrations, struggles and failures. The Psalmist says that it is vain to attempt to do anything without divine help. Our first commitment should be to hear God, obey Him and do His will (Deuteronomy 10:12-13), because we cannot succeed without Him. There is a way that seems good in the eyes of a man but the end of it is death (Proverbs 14:12). Disobedience ends in destruction. The best decision we can ever make is committing every aspect of our lives to Him.

Further Reading: **Psalm 127:1; Psalm 124:1-6**
Prayer for the Day: **Father, I commit my life and all my endeavours to You. Oh God guide me in everything, Amen.**

29th August

Determination is Powerful

"Be diligent in these matters; give yourself wholly to them, so that everyone may see your progress" (1 Timothy 4:15)

Some apportion blame to parents, friends, enemies or even Satan for their undesirable outcomes in life. In many instances, we are responsible for the hardship we go through because we are not determined enough to act on them. When we are fully determined to pursue something in life, no opposing force can stop us. Our enemies can perceive how devoted we are to the things we do and quit if we refuse to relent in pursuing what God has promised. The enemies of our destinies are opportunistic; they look for chances to derail us especially if we yield to discouragement and stop pursuing His purposes. After unsuccessfully tempting Jesus three times, he left Him to wait for an opportune time (Matthew 4:11). He does the same with us.

Nothing is impossible for a person who is wholeheartedly devoted to a cause. Scripture assures us that our progress will be evident to all if we spare no effort in doing what God has called us to do.

Greatness is a product of determination. Have you given yourself fully to pursue your destiny? Are you determined to become the person God created? Be a realist and stop wishing for things to happen; make them happen through the power of determination.

Further Reading: Genesis 11:5-6; Luke 9:62
Prayer for the Day: Dear God, may thy grace which is always sufficient for me, enable me pursue my destiny with determination, Amen.

Ezekiel 9-12

30th August

Have Confidence in God

"If we are thrown into the blazing furnace, the God we serve is able to save us from it, and he will rescue us from your hand, O king. But even if he does not, we want you to know, O king, that we will not serve your gods or worship the image of gold you have set up" (Daniel 3:17-18).

King Nebuchadnezzar commanded that a golden statue be erected and everybody under his authority to worship it. Three young men Meshach, Shadrach and Abednego refused to bow down to that idol. Furious, Nebuchadnezzar ordered they be thrown into a fiery furnace. The furnace was heated seven times more than normal but the young men did not change their minds because they had great confidence in God.

They were not burnt. The Son of God joined them and they praised God in the midst of the fire. They were divinely exempted from death. When we have confidence in God, all situations co-operate with us. Things meant to destroy us fail to do so as God turns them around for our good because of our faith in Him. Our confidence in God should be based on who He is and not only what He can do. The word of God offers us a sure foundation on which we can build our confidence in God.

Further Reading: Hebrews 10:35; 1 Timothy 1:12
Prayer for day: O God, help me have total confidence in You today and in all my life, in Jesus' name, Amen.

Ezekiel 13-15

Day 243

31st August

Growing in the Kingdom of God Takes Time

"The kingdom of heaven is like a mustard seed, which a man took and planted in his field. Though it is the smallest of all your seeds, yet when it grows, it is the largest of garden plants and becomes a tree, so that the birds of the air come and perch in its branches" **(Matthew 13:31-32).**

Jesus used the parable of the mustard seed to explain some of the mysteries of the kingdom of God. A mustard seed is not only the smallest seed but also takes time to grow. The growth process is so slow that it is impossible to observe it with our naked eyes. Since God is not limited by time, we sometimes feel like He is taking too long to fulfill His promises. However, understanding how He views time can help us wait upon Him without losing heart. God is not slow but patient so that all people may turn to Him by faith.

Sometimes we pray, fast, and wait upon God to do things as fast as we wish, but little seems to happen. However, God is always at work even when we cannot perceive it. As such, we must allow God to transform our lives in His time, or else we will be discouraged.

The kingdom of God demands that we train ourselves to trust the process of gradual progression that God may choose to take us through. Once the product is finished, we are able to proclaim that it is the doing of the Lord, and it is marvelous in our eyes.

Further Reading: 2 Peter 3:8-9; Mark 4:26-27
Prayer for the Day: Oh God, help me to be patient with you even as you work all things out for my good, halleluiah.

Day 244 — Ezekiel 16-17

1st September

The Kingdom of Small Beginnings

"Who despises the day of small things?" (Zechariah 4:10a).

The word of God admonishes us not to despise small beginnings. This is because the kingdom of God is characterized by small beginnings, regardless of how far a person is destined to go. Each saint must agree with the will of God to grant gradual increase from humble beginnings to the attainment of one's destiny. Some of the prophetic revelations believers receive from God appear too grand to be true especially when we consider their low states. However, through divine enablement and the working of the grace of God, they become increasingly manifest as one walks with God and depends on His help. God requires that we continually trust Him and be patient as He increases us from one level of glory to another.

Sometimes, the kingdom of God seems inconsequential or insignificant the same way a mustard seed appears tiny when sown (Mark 4:30-32). At times, God may instruct an individual to start something that may seem insignificant or of little meaning to many. If one obeys, they experience a supernatural harvest and great breakthrough to the amazement of observers. Most success stories in ministry, career, business and leadership had small beginnings but grew when they were cultivated with God's help and discipline. Accepting small beginnings is a sign that you have faith in God who makes us prosper. Be willing to start small and let God unfold your destiny.

Further Reading: Job 8:7; 2 Corinthians 3:18
Prayer for the Day: My Father and my God, help me not to despise small beginnings but trust in you for enablement to grow from glory to glory, Amen.

Ezekiel 18-19

2nd September

The Process of God's Making

"Come, follow me," Jesus said, "and I will make you fishers of men" (Mark 1:17).

The kingdom of God is systematic and procedural. God has made great and precious promises to His people but between the promises and their fulfillment, there is a process. God may call and show you the great destiny He has ordained, but you have to go through a process to become the minister, career person, businessperson or leader He desires.

Before Jesus told His disciples: *"Go ye therefore…"* (Matthew 28:19, KJV), He had earlier told them, "Come ye after me, and I will make you…" The Lord had first to make them. They needed to be transformed from fishermen to fishers of men. God takes time to make a sermon out of our lives since our lives minister more than words. Walking with God daily, listening and knowing Him transforms us into competent vessels He can entrust with power and authority.

When God calls us, we may appear different from what He desires us to be. However, as we cooperate with Him, He increasingly clothes us with His power and glory until we become the people He desires. The duration of the preparation process varies from one person to another. Some take longer than others do before they see fruits in their calling. If one is not ready to go through the process of making, He cannot co-work with God to advance His kingdom on earth.

Further Reading: Isaiah 66:8; Romans 8:30
Prayer for the Day: My God I pray that You may help me endure as I go through Your process of making, amen.

Day 246 — Ezekiel 20-21

3rd September

God Walks with Us and Dwells in Us

"For you are the temple of the living God. As God has said: I will dwell in them and walk among them. I will be their God, and they shall be My people" *(2 Corinthians 6:16, NKJV).*

God delights in walking and dwelling among His people. Enoch walked with God for centuries (Genesis 5:21-24). Subsequently, beginning with Abraham, God walked with the patriarchs. God promised that He would be with them and protect them wherever they went. God's presence was with them during the journey from Egypt to the Promised Land, building of the tabernacle and rebuilding the temple. His manifest presence was in the tabernacle and in the temple to give safety, protection and peace.

The Bible teaches us that all these were shadows of what would happen in the New Testament (Colossians 2:17; Hebrews 8:5; 10:1). The reality though, is in Christ Jesus. God was pleased to have all His fullness dwell in Christ (Colossians 1:19).

In the New Testament, God makes His dwelling in the hearts of the saints. Our bodies are the temples of the Holy Spirit. God no longer lives in man-made temples but dwells in the hearts of believers. God desires to live and walk with us. For God to walk with us, He must live in us and we must offer our bodies as His dwelling place.

Further Reading: **1 Corinthians 6:19-20**
Prayer for the Day: **Lord, I offer my body as a temple to Your Spirit that You may dwell in me, Amen.**

Ezekiel 22-23

Day 247

4th September

The Blessing of God Abiding in Us

The ark of the Lord remained in the house of Obed-Edom the Gittite for three months, and the Lord blessed him and his entire household. Now King David was told, "The Lord has blessed the household of Obed-Edom and everything he has, because of the ark of God" (2 Samuel 6:11-12).

The Ark of the Covenant was a portable chest with two related items - the mercy seat and the cherubim. In the history of Hebrews, it was the most important sacred object during the wilderness sojourn. It represented God's presence among His people.

An interesting experience is recorded about the Ark of the Covenant, which was taken to the house of Obed-Edom the Gittite. He experienced immense blessings because of its presence. It stayed in the house of Obed-Edom for three months and during that time, he was blessed in every possible way. The same thing happens to those who walk with God; they are blessed in every aspect of their lives.

Allowing God to dwell in us helps attract His blessings. We should not mechanically seek blessings while ignoring God who owns all. Our primary interest should be seeking God because when we find Him, we get everything else. All glory, power, riches, wisdom, strength, honour and blessings belong to Jesus. Thus, Christ is everything many are busy chasing after.

Further Reading: Revelation 5:11-13; Ephesians 1:3
Prayer for the Day: God, I make room for you in my life by the help of Your Spirit that You may abide in me, Amen.

Day 248 — Ezekiel 24-27

5th September

Biblical Definition of Humility

And be clothed with humility, for "God resists the proud, but gives grace to the humble." Therefore humble yourselves under the mighty hand of God, that He may exalt you in due time (1 Peter 5:5b-7).

Humility is freedom from arrogance that grows out of recognizing that who we are and what we have comes from God. Some people despise humility because they mistakenly perceive it as a sign of inadequacy, lack of dignity and worthlessness. This is inaccurate because true greatness lies in humility. Jesus is the supreme example of humility (Matthew 11:29; Mark 10:45; John 13:4-17; Philippians 2:5-8). He is adequate and infinite in dignity and worth. Biblical humility is not belittling oneself but exalting others especially God and Christ (John 3:30). A humble person focuses more on God and others than on self.

Biblical humility is also recognizing that by ourselves, we are inadequate and worthless. Yet, because we are created in God's image and are believers in Christ, we have infinite worth and dignity (1 Corinthians 4:6-7; 1 Peter 1:18-19). True humility produces gratitude. Since God is both Creator and Redeemer, our existence and righteousness depend on Him (John 15:5; Acts 17:28; Ephesians 2:8-10). The opposite of humility is pride. Pride is a haughty attitude shown by somebody who believes, often unjustifiably, that he or she is better than others. Proud people seek to glorify themselves, and not God. The Bible says that God gives grace to the humble but opposes the proud.

Further Reading: Philippians 2:3-4; Psalm 147:6, Acts 17:28
Prayer for the Day: Oh God, grant me the ability to walk in true humility so that I may receive Your grace and lifting, for Your name's sake, Amen.

Ezekiel 28-31

Day 249

6th September

Pride Comes Before Destruction

"Pride goes before destruction, a haughty spirit before a fall" (Proverbs 16:18).

Pride can be defined as a haughty attitude shown by somebody who believes, often unjustifiably, that he or she is better than others. Proud people are interested in glorifying themselves instead of God. They consider themselves better than others.

God rejected King Saul when he exhibited pride especially after his victory over the Amalekites. He did not give glory to God (1 Samuel 15:10-15). Saul sinned against God by sparing the things God commanded him to destroy. As if that was not enough, he built a monument for himsef as a memorial for the victory. He was disobedient even after God fought for him and took the glory himself. While erecting the monument, Saul failed to ascribe the glory to God as Samuel had done earlier when he said, "This far the Lord has helped us" (1 Samuel 7:12). When Samuel confronted him about his sin, Saul did not repent. Instead, he gave excuses and tried to justify why he had done so. Eventually, God rejected him as king of Israel.

Pride prevents us from walking with God because of its unrepentant nature. When Satan exalted himself, God threw him down together with other proud and disloyal angels. Satan cunningly employs the same strategy to tempt servants of God. He knows that those who entertain this sin will meet the same fate; falling. Do not fall for his bait!

Further Reading: James 4:6; Daniel 4:28-33
Prayer for the Day: Oh Lord, help me deal with the spirit of pride in my life. I pray for the grace to walk in humility Lord, for You exalt the humble and reject the proud.

Ezekiel 28-31

7th September

The Danger of Self-glorification

Twelve months later, as the king was walking on the roof of the royal palace of Babylon, he said, "Is not this the great Babylon I have built as the royal residence, by my mighty power and for the glory of my majesty?" (Daniel 4:29-30).

Self-glorification is taking God's glory. God has forbidden man from glorifying himself. Unfortunately, many people have disregarded this command and suffered destruction. In some of the testimonies believers share concerning what God has done, they deflect attention from God to themselves. Instead of directing people towards God, they exalt themselves, their achievements, ministries or careers. As a result, people focus on them rather than God. God does not allow such people to prosper but judges them for not giving praise to God (Acts 12:23).

Nebuchadnezzar reigned over Babylon when the Israelites were in exile. He dreamt of a big tree being cut down and when he sought for interpretation, Daniel informed him that he was that tree and that God would judge him. Daniel entreated him to repent so that the intended evil would not be brought upon him. However, his pleas were ignored. After a year, the prophetic word of God was fulfilled. Nebuchadnezzar attributed the success and splendor of Babylon to his own efforts and greatness, power and might; he did not honour God. He usurped the glory of God and was judged. God frowns at pride. We should never entertain it in any of its various forms.

Further Reading: *Proverbs 16:18; Isaiah 42:8*
Prayer for the Day: *Oh God, deliver me from every form of self-glorification. Receive all glory and honour forever and ever, Amen*

Ezekiel 35-37

Day 251

8th September

Do Not Touch God's Glory

On the appointed day Herod, wearing his royal robes, sat on his throne and delivered a public address to the people. They shouted, "This is the voice of a god, not of a man." Immediately, because Herod did not give praise to God, an angel of the Lord struck him down, and he was eaten by worms and died (Acts 12:21-23).

The God of Israel demands humility from man. Those who exalt and glorify themselves incur His wrath because He jealously guards His glory. God expects those who claim to know Him to honour Him in a manner commensurate with their level of knowledge. God holds us accountable for our actions in proportion to the revelation He has given. The more we know Him, the more privileges we enjoy, but the more accountable we should be to the truth we know.

Herod did not speak blasphemous words. However, he felt self-important when the people praised him and made comments that ascribed glory to him. Instead of glorifying God, he delighted in the blasphemous words the people spoke. The angel of the Lord struck him and he was immediately eaten by worms and died.

We owe everything we are, have or have accomplished to God. Our intelligence, good planning and efforts cannot give victory. We ought to take our rightful position in humility and give all glory to God Almighty. When we glorify Him, we enjoy blessings and maintain our victory.

Further Reading: Proverbs 16:18; Daniel 4:28-33; John 3:30
Prayer for the Day: O God, help me never to take the glory that You deserve, receive it all forever, Amen.

Ezekiel 38-39

9th September

Make Effort to Meet God's Standards of Righteousness

"Woe to me!" I cried. "I am ruined! For I am a man of unclean lips, and I live among a people of unclean lips, and my eyes have seen the King, the Lord Almighty" *(Isaiah 6:5).*

Repentance is God's gift to man to enable him walk with Him. God's standards of holiness are too high for man to attain. Therefore, we need to repent continuously so that we can have continuous fellowship with Him. God reveals our true character as we walk with Him. We might mistakenly assume that we are holy but when God's light shines upon our hearts, we discover that we are wanting. Isaiah did not know the uncleanness of his heart until he saw the glory of God. It is worth noting that until this time, Isaiah had been prophesying God's messages but not with the level of holiness God requires.

Many believers are mistakenly satisfied by the standard of righteousness they operate in. However, when we continue walking intimately with God, we identify the areas in which we need to offer repentance to be truly free. Repentance is key in walking with God. Apostle John reiterates that if we claim to be without sin, we make God to be a liar and His truth is not in us (1 John 1:8). We need to make it our goal to seek the highest levels of God's righteousness by repenting all manner of sin so that we can maintain our fellowship and right standing with God.

Further Reading: Romans 3:23; Jeremiah 17:9-10
Prayer for the Day: God, I pray that You may grant me a repentant heart and help me live up to Your standards of righteousness, in Jesus' name, Amen.

Ezekiel 40-41

Day 253

10th September

Build Your Spiritual Hedge through Repentance

When a period of feasting had run its course, Job would send and have them purified. Early in the morning he would sacrifice a burnt offering for each of them, thinking, "Perhaps my children have sinned and cursed God in their hearts." This was Job's regular custom (Job 1:5).

Sin does not only separate us from God but also breaks the protective hedge that surrounds us. This makes any person who commits sin vulnerable to attacks of the enemy. Job understood the power of repentance as a way of protecting his children. He offered sacrifices for them whenever they went feasting because he felt that they could have sinned against God during the merry-making. He was a wise spiritual builder and his prayer maintained a spiritual wall around his family and property. This made it difficult for Satan to just attack his family at will.

Parents have authority over their children and should offer repentance on their behalf. Many young people engage in ungodly activities that expose them to divine judgment. Repenting on their behalf can secure and lead them to salvation, because God is merciful and desires that all people should be saved.

As believers, we sometime have premonitions about our lives and those of people close to us. This often implies that they are spiritually exposed and lack a spiritual cover since their spiritual walls may be broken. Through repentance, one can deal with satanic tides that would otherwise destroy a person, family or nation.

Further Reading: Ezekiel 22:30; Ecclesiastes 10:8b
Prayer for the Day: My God in Jesus' name, I ask for the grace of a spiritual builder, that I may be safe from spiritual attacks, Amen.

11th September

True Repentance Precedes Revival

"Repent, then, and turn to God, so that your sins may be wiped out, that times of refreshing may come from the Lord" (Acts 3:19).

Revival is always a product of repentance. Biblical and human history indicates that all spiritual awakenings were preceded by deep repentance. Sin acts as a barrier between God and man. It turns His ears away from the cry of the wicked. Man has to deal with sin first before he can encounter God. In ancient Israel, before God met His people, He often commanded them to wash their garments. In this dispensation, this corresponds to the cleansing achieved through the blood of Jesus Christ. Before we invite God, He requires us to be washed by the blood of His Son Jesus Christ.

Repenting and cleansing ourselves in preparation to receive God's presence is exemplified in 2 Chronicles 5:11-14. Before the glory of God came down, the priests sanctified themselves. In these end-times, God will release His Spirit without measure to those who yield to the cleansing work of the cross. Repentance and living holy lives are key in walking with God and experiencing revival. People who walk with God will do exploits. Our God is holy and we cannot walk with Him if we entertain sin. The Lord is a consuming fire; His presence cannot withstand sin. He requires us to emulate His character by walking in purity.

Further Reading: *Joshua 24:19; Matthew 4:17*
Prayer for the Day: *Oh God, cleanse me and give me the ability to live a holy life that I may experience Your times of refreshing, Amen.*

Ezekiel 44-45

Day 255

12th September

True Worship is based on Right Knowledge of God

"If we are thrown into the blazing furnace, the God we serve is able to save us from it, and he will rescue us from your hand, O king. But even if he does not, we want you to know, O king, that we will not serve your gods or worship the image of gold you have set up" (Daniel 3:17-18).

Ignorance is one of the greatest hindrances to true worship of God. Some people know God in a limited way; only as a problem solver, a deliverer, provider or giver of peace, but they have no knowledge of Him as a saviour, healer and Father. To enjoy dominion and attain the fullness of our destinies, we must have the right knowledge of who He is. We must see Him in the light of His eternal nature and unlimited power.

Many people fail to worship God in the full splendor of His glory because their worship is dictated by what they think He does or does not do. This makes them deny Him the glory He deserves. The three Hebrew men knew the greatness of God is not determined by Him performing miracles or not. They refused to allow their circumstances dictate their worship of God, which they did in truth and in spirit.

To become true worshippers, we must be prepared to worship God in the good and bad things. A true worshipper always sets his heart on worshipping God, whether things work for or against him.

Further Reading: Habakkuk 3:17-18; John 4:23-24
Prayer for the Day: Oh Lord, help me to always worship You in truth and in spirit, regardless of the challenges that may come my way, Amen.

Day 256 — Ezekiel 46-48

13th September

God Seeks True Worshippers

"But the hour is coming, and now is, when the true worshipers will worship the Father in spirit and truth; for the Father is seeking such to worship Him. God is Spirit, and those who worship Him must worship in spirit and truth" (John 4:23-24).

Few people worship God in a worthy manner. Even fewer know how to honour, extol and glorify Him. Some humble themselves before Him out of fear of eternal judgment while others are driven by a desire to receive signs, miracles and wonders. Their motivation for seeking God in reading the word, fellowship and prayer is not in the perfect will of God. Those who worship God outside the way He has prescribed forsake Him when He fails to meet their carnal desires.

True worshippers are sincere and do not engage in hypocrisy. The kind of worshippers God is looking for are those who will worship Him, not in buildings or mountains, but in truth and spirit. Worshipping God in truth is worship based on true knowledge of who He is, in sincerity of heart without hypocrisy. Worshipping God in spirit is doing so from the depth of the heart. Remember it is our spirit that communes with God - who is also a Spirit. As such, complete worship should involve our spirits being united with the Spirit of God in deep communion. We should therefore purpose to worship Him with all our hearts.

Further Reading: **Psalm 93; Psalm 95:6-7; Daniel 3:17-18**
Prayer for the Day: **Oh God may You fill me with Your Spirit a fresh that I may worship You in Spirit and in truth, in Jesus' name, Amen.**

Joel 1-3

Day 257

14th September

God Delivered Us to Worship Him

Then say to him, "The Lord, the God of the Hebrews, has sent me to say to you: Let my people go, so that they may worship me in the desert" (Exodus 7:16).

God delivered the Israelites from Egypt so that they could be free to worship Him. We too, are delivered to worship Him. While in bondage, the Israelites served oppressive and thankless masters who made them work as slaves. When they cried out to God in their desperation, He heard and sent Moses with a message to Pharaoh to let His people go.

Like the Israelites, we who are in Christ were delivered from the dominion of darkness so that we could worship and serve God. To please God, we need to serve Him unconditionally. God paid for our redemption through the sacrifice of His Son. We should thus not attach our worship to the gains we expect from Him. The Lord deserves our worship at all times.

By His grace, God redeemed us from all iniquity and purified us with a view of making us zealous for good works. We should therefore allow the word of God to transform our mindset so that we can serve the purposes for which He created us. We should understand that we were created for worship, and were redeemed to worship Him.

Further Reading: Colossians 1:12-14; Titus 2:12-14
Prayer for the Day: Oh God, You created, saved and called me that I may worship You. Help me to offer my true worship to You at all times, Amen.

Day 258 — Daniel 1-3

15th September

True Worshippers Receive Abundant Blessings

"But seek first the kingdom of God and His righteousness, and all these things shall be added to you" (Matthew 6:33).

Our primary motivation in life as disciples of Christ is to serve and please God. We do not worship God for gain but the Scriptures teach us that God abundantly blesses true worshippers. As such, God desires that we deny ourselves and pay allegiance to Him.

When we make seeking the kingdom of God and His righteousness our priority, He provides everything we need to live comfortably. As we become intimate with God, He reveals the secrets of His kingdom. The word of God promises that we shall enjoy abundant divine provision if we align ourselves with God's interests. David walked closely with God because he had a heart of worship. Though he began as a poor herd's boy, God gradually elevated him to greatness and greatly blessed him. By the time he handed his throne to Solomon his son, he had accumulated enough wealth both for his children and for building the temple. He worshipped God with sincerity and He rewarded him greatly. At the end of his life, the Bible records, "…So he died in a good old age, full of days and riches and honour"(1 Chronicles 29:27-28).

Abraham, Isaac and Job are some of the other worshippers whom God blessed richly. Their experiences demonstrate that there is a close relationship between true worship and wealth. God honours true worshippers with long life, wealth and honour.

Further Reading: Psalm 37:4; Psalm 91:14-16; Exodus 23:25
Prayer for the Day: Dear God, help me to seek Your kingdom first, as commanded in Your Word. Grant me the grace to become a true worshipper.

Daniel 4-6

Day 259

16th September

True Worship Has a Cost

Sometime later God tested Abraham…Take your son, your only son, Isaac, whom you love, and go to the region of Moriah. Sacrifice him there as a burnt offering on one of the mountains I will tell you about" …and said "I swear by myself, declares the Lord, that because you have done this and have not withheld your son, your only son, I will surely bless you… (Genesis 22:1a-2, 16-17a).

True worship is costly but pays handsomely. It demands that an individual should not be attached to anything, but wholeheartedly pay allegiance to the living God. The Lord our God is a jealous God and does not allow anything to take His place in our lives. God called Abraham from his father's land where the people worshipped other gods. God called him to set himself apart and worship Him alone, promising to bless and make a nation out of him (Genesis 12:1-3).

God blessed Abraham and made him exceedingly wealthy. However, it is worth noting that this greatness came at a cost. God subjected Abraham to one of the greatest tests any man has ever faced. The Lord asked him to offer his only son as a burnt offering. Abraham was a worshipper and obeyed God. In return, God confirmed the covenant of His blessings upon him (Genesis 22:15-18). Like the patriarchs, we must be ready to pay the cost of our worship because there is no worship without sacrifice.

Further Reading: Luke 14:25-33; 2 Samuel 24:24
Prayer for the Day: Dear Lord, I thank You for helping me understand that, 'there is no worship without sacrifice.' I pray for the grace and willingness to pay the cost of true worship, Amen.

Day 260 — Daniel 7-9

17th September

The Test of True Worship

"Naked I came from my mother's womb, and naked I will depart. The Lord gave and the Lord has taken away; may the name of the Lord be praised." In all this, Job did not sin by charging God with wrongdoing (Job 1:21-22).

Job is an example of a true worshipper. By faith in God, he overcame great adversity and maintained his integrity despite facing severe trials. He remained steadfast in his faith in God and even after his wealth and family were decimated, he still worshipped God. After calamities struck, he bowed and worshipped him. Unfortunately, many people – believers included – grumble, murmur or complain to God when they face hardship and trials, instead of worshipping Him. We pass the test of true worship when our allegiance to God is not affected by the things we go through.

It takes a heart of worship to thank God sincerely when you lose your possessions, spouse or children. When we become authentic worshippers, lack, misfortune, hunger, thirst and loss drive us closer to God rather than away from Him.

Such people are rare. They are the worshippers the Spirit of God desires to find. They love God without question. To fit in this category of worshippers, we need to stop asking Him questions and worship Him as the Almighty and sovereign of the universe. We must allow God's Spirit to transform us into true worshippers.

Further Reading: John 4:23-24; Habakkuk 3:17-19
Prayer for the Day: My God and my Father, Fill me with Your Spirit and grant me strength to pass the test of loyalty to You, Amen.

Daniel 10-12

18th September

Understand Wisdom in the Biblical Perspective

"When all Israel heard the verdict the king had given, they held the king in awe, because they saw that he had wisdom from God to administer justice" (1 Kings 3:28).

Wisdom can be defined as applied knowledge. Wisdom is different from knowledge which refers to general awareness or possession of information, facts, ideas, truth or principles. Having knowledge alone does not guarantee success. Each of us must have seen a person whom they considered knowledgeable but did indiscreet acts. Many intelligent people do not do right because they are spiritually weak and incapable of putting the knowledge they have to work.

Biblically, wisdom can be described as the ability to "see." That refers to making sound judgement and following the best course of action based on understanding. Wisdom helps us clearly perceive things which others find difficulty in. Solomon was able to settle a dispute between two mothers about their babies because he was divinely empowered to administer justice. He demonstrated great understanding and good judgment.

Old Testament prophets were referred to as seers because they could see into the future. They also had special insight into issues that people could not easily perceive. Consequently, they could counsel God's people. Wisdom gives a person the ability to see life's issues clearly. It gives guidance in making the right choices when faced by dilemmas. Godly wisdom enables one to see the purposes of God in their lives, understand their requirements as well as the path they should follow to attain their destiny.

Further Reading: James 1:5; Ephesians 5:17-18; James 3:13-17
Prayer for the Day: Oh God, like Solomon, I ask for Your wisdom so that I can understand and serve Your purposes, Amen.

Day 262 | Ezra 1-3

19th September

Godly Wisdom is Manifested in Our Actions

"Who is wise and understanding among you? Let him show it by his good life, by deeds done in the humility that comes from wisdom" *(James 3:13).*

Godly wisdom is seen when we walk our talk. It is manifested in thought and good deeds. Knowledge operates in the realms of thought but wisdom is demonstrated in the things we do. We can tell that we have received divine wisdom when we live according to His revealed word. Our words and actions please God when they are guided by spiritual wisdom and understanding. The Bible says, "the fear of the Lord is the beginning of wisdom; a good understanding have all those who do His commandments (Psalm 111:10). Some people are knowledgeable and great thinkers. They can teach others what they know and answer any question. However, their actions are ungodly and this makes them miss the mark of divine wisdom.

Some people have a wide acclaim in scholarly achievements, sports, arts and business. They have accomplished great things through hard work but deep within, they are empty because they have little heavenly wisdom. However hard they try, they are unable to have abundant lives that only Christ can offer to those who commit to doing the will of God. True wisdom is manifested in good deed and comes from God. When you live according to God's word, you walk in heavenly wisdom and God blesses you.

Further Reading: *Proverbs 9:10; Matthew 11:19b*
Prayer for the Day: *Dear God, fill me with Your wisdom that I may walk and live in it, in these evil times, Amen.*

20th September

Wisdom Helps Us Retain God's Glory

"Like a gold ring in a pig's snout is a beautiful woman who shows no discretion" *(Proverbs 11:22).*

Acquiring spiritual treasures is relatively easy but maintaining them is hard work. The Bible likens a beautiful woman who lacks wisdom to a gold ring in a pig's snout. Gold represents wealth or glory and a beautiful woman is an image of the church - the bride of Christ. A pig is a dirty animal and cannot comprehend the value and significance of a gold ring. Therefore, it can neither appreciate it nor care for it. Despite having it on its snout, it will wallow in the mire. The same is true of a believer who lacks wisdom. Such a person does not appreciate the glory of God he or she carries, and would consequently not restrain himself or herself from doing things that are defiling, thus dishonouring God.

A person who lacks wisdom cannot care for or handle the treasures given by God. When we enter the kingdom of God, He deposits great treasures into our lives and the enemy viciously pursues them to destroy or steal them. If he succeeds, he can make us unfruitful and our walk of faith ineffective. This is why we must yield to God so that we can resist the enemy.

Some of us carry revival, healing for the nations and deliverance for cities. We must therefore treasure divine wisdom as it enables us actualize our God given visions.

Further Reading: 2 Corinthians 4:7; 2 Timothy 1:14
Prayer for the Day: *Dear God, grant me the wisdom to help me guard the treasures You have entrusted me, in Jesus' name, Amen.*

Haggai 1-2

21st September

Live as a Wise Person

"Be very careful, then, how you live - not as unwise but as wise, making the most of every opportunity, because the days are evil. Therefore do not be foolish, but understand what the Lord's will is" **(Ephesians 5:15-17).**

Most people live unwisely. They do not discern their seasons of life. Consequently, they miss the opportunities God presents and sabotage their temporal and eternal destinies. Paul warns us not to live ignorant of the will of God.

One characteristic of wisdom is making the most of every opportunity. God desires that we understand seasons in life and maximize every opportunity each season offers us. A wise farmer does his work wisely; he knows when to till the land, sow, weed, allow crops to grow and harvest his crop. When he makes the most of every season, he receives a bumper harvest. As believers and sons of God, we need to have the same wisdom in our walk of faith.

Lack of wisdom makes people complain about almost everything instead of making the necessary adjustments in each new season. Some complain of cold and wetness during the rainy season while others complain of heat during the hot season. This should not be the case because the Bible is definite that seasons are inevitable (Genesis 8:22). Besides spiritual understanding, we need to know the things to expect in each season not to sabotage our destinies by negative speech. Having divine wisdom can enable us benefit maximally from every season of our physical and spiritual lives.

Further Reading: *1 Chronicles 12:32; Ecclesiastes 3:1*
Prayer for the Day: *Dear God, I pray for wisdom that I may understand my seasons in life and make the most of every opportunity availed to me, in Jesus' name, Amen.*

Zechariah 1-7

22nd September

Strive to be in the Right Position

Then the Lord God called to Adam and said to him, "Where are you?" (Genesis 3:9).

When a teacher asks a student a question, he already knows the answer. Similarly, when God asked Adam where he was after eating of the fruit of the forbidden tree, He knew exactly where Adam was. He is all-knowing and nothing is hidden from Him. Adam hid himself because he was guilty of sin. In God's plan, we are supposed to be in a particular place at a specific time. God designed us to function in His perfect will which is only possible when we are in the right place, at the right time and doing the right thing.

The will of God is geographical. To receive our blessings, we should be where He desires us to be at a particular time. Unfortunately, some people leave those positions when they face challenges, discouragement, and despair. Others become impatient and move before God signals them to move. When God called Adam asking where he was, He expected him to be in a specific position He had assigned him. In the assigned position, Adam could have exercised power and authority over all creation and God would have fulfilled His promise to him.

Like Adam, many have left the positions God assigned them. Whenever He comes to reward them, He does not find them where He ordained them to be. God's promises are conditional; He fulfills them as man takes his rightful position.

Further Reading: Acts 17:26; Isaiah 1:19-20
Prayer for the Day: Oh Lord, help me to always take my rightful position to the glory of Your Holy Name, Amen.

Day 266 | Zechariah 8-14

23rd September

Understand the Seasons of Your Life

"To everything there is a season, a time for every purpose under heaven" (Ecclesiastes 3:1).

Our lives are divided into seasons. Each of us is in a unique season at a particular time. The word of God teaches that there is a season for everything. God allows adequate time for a season of preparation, time which plays a role in determining a person's success. Those who squander the opportunities the seasons offer end up failing because success only manifests when opportunities meet preparedness. This truth applies to the spiritual as well as our physical lives.

God allows His people to go through hardship, pain and suffering during their season of preparation. Understanding your season is critical because it helps you maximize opportunities. Many waste opportunities because of ignorance. It is instructive to understand that the opportunities we have today will not last a lifetime. A student must understand that he or she will not always have the opportunity to study. Unless they make use of their time now and study seriously, they may find it impossible to rise to certain levels.

God changes seasons. We can therefore trust Him to help us transition from seasons of lack, adversity and sowing to seasons of plenty and victory. He desires that we agree with Him as He systematically ushers us into new seasons at the right time. If we walk in wisdom, we will put much effort in our endeavours even if there is no immediate outcome.

Further Reading: *Ecclesiastes 9:10-11; Isaiah 48:10*
Prayer for the Day: *My God in Jesus' name, fill me with Your Spirit afresh that I may always understand the seasons of my life, Amen.*

Esther 1-5

24th September

Stand Firm in Your God-ordained Position

"But when Sanballat, Tobiah, the Arabs, the Ammonites and the men of Ashdod heard that the repairs to Jerusalem's walls had gone ahead and that the gaps were being closed, they were very angry. They all plotted together to come and fight against Jerusalem and stir up trouble against it. But we prayed to our God and posted a guard day and night to meet this threat" (Nehemiah 4:7-9).

The fact that God has positioned you in a particular place does not mean that you will not face challenges. In the Scriptures, every person who was used of God went through challenges. They endured hardships and trusted God despite their situations. Consequently, God helped them attain their destinies. If you do not face challenges, chances that you are going the same direction with the world are very high. Discouraging situations will come your way even when God has called you.

Nehemiah received a divine burden to rebuild the wall of Jerusalem. He had to leave his work as the king's cupbearer in Persia and return to Jerusalem to embark on it. However, when he started, he faced opposition (Nehemiah 4). Despite the opposition, he stood firm through prayer and focused on the work until he finished it.

As we depend on the Spirit of God to empower us serve God's purposes, He gives the wisdom and tenacity we need to keep going despite facing resistance from the kingdom of darkness and the world.

Further Reading: Habakkuk 2:1a; 2 Chronicles 20:17; James 4:7
Prayer for the Day: Dear God, I pray for the grace to remain steadfast in my God-ordained position in spite of the challenges that come our way in our walk with You, Amen.

Day 268 — Esther 6-10

25th September

Do Not Enter a Comfort Zone

'Then he said, 'This is what I'll do. I will tear down my barns and build bigger ones, and there I will store all my grain and my goods. And I'll say to myself, "You have plenty of good things laid up for many years. Take life easy; eat, drink and be merry."' "But God said to him, 'You fool! This very night your life will be demanded from you. Then who will get what you have prepared for yourself?'" (Luke 12:18-20).

The will of God is progressive. He desires that we move from one level of glory to another until we attain everything He has written in the books of our destinies. Destiny is multifaceted and we should make sure that we attain every aspect of it. Our spiritual and physical aspects matter to God and we need to constantly monitor our progress.

The rich fool wrongly thought that he had all the wealth he needed although his relationship with God was wanting. He made elaborate plans on how to please himself unaware that his time on earth was short. He settled for deceptive material possessions at the expense of his eternal soul. One of our greatest enemies is average. We must resist it in order not to give the enemy an opportunity to derail us from attaining our destinies. Strive for more as there is always a higher level of attainment for everyone, irrespective of what one may have achieved at a particular time in life.

Further Reading: Philippians 3:12; Zephaniah 1:12
Prayer for the Day: *Oh God, help me not to settle for less than that which You created and called me for, 'Your best', in Jesus' name, Amen.*

Esther 6-10

26th September

Deal with the Spirit of Discouragement

"Have I not commanded you? Be strong and courageous. Do not be terrified; do not be discouraged, for the LORD your God will be with you wherever you go" (Joshua 1:9).

The life of a believer is a battle fought or won in the spiritual realm. Man is a triune being with a spirit, soul and body. The most intensive spiritual battles happen in the unseen realm of the spirit. Discouragement is one of the weapons Satan uses to resist the saints and hinder them from serving God's purpose. Many people have made unwise decisions or taken their own lives as a result of discouragement.

God instructed Joshua to take heart when he took over the role of leading the Israelites from Moses. To be successful in that assignment, Joshua needed to be strong in the Lord as he led them to the Promised Land. Today, God gives us the same command because discouragement is a weapon the devil unleashes on many saints. It makes people give up and break the momentum in making progress. We need to be aware of the devices the enemy uses so that we can take our stand against him. Our father of faith Abraham refused to be discouraged and remained steadfast in his faith in God's promise of a son. He did not waver in unbelief because he considered God faithful (Romans 4:18-22). This was credited to him as righteousness.

Further Reading: 2 Timothy 1:7; 1 Thessalonians 5:14; Titus 2:6; 1 Samuel 30:6-8

Prayer for the Day: Today, in the name of Jesus Christ, I resist the spirit of discouragement in my life and declare that I will remain steadfast in God's promises no matter how long they may take, amen.

Esther 6-10

27th September

Bad Choices Lead to Suffering

"…when that day comes, you will cry out for relief from the king you have chosen, and the LORD will not answer you in that day. But the people refused to listen to Samuel. "No!" they said, "We want a king over us. Then we will be like other nations, with a king to lead us and to go out before us and fight our battles" **(1 Samuel 8:18-20).**

God settled on Israel from among the nations to be His chosen people. His intention was for them to be a peculiar people, set apart for God to carry His name and showcase His glory. He made this promise to the patriarchs and was committed to keeping it as long as they were faithful to Him (Deuteronomy 7:6). Israel was called to be His holy people and the Lord was devoted to reigning over them in righteousness and justice.

However, Israel did not share in God's vision and they blindly desired to be like other nations. They disregarded God's warnings (1 Samuel 8:10-17). Consequently, they faced great troubles as a result of that decision.

God has given us the right to make choices. He gives us the liberty to either accept or reject His will. Wrong choices expose us to punishment and hinder us from attaining the destinies God created us to manifest. We need to depend on the guidance of the Holy Spirit so that every decision we make is in the perfect will of God.

Further Reading: Deuteronomy 30:19
Prayer for the Day: Holy Spirit, help me make right choices and do the will of my Father, in Jesus' name, Amen.

Nehemiah 6-7

Day 271

28th September

Christ Humbled Himself for Us

"Your attitude should be the same as that of Christ Jesus: who, being in very nature God, did not consider equality with God something to be grasped, but made himself nothing, taking the very nature of a servant, being made in human likeness" *(Philippians 2:5-7).*

Jesus Christ was God in the flesh. He went through the natural process of birth and took the human nature. He set aside His Heavenly glory as God and humbled Himself taking the form of a slave. He did this to take our place as sinners and restore us to God. He also came to restore to man the dominion he lost to the enemy after the fall. He is our High Priest for He went through physical and emotional pain like we do yet without sin (Hebrews 4:14-15). As a result, we can approach Him with confidence for He is our advocate before the Father (1 John 2:1).

As believers, we ought to walk with the full awareness of the work of the cross and Christ's selflessness and humility that made it possible. Unfortunately, the enemy deceives many into believing that Christ is distant and unapproachable. He makes people believe false things about the love and gentleness of Christ towards all who call on Him. With the knowledge of God's word and His character, we can confidently emulate Christ and bear lasting spiritual fruit.

Further Reading: Colossians 2:14; Hebrews 10:5, 8-10
Prayer for the Day: Oh Lord, help me to emulate the example of humility you set by offering your life for me. Help me do the same for my brethren in your holy name. Amen.

Day 272 — Nehemiah 8-10

29th September

Divine Knowledge is Priceless

He replied, "The knowledge of the secrets of the kingdom of heaven has been given to you, but not to them" (Matthew 13:11).

Knowledge is the psychological result of perception, learning, and reasoning. Divine knowledge is having an understanding of Godly and spiritual things. This kind of knowledge enables believers to have a deep understanding of things that are unfathomable in the natural realm. God has granted believers access to the knowledge of divine mysteries.

Our Lord Jesus came full of knowledge, grace, and truth. It is this truth that sets people free when they believe and accept Him. This key of knowledge gives access to the vast possibilities in Christ. Lack of it is like standing before the entrance of a big mansion but not being able to enter. Every mystery in the Kingdom requires a prerequisite knowledge of the same.
Unfortunately, the spirit of religion denies people the key to knowledge. Jesus accused the Pharisees of being hypocritical and denying people access into the kingdom while they themselves did not enter (Matthew 23:13). This means that the Pharisees denied people access to knowledge that was essential for freedom.

Divine knowledge brings preservation in times of peril. As believers, we ought to give ourselves to reading the word of God and other relevant materials for a victorious Christian living. God detests lack of knowledge (Hosea 4:6).

Further Reading: 2 Peter 1:2-3; Proverbs 23:23; James 1:5
Prayer for the Day: Lord, I pray for divine knowledge to understand the mysteries of your kingdom. Amen.

Nehemiah 11-13; Psalm 126 — Day 273

30th September

Do Not Take God's Glory

You said in your heart," I will ascend to Heaven; I will raise my throne above the stars of God; I will sit enthroned on the stars of God; I will sit enthroned on the mount of assembly, on the utmost heights of the sacred mountain. I will ascend above the tops of the clouds; I will make myself like the Most High." But you are brought down to the grave, to the depths of the pit (Isaiah 14:13-15).

A believer's foundation for seeking and serving God should be to bring God all the glory. God pours His enabling grace on His people to enable them do exploits in His name with the expectation that they will return all the glory to Him. When this is not done, destruction inevitably follows.

The anchor verse depicts the fall of Lucifer, who attempted to take God's position and glory. Consequently, he was cast out of Heaven even though he was chief among the angels. Throughout generations, the enemy has been inciting men to commit the same sin he did, and many have fallen prey.

The same happens when after a person has fulfilled the purposes of God, he or she exalts himself or herself thereby robbing God of His glory. As believers, we ought to examine our motives of serving God. Pride is the very foundation of sin, and we need to overcome it by dying to self and crediting all the glory to God, even after great achievements.

Further Reading: Isaiah 42:8; John 12:24
Prayer for the Day: Oh Lord, I pray that I may die to self and remain humble before you. Help me never to take your glory. Amen.

Day 274 — Malachi 1-4

1st October

Jesus Offers Healing of the Inner Man

"The Spirit of the Sovereign LORD is on me, because the LORD has anointed me to preach good news to the poor. He has sent me to bind up the brokenhearted, to proclaim freedom for the captives and release from darkness for the prisoners" (Isaiah 61:1).

One of the mandates of Jesus is to heal the brokenhearted. Hearts of many people have been broken and God in His great love desires to heal their inner wounds. That way, they can align themselves with His will and great things will happen. Whenever God desires to accomplish great things, He seeks men with whom to partner. He works on their hearts by healing their deepest wounds so that they can become worthy vessels to partner with Him. It is very difficult for people who are wounded and hurting to do divine assignments which require inner strength and physical stamina.

The inner man can be wounded by different things. These include sin which gives the enemy legal right to oppress a person. The challenges one goes through in life can leave deep seated wounds in their heart and make it impossible to serve God effectively. Having one's hope deferred can also make the heart sick (Proverbs 13:12).

Jesus is the Great Physician; He not only came to bring mankind good news but also makes healing of the inner man available to all who approach Him by faith. We are His co-workers and He can use us to minister inner healing to believers.

Further Reading: Revelation 5:11-12; 1 Peter 2:8
Prayer for the Day: Holy Spirit, reveal any wounds in my life and heal me, Amen.

Luke 1; John 1:1-14

Day 275

2nd October

The Lord Can Heal a Crushed Spirit

"A man's spirit sustains him in sickness, but a crushed spirit who can bear?" (Proverbs 18:14).

As followers of Christ, we are in a battlefield pitted against demonic powers determined to destroy our destinies. The enemy is a schemer and intentional in weakening us by inflicting wounds. Our spirit is our inner man breathed into us by God himself. It comprises perception, conscience and communion. Perception is the ability to see things beyond face value. A healthy perception facilitates a high level of discernment. We are also able to operate in the gifts of the Holy Spirit when our perception is healthy.

Conscience refers to the ability to distinguish between right and wrong. The conscience enables us to understand God's moral law and receive conviction of sin, righteousness and judgment. Communion refers to the ability to fellowship with God who is Spirit (John 4:24). Sickness is an enemy believers encounter consistently. When one's spirit man is healthy and vibrant, recovering from malaise is quick and effective. However, the process of recovery can be hampered by a negative mindset. If one's spirit is crushed, it becomes impossible to face and successfully overcome challenges.

Thus, we should care about our spiritual health by feeding the inner man on the Word of God. In addition, we should exercise our faith.

Further Reading: Proverbs 4:23; Psalm 147:3
Prayer for the Day: *Holy Spirit, heal every part of my spirit man so that I can be healthy to pursue my destiny, Amen.*

3rd October

Knowing God Inspires Confidence

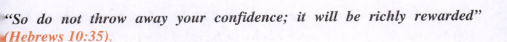

"So do not throw away your confidence; it will be richly rewarded" (Hebrews 10:35).

Confidence is one of the characteristics displayed by people who know God. Such people have great faith in God because they are aware of His dependable and unfailing nature. Scriptures were written to help us believe in God and partake of His divine nature. We cannot have this confidence without daily meditating on God's word. The saints in the first century church went through trying times. They were afflicted, ostracized, misunderstood, persecuted and killed. However, because their faith was firmly rooted in Christ, they still stood their ground and overcame all the battles they faced.

The main challenge we have in the church today is that many believers are not confident about their faith in God. If left unchecked, this can be a hindrance to the move of God in the world because He works through men of faith. We cannot become carriers of revival if we are not fully persuaded of God's power and plan for our lives. When someone is not confident in God, their works convey doubts and unbelief.

Shadrach, Meshach and Abednego were confident in God. They refused to worship the idol Nebuchadnezzar erected and remained faithful to their God. When he faced Goliath, David had total confidence in the Lord his God and this made him triumphant.

Further Reading: Daniel 3:5-20; 1 Samuel 17:41-52
Prayer for the Day: Dear God, deliver me from every form of fear so that I can walk in confidence as I trust You, in Jesus' name, Amen.

Matthew 2; Luke 2:39-52

Day 277

4th October

God is Concerned for Foreigners

"The alien living with you must be treated as one of your native-born. Love him as yourself, for you were aliens in Egypt. I am the LORD your God' (Leviticus 19:34).

The Lord our God is concerned about people who leave their nation and settle elsewhere. In His wisdom and foreknowledge, God planned the time of our birth and the places we live in (Acts 17:26). He also planned beforehand where people would live, work and minister in, away from their places of birth.

The Lord exercises sovereignty over human beings and can cause people to move to different nations to serve His purposes for His glory. He caused Israel to move to Egypt after which He delivered them with a mighty hand. He released judgment on the idolatrous nation of Egypt whose leaders were determined to oppress the people He had chosen to be His special possession and royal priesthood. The miracles, signs and wonders He performed through Moses manifested His power and spread His fame to all the earth.

God understands what it means to be a foreigner. He knows that sometimes foreigners are mistreated (Deuteronomy 10:19), and states that a curse befalls those who mistreat them. God is merciful and defends the rights of the most vulnerable members of society. We too should be kind towards people from other nations. We should not practice partiality.

Further Reading: Deuteronomy 27:19; Psalm 146:9
Prayer for the Day: Oh God, I pray that thy grace may locate foreigners wherever they are in the world, and show them mercy. Amen.

Day 278 — Matthew 3; Mark 1; Luke 3

5th October

You are Not Alone

Then Jesus came to them and said, "All authority in heaven and on earth has been given to me. Therefore go and make disciples of all nations, baptizing them in the name of the Father and of the Son and of the Holy Spirit, and teaching them to obey everything I have commanded you. And surely I am with you always, to the very end of the age" (Matthew 28:18-20).

Man was created a social being and desires to enjoy the company of others. As believers, we have a desire to host the presence of God wherever we go as His ambassadors on earth. Our Lord Jesus Christ assured His disciples – and that includes us – that He will be with us till the end of the age. He promised His disciples that upon His ascension, He would not leave them as orphans (John 14:18). Assured of God's presence with us, we are able to serve our divine mandates.

Servants of God who served Him effectively knew the power of His presence. Moses knew that the secret of his success in carrying out His divine assignment was the presence of God (Exodus 33:15). He knew that the presence of God is what made the difference between success and failure. The Psalmist knew that irrespective of the magnitude of the challenges he faced, he could rely on God who is the ever-present help in times of trouble (Psalm 46:1).

Further Reading: *Psalm 55:4-16; Revelation 3:20*
Prayer for the Day: *Thank you God for Your abiding presence in my life. Help me weather every storm by having faith in You, Amen.*

Matthew 4; Luke 4-5; John 1:15-51 — Day 279

6th October

God's Grace is an Agent of Transformation

"For the grace of God that brings salvation has appeared to all men. It teaches us to say "No" to ungodliness and worldly passions, and to live self-controlled, upright and godly lives in this present age" **(Titus 2:11-12)**.

The grace of God is effective in changing the lives of those who walk by faith. It refers to unmerited favour which makes it possible for us to access what we do not deserve. It enables us access God's divine power to live above ungodliness and worldly passions. One of the greatest blessings we receive by God's grace is His transformative power. We are weak and cannot change our character without divine enablement. God loves us despite our sinful background and will not leave us the way we are. He desires we become godly, spiritually fruitful and faithful ambassadors of His eternal kingdom.

Grace is multifaceted; it saves, secures, sustains and helps us to be effective in ministering to the needs of others. To attain the fullness of our destinies, we require different forms of grace (Hebrews 4:16). The grace that transforms people from their older versions to the version God desires is readily available to all believers and it makes them reflect more of God's glory as they continue beholding His power. We need the ability to surrender to God so that He can transform us. In addition, we need to be continually renewed so that we can completely shed off the old sinful nature.

Further Reading: *2 Corinthians 3:16-18; Isaiah 41:8-15*
Prayer for the Day: *Oh God, release grace to transform me so that I can fulfil my divine purpose, Amen.*

7th October

Do Not Be Afraid; God is with You

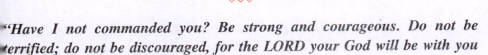

"Have I not commanded you? Be strong and courageous. Do not be terrified; do not be discouraged, for the LORD your God will be with you wherever you go" (Joshua 1:9).

Many people do not pursue what God has called them to do because they lack confidence. They keep asking if the things God has promised them will happen. They feel spiritually weak and discouraged because they do not have enough confidence in God's power. God is pleased by people who are confident, for He is able to accomplish everything He has committed to doing.

He likens himself to different animals such as the lion and the eagle. The lion is not the biggest animal but it rules the jungle because it is brave and confident. The eagle has a powerful vision and spots prey several kilometers away. We need to emulate the Lord in these respects as this can make us confident of walking in victory. Our speech, actions and emotions should be so focused on Him that we see through our inner eyes the possibilities in Christ, and have faith that they will become a reality as we trust Him.

God rewards the confident one (Hebrews 10:35). Even though our beginning might be small, we can be sure that as we trust God, our end will be great. He performs great signs, miracles and wonders for those whose trust Him. He makes a way where there is none through His great power which equals none.

Further Reading: *Judges 7:3; Job 8:7; Jeremiah 1:12*
Prayer for the Day: *Today, I renounce every form of fear and declare that I have confidence in God. Amen.*

8th October

Taking Responsibility is the Key to Greatness

"When the woman saw that the fruit of the tree was good for food and pleasing to the eye, and also desirable for gaining wisdom, she took some and ate it. She also gave some to her husband, who was with her, and he ate it. Then the eyes of both of them were opened, and they realized they were naked; so they sewed fig leaves together and made coverings for themselves" (Genesis 3:6-7).

Shifting blame is characteristic of many people as they also shift responsibility to others especially where wrongdoing is involved. Few people readily admit their wrongdoing and ask for forgiveness. Those who fail to do so in most cases experience failure in accessing God's grace and mercy. It reduces people who were meant to be great to weaklings and losers, since God always ensures that justice is done and that people reap what they sow.

To attain our God-given destinies, we need to mature to the point that we take personal responsibility as is expected by God. In the Garden of Eden, Adam and Eve demonstrated their inability to take responsibility by pointing fingers at each other instead of acknowledging their rebellion to God's command. Unfortunately, many people get stuck in the wrong because they are unwilling to ask for mercy and forgiveness.

Taking responsibility is the key to greatness. To manifest all the potential God has deposited in your life, be proactive and admit your wrong doing. We cannot control what happens to us but we can determine how we respond to the things that happen.

Further Reading: Exodus 32:1-24; 1 Kings 20:39-40
Prayer for the Day: Dear God, I pray that You may enable me take responsibility over my actions always in my walk with You and in my daily endeavours. Amen.

Day 282 | John 5

9th October

Align Yourself with God's Purpose

'For we are God's workmanship, created in Christ Jesus to do good works, which God prepared in advance for us to do" *(Ephesians 2:10).*

God has preserved us because He has a specific purpose He desires us to accomplish. The greatest achievements we can have are discovering our purpose and striving to fulfill it. The sweetest thing in life is to discover your purpose. We need to be faithful to God as our level of commitment to Him determines the impact we will have in life. We need to seek and pursue our divine purposes so well that at the end of our lives, we will look back and rejoice that we lived as God desired. Sadly, many people do not do this.

God has given us the privilege to live in this dispensation for a special purpose. He has intricately configured us in a way that we can face and overcome all challenges, and take advantage of the opportunities He has prepared. God looks for people who are committed to His purposes and upholds them by their mighty hand. David was devoted to serving God's purpose and kept calling on Him until he fulfilled his purpose. God kept him safe from his enemies (Psalm 57:2-3).

When you align yourself with God's purpose for your life, your enemies have no power over your life. This is so because God offers protection and provision to those who wholeheartedly serve His purposes. We need to be aware that serving God's purpose comes at a cost and we must die to self to become what God desires.

Further Reading: John 4:32; Ephesians 1:4
Prayer for the Day: Dear God, grant me grace to fulfill your divine purpose, to the glory of Your Holy Name, Amen.

Matthew 12:1-21; Mark 3; Luke 6

10th October

The Kingdom of God Manifests Power

"For the kingdom of God is not a matter of talk but of power" (1 Corinthians 4:20).

The power of God is like a magnet. It has the ability to attract all the people you require to fulfil God's purpose in the attainment of your destiny.

God created us with capacity to hunger and thirst for His power. When we have a high appetite for His power, He draws us to Himself and imparts His power into our lives. The kingdom of God is characterised by great power which is generated through communion with the Holy Spirit.

During His ministry on earth, Jesus spent quality time in prayer. He modeled a lifestyle of consistent prayer for His disciples and He expects us to seek divine power with the enablement of the Holy Spirit. His life was characterised by great works of power because He was anointed by the Holy Spirit (Acts 10:38). When the disciples sought God in prayer, He worked great wonders through their ministries. They turned people from the power of darkness to the kingdom of light. The lives of their hearers were transformed by God's power.

All things serve God. His power mobilizes and avails all the resources we need to attain our destinies and serve our purpose. When we make seeking His kingdom our priority, He takes care of all our needs (Matthew 6:33). We need to do this by divine revelation, not just to satisfy our religious consciences.

Further Reading: Isaiah 2:2; Haggai 2:7
Prayer for the Day: Oh God, I pray that I may be able to pay the cost for the manifestation of Your power in my life, for Your Name's sake, Amen.

Day 284 | Matthew 5-7

11th October

God Speaks in Different Ways but Few Comprehend

"For God does speak - now one way, now another - though man may not perceive it. In a dream, in a vision of the night, when deep sleep falls on men as they slumber in their beds" (Job 33:14-15).

Hearing from God is a treasure that every believer should desire to cultivate. There is a direct correlation between divine prosperity and hearing from God. According to Jeremiah 10:23, God desired to continue fellowshipping with man whom he denied the ability to chart his own path. He instead availed the privilege of prayer through which man communes with Him, and gets to know His will.

God reveals His will through His word and communicates to many people through dreams. Most dreams have a supernatural element. They reveal information one could not have known in any other way. Dreams that carry divine messages are often a continuation of a conversation one has had with God. Most dreams are confirmed through closely related divine messages.

God delights in communicating to His people and uses many different ways some of which many people do not understand. To attain our destinies, we need to incline our ears to God's voice and allow Him to speak to us through different channels. This includes messages of guidance, help, rebuke, correction and instruction. God is not limited in the ways He speaks to us. His Spirit enables us decode the messages we receive in dreams.

Further Reading: John 10:27; Matthew 2:13; Genesis 20:3
Prayer for the Day: Dear God, give me a hearing ear and activate the dream realm in my life, Amen.

Matthew 8:1-13; Luke 7

12th October

Deal with Causes of Barrenness

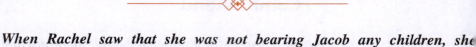

When Rachel saw that she was not bearing Jacob any children, she became jealous of her sister. So she said to Jacob, "Give me children, or I'll die!" Jacob became angry with her and said, "Am I in the place of God, who has kept you from having children?" (Genesis 30:1-2).

Barrenness has different causes. God desires that people get into a covenant with Him so that they may be fruitful both spiritually and physically. This is what happened with Samuel's mother Hannah, whose solemn vow to God that she would raise her son in God's house activated the fruit of the womb (1 Samuel 1:10-18). Entering into such an agreement with God catalyzes fruitfulness in a person's life as was Hannah's case.

Despising servants of God causes barrenness. Michal did not bear any children because she despised David when he danced before the Lord as a common man (2 Samuel 6:14-23). This can be avoided by maintaining a non-judgmental attitude towards servants of God. Family members need to accept and honour those who have been called by God among them. Doing this attracts God's favour to the family and causes Him not close the door of His blessings for them.

Abraham's experience teaches us that barrenness may come from one's lineage (Genesis 25:21). This makes it is necessary to undertake a spiritual diagnosis on the cause of unfruitfulness in life.

Further Reading: Genesis 20:18; Isaiah 51:1-2
Prayer for the Day: *Oh God, there are many areas in my life where unfruitfulness has taken root. Today in Jesus' name, I uproot everything that was not planted by my Father and declare fruitfulness in Jesus' name, Amen.*

13th October

Jesus Identifies with Our Suffering

"Since the children have flesh and blood, he too shared in their humanity so that by his death he might destroy him who holds the power of death - that is, the devil - and free those who all their lives were held in slavery by their fear of death" (Hebrews 2:14-15).

Our Lord and Saviour Jesus Christ identifies with our humanity. He knows all our weaknesses and propensity to fall into temptation because He took on the form of a man and was tempted in all ways as a man. The enemy and fallen angels create a false and misleading impression that Jesus is unapproachable to keep people from going to Him for help in prayer. However, Jesus invites us to approach Him directly at any time of weakness, because through His death, we have access to the holy of holies (Matthew 27:50-51).

Jesus identifies with family relationships as He had an earthly family (Matthew 13:55-56). Since He was born and raised in one, He understands the challenges families face which may include disunity, misunderstanding and betrayal. Jesus understood work related issues. He knew that one could work for others only for the payment to be withheld. He understood payment of taxes (Matthew 17:24-27). According to Isaiah 53:6-10, He understands pain and suffering. He went through emotional and physical suffering. He was rejected and crucified by the people He came to save. Most of the people God uses to do wonders went through diverse forms of suffering which moulded them for service.

Further Reading: Hebrews 4:14-15; Matthew 27:46
Prayer for the Day: Thank you Lord for identifying with my humanity. I ask You for wisdom to help people going through challenges, Amen.

Matthew 12:22-50; Luke 11 — Day 287

14th October

Become a Spiritual Craftsman

Then the LORD showed me four craftsmen. I asked, "What are these coming to do?" He answered, "These are the horns that scattered Judah so that no one could raise his head, but the craftsmen have come to terrify them and throw down these horns of the nations who lifted up their horns against the land of Judah to scatter its people" (Zechariah 1:20-21).

The world is controlled from the spirit realm which is stronger than the physical. The physical originated from the spiritual. Therefore, the unseen is superior to the seen (Hebrews 11:3). Many undesirable things that happen in the world are a result of evil spiritual programming. However, that programming can be destroyed by the power of prayer. Every believer must understand that victory depends on the ability to do spiritual transactions. In the above Scripture, horns are a symbol of authority and power. When it is used for evil purposes, it can scatter marriages, businesses, callings, nations.

Those who find themselves stagnant and unable to make progress are under the power of evil horns, which introduce limitations that make attaining one's destiny difficult or impossible. One of the most effective ways of becoming a spiritual craftsman is paying attention to the prophetic words from God. We can only witness the fulfillment of prophecy if we engage in warfare (1 Timothy 1:18). Many believers who have received powerful prophecies are unable to actualize them because they are not willing to play their part as spiritual builders and craftsmen.

Further Reading: Zechariah 1:14-19; Ephesians 3:10
Prayer for the Day: Today in Jesus' name, I wage warfare against every evil horn that hinders my progress. Amen.

Matthew 13; Luke 8

15th October

Give Prayers as A Gift

Now Naaman was commander of the army of the King of Aram. He was a great man in the sight of his master and highly regarded because through him, the LORD had given victory to Aram. He was a valiant soldier, but he had leprosy. Now bands from Aram had gone out and had taken captive a young girl from Israel and served Naaman's wife. She said to her mistress," If only my master would see the prophet who is in Samaria! He would cure him of his leprosy" **(2 Kings 5:1-3).**

Praying for people is one of the greatest gifts we can offer them. The society is stratified into different social classes. When we desire to be charitable, we may be at a loss of what to give those endowed with financial resources. The good news is that we can offer prayers as a gift because not every problem can be solved by money.

Naaman's illness gave him a hard time despite being a person of means and status. He had favour with the king but he needed someone who could give him the gift of prayer. This gift came through a slave girl who had been captured from Israel. When he was directed to the man of God in Samaria, his sickness was incurable unless through divine means was instantly healed. His riches and high status in society could not help him. We can offer this gift freely to everyone irrespective of their socio-economic status.

Further Reading: Philippians 1:4; Colossians 1:9
Prayer for the Day: Oh Lord, give me the grace to give the gift of prayer to everyone who needs it. Amen.

Matthew 8:14-34; Mark 4-5

16th October

God Exempts His People

"There will be loud wailing throughout Egypt-worse than there has ever been or ever will be again. But among the Israelites, not a dog will bark at any man or animal. Then, you will know that the LORD makes a distinction between Egypt and Israel" **(Exodus 11:6-7).**

Exemption is the state of being free from an obligation or liability imposed on others. This often applies to the payment of taxes. When David defeated Goliath, his family was exempted from paying taxes. In the same way, people are exempted in the natural realm, they can also be exempted in the spiritual realm.

God exempts His people from various problems that plague mankind. Pharaoh refused God's command to let His people go and worship Him. In return, God sent ten deadly plagues to Egypt. The last and most devastating was the death of all the firstborns belonging to the Egyptians. Every household in the land mourned and the outcry in the land was great. However, Israel was spared by the angel of death.

Egypt represents the world, and the Israelites represent believers. We live in this world but through God's power, the challenges that plague others will not affect us. The Lord promises to make a clear distinction between His people and the world and exempts them from sufferings common to others.

Further Reading: Exodus 8:22; Ezekiel 9:3-6; Psalm 91:1-6; Malachi 3:18
Prayer for the Day: Dear Lord, I thank you for promising to make a distinction between your people and the world. I ask for your help to walk with this revelation in Jesus' name. Amen.

Day 290 — Matthew 9-10

17th October

God Uses Ordinary Men

"When they saw the courage of Peter and John and realized they were unschooled, ordinary men, they were astonished, and they took note that these men had been with Jesus" **(Acts 4:13).**

The Bible is full of possibilities and nothing is impossible with God. It records many instances when God did the unexpected through His miracle-working power. God often works through ordinary people to fulfill His plans and purposes. In His unsearchable wisdom, God chose the foolish and weak things of the world to shame the strong. Weak and seemingly undeserving people glorify God most since their exploits manifest His power and grace.

The disciples of Jesus were ordinary men who were fishermen before He called them. After three years, He turned them into mighty men who performed great signs and wonders. They stood out for their courage and clarity of purpose as they preached the good news in the first century and the people in their generation could not help but notice that they had been with Jesus.

God does not call the qualified but rather qualifies those He calls. This should encourage us that even though we may not be qualified according to human standards, God can still use us. We should not disqualify ourselves or let the enemy deceive us that God cannot work in and through us. We ought to put our trust and faith in Jesus for in Him lies our ability to do exploits.

Further Reading: *1 Corinthians 1:27; Acts 19:11-12*
Prayer for the Day: *Lord, I thank you for I know that you use ordinary men to do exploits in your name. I pray for more grace to serve you effectively. Amen.*

Matthew 14; Mark 6; Luke 9:1-17

18th October

God's Grace Brings Transformation

"For the grace of God that brings salvation has appeared to all men" (Titus 2:11).

The greatest need of every believer is to be transformed into the likeness of Christ. The above Scripture is usually quoted when preaching salvation to unbelievers. However, the word salvation used in the passage is "sozo" in Greek. It is translated to several words which include: saved, made whole, restored, healed, delivered, preserved and rescued from danger. God's grace is able to holistically change a believer in all spheres of life.

God's grace has transformative power and begins working in us the moment we receive Christ as Lord and Saviour. The process of transformation is continuous and lasts the entire lifespan of a believer. The grace of God brings sufficiency in provision and divine empowerment. It makes us effective as we serve Christ as His ambassadors. The transformation we receive manifests His glory through our lives.

As we walk with Christ, we need to yield to Him and allow His grace to work in us continually and transform us to the level where we attain the stature of Christ. That way, we can walk in maturity and unity with Christ which is His desire for us. When believers are fully transformed, they impact the world positively and reveal the glory of God through their lives.

Further Reading: 2 Corinthians 9:8; 2 Corinthians 3:18
Prayer for the Day: Father, I pray that your grace may continually work in me to bring transformation that I may radiate your glory and impact the world and those around me positively. Amen.

19th October

Seek Spiritual Backing in Your Endeavours

'But by the grace of God I am what I am, and his grace to me was not without effect, no, I worked harder than all of them - yet not I, but the grace of God that was with me" **(1 Corinthians 15:10).**

Backing is offering support to someone or something. Spiritual backing is divine help rendered to believers to enable them do things with ease. This is the portion of every believer and is God's will for all His children. Apostle Paul achieved more in ministry than all the other apostles. He admits that he worked harder than them. However, he notes that everything he did was powered by the grace of God. Everything he did was backed by God, who granted him victory.

Like Paul, Nehemiah received spiritual backing and rebuilt the walls of Jerusalem in a record time of fifty-two days. This filled the hearts of the enemies of Israel with fear because they acknowledged that the work had been done with the help of the Lord (Nehemiah 6:16).

As believers, we ought to understand that we need this backing to overcome opposing demonic forces. Our warfare is not carnal and the weapons we use are mighty through God to overcome every opposition. We need supernatural backing to secure victory and maintain the territory we have recovered.

Further Reading: **Philippians 4:13; Colossians 1:29; Ephesians 3:20**
Prayer for the Day: **Dear Lord, I pray that you may activate your grace of spiritual backing in my life today. Amen.**

Matthew 15; Mark 7

20th October

The Church Was Birthed by the Supernatural

"Suddenly, a sound like the blowing of a violent wind came from heaven and filled the whole house where they were sitting. They saw what seemed to be tongues of fire that separated and came to rest on each of them. All of them were filled with the Holy Spirit and began to speak in other tongues as the Spirit enabled them" **(Acts 2:2-4).**

The church of Jesus Christ is not a building but a community of believers who live and walk by faith in the Son of God. The Greek word of the church is "ecclesia" which means the "called out ones." As believers, we have been called out of the world to live holy lives that glorify God. As we walk with God, He builds us as we continually accept, follow and teach His word.

This church was birthed on the day of Pentecost when the disciples were gathered in the upper room. They were filled with the Holy Spirit and began speaking in new tongues. Since then, the church started walking in extraordinary signs and wonders.

The Lord desires to restore the supernatural in the church. The Bible is full of supernatural occurrences of judgement and deliverance. As members of the universal body of Christ, we need to pray for the restoration and increase of this power. The world needs to witness the unfathomable wonder-working power of God to be won to Christ. The church has the mandate to do this assignment.

Further Reading: Job 9:10; Ephesians 2:20
Prayer for the Day: *Dear Lord, I pray that you may release your supernatural power to the church through the Holy Spirit. Amen.*

Day 294 — Matthew 16; Mark 8; Luke 9:18-27

21st October

The Prayer of the Righteous Avail Much

'Elijah was a man just like us. He prayed earnestly that it would not rain, and it did not rain on the land for three and a half years" (*James 5:17*).

Efficacy is the ability to produce a desired effect or result. Prayer has the ability to make even the weakest believers produce supernatural results through communion with God. This is so because it does not depend on man's effort but on God's grace and mercy (Romans 9:16).

The anchor verse expounds on the exploits of Elijah. It is important to note the emphasis laid in the first part of the Scripture that Elijah was a man like us. This means that he was prone to everything that we go through like anger, exhaustion and discouragement. However, the Scripture also states that he did the supernatural through prayer. Elijah knew that he had a mighty God whose power is unlimited, and who delights in answering the prayers of His people.

As we continue striving to fulfill our destinies, we ought to have this understanding of prayer. We may be mere men but we are able to connect with God and activate His power any time through prayer. We do not make things happen but God acts in response to our prayers. This admonishes every believer to continue tarrying in prayer, and many great and wondrous things will be birthed as happened through Elijah.

Further Reading: *Luke 18:1; 1 Kings 18: 42-45*
Prayer for the Day: *Lord, I pray that my prayers may produce great results to the honour of your name. Amen.*

22nd October

The God Kind of Life

"In him was life, and that life was the light of men" (John 1:4).

The New Testament was translated from Greek. As a result of the translation, three different words were translated to life but have different meanings. These words are bios, psuche and zoe. Bios means the life of the physical body; psuche means the psychological life of the human soul, while zoe is the divine life uniquely possessed by God. Scripture describes zoe which encompasses God's fullness of love, joy, power and ability.

This Scripture describes the kind of life the Lord Jesus possesses which is the light of men. Thisgives life to everything that is dead. It brings wellness, restoration, increase and eternal life. Itbrought life to dry bones (see Ezekiel 37). Jesus came to offer this life to all men who believe and accept Him as Lord and Saviour.

Disconnecting something from its original source implies taking life out of it just as taking a fish out of water causes its death. When man was banished from the Garden of Eden, he was disconnected from zoe and death crept in. This life is now offered to us through the person of Jesus Christ. As believers, we ought to remain connected to Christ's indestructible life by the help of the Holy Spirit.

Further Reading: John 10:10; John 5:26; Ezekiel 37:4-5, 9
Prayer for the Day: Dear Lord, I pray that I may receive and remain connected to your kind of life through the Holy Spirit. Amen.

23rd October

Understand How the Holy Spirit Works

"Now the earth was formless and empty, darkness was over the surface of the deep, and the Spirit of God was hovering over the waters" (Genesis 1:2).

The Holy Spirit is the third person in the God-head. He is responsible for the process of conviction of sin, righteousness and judgment. He is also the chief agent of our sanctification so that we can share in God's holy character. He acts as a comforter, helper, advocate and intercessor (John 14:26 AMP). He enables Christians to have a right standing with God. He was the gift Jesus promised to the disciples and those who will believe their message.

The above verse describes the presence and participation of the Holy Spirit during creation. It helps us perceive Him as an equal partner in the work of redemption. In God's redemptive plan, Jesus came into the world and died for our sins. However, before He begun ministry, He had to be anointed by the Holy Spirit (Luke 4:18). After His ascension, His disciples tarried in Jerusalem until they were filled with the Holy Spirit. The Holy Spirit is the carrier of creative power and is responsible for the manifestation of the power of the cross.

Unfortunately, the Holy Spirit is least understood today. Some Christians do not acknowledge Him. As a result, there is more talk in the church but minimal results. Believers who understand and have the Spirit of God walk with great power as they manifest the works of God in their lives.

Further Reading: *John 16:7; 1 Corinthians 1:17*
Prayer for the Day: *Help me, oh Lord, to understand the work of the Holy Spirit and to acknowledge Him as an equal partner in the work of redemption, Amen.*

John 7-8

24th October

Unconditional Prophecies Must be Fulfilled

"The reason the dream was given to Pharaoh in two forms is that the matter has been firmly decided by God, and God will do it soon" (Genesis 41:32).

Prophecies are predictions uttered under divine inspiration. They are knowledge of the future obtained from a divine source. Prophecies are used to encourage or warn believers helping them be at par with what God intends to do. Joseph gave an interpretation to two dreams that Pharaoh had. The dreams were similar and warned of an impending danger on the land. There was to be a seven-year period of plentiful harvest followed by a similar period of famine. The matter was decided by God and was bound to happen irrespective of how people would respond. Prayers and repentance were inconsequential; the only possible mitigation was to come up with strategies that would help Egypt avert the consequences of the famine.

Jesus told His disciples the things that must happen before the end of this age. Nothing can be done to stop them. However, we can face the future confidently and come up with strategies on how to stay safe the same way Joseph's foresight saved Egypt from famine. God desires us to be aware that we are living in a season when prophecies will be fulfilled rapidly. We can escape all negative consequences of the things that are going to happen as we seek and activate the grace of divine exemption.

Further Reading: Matthew 24:3-6; 1 Timothy 4:1; 2 Timothy 3:1-5
Prayer for the Day: Dear Lord, I pray for divine exemption even in the fulfilment of unconditional prophecies. Amen.

John 9:1-41; John 10:1-21

25th October

Access to the Grace of God

"From the fullness of his grace we have all received one blessing after another. For the law was given through Moses; grace and truth came through Jesus Christ" (**John 1:16-17**).

The grace of God carries divine power to transform us. Looking at our lives closely can help us identify the kind of grace God has given us. The things we have done successfully point to the divine enablement we have already received from God.

The sacrificial death of Jesus on the cross paid the price of our redemption and granted us access to the grace of God. All the possibilities in Christ become realities through the grace of God (2 Corinthians 9:8). Although God loves us equally, we walk in different dimensions of power and manifestation depending on the grace we have received. We should not be deceived into thinking that all things will be possible in our lives because of God's love. The results we receive are proportional to the measure of revelation and knowledge of God's grace we have received.

According to Acts 20:24, the gospel is the good news of the grace of God. This is because the grace of God avails power to live as God intended and makes possibilities that are in Christ Jesus to become realities in our lives. Failure to witness the manifestation of the promises of God is an indicator that we are lacking in grace because all the promises of God are "yes" and "Amen" in Christ Jesus (2 Corinthians 1:20).

Further Reading: *1 Corinthians 1:4; 2 Timothy 1:9; 2 Corinthians 8:9*
Prayer for the Day: *Oh God, may thy grace that brings transformation, be upon my life, in Jesus' name, Amen.*

Luke 10-11; John 10:22-42

26th October

Be a Faithful Steward of God's Gifts

"Now it is required that those who have been given a trust must prove faithful" (1 Corinthians 4:2).

The Lord has given believers diverse gifts for the benefit of His body, the church. His desire is for us to be faithful stewards of all the gifts and grace He has entrusted us. God has called us to partner with Him in different areas of influence – giving, administration, encouragement or prophesying (see Romans 12:6-8). He requires that we become faithful in dispensing every gift He has given. The more we serve faithfully, the more power and grace we receive to continue ministering to the needs of the saints.

Irrespective of the area of service God has called us to, we need to be faithful and glorify Him in everything. Faithfulness is a fruit of the Spirit. Authentic believers do their best to be faithful to God and man as that is part of the many blessings and privileges we have received through our knowledge of the Lord. God honours the faithful by promoting them once they demonstrate faithfulness in the little they have been given (Luke 16:10).

It is unfortunate that many believers use the graces God has given them for selfish gain. The word of God warns us against the love of money and we must therefore resist the temptation to peddle the gospel for profit. God will reward us in time and eternity if we serve Him as His holy word prescribes.

Further Reading: 1 Timothy 1:12; 1 Corinthians 4:17; Hebrews 3:5
Prayer for the Day: Dear God, help me be faithful in everything You have entrusted me, in Jesus' name, Amen.

Luke 12-13

27th October

Honouring Vows is Powerful

"Jephthah made a vow to the Lord: 'If you give the Ammonites into my hands, whatever comes out of the door of my house to meet me when I return in triumph from the Ammonites will be the Lord's, and I will sacrifice it as a burnt offering'" (Judges 11:30-31).

The story of Jephthah illustrates the weight of fulfilling vows to God. He pledged to offer the first thing that would meet him at his door after victory. After God made him successful, his only daughter was the first person to meet him and because he was committed to doing what he had promised, he offered her as a sacrifice. His unwavering commitment reveals how God expects us to honor our vows. Unfortunately, most people relax the intensity of their vows after God answers their prayers. They slacken the commitments undermining their integrity.

The pledges we make in church require commitment and sincerity. Many believers commit to offer support but end up failing. Ecclesiastes 5:6 warns against arousing God's anger against the work of our hands by breaking our promises. It is better not to vow than to do so and fail to honour.

Our vows mirror our devotion and trust in God. They are an avenue God uses to grow our faith. We should not regard our vows as a burden but as avenues of entering higher levels of walking with God. Making vows and observing the discipline of honouring them however demanding they might be can fortify our bond with God.

Further Reading: **Psalm 61:8**
Prayer for the Day: Dear God, help me grasp the significance of honouring my vows to you. Strengthen me to fulfill the vows I make to you, in Jesus' name. Amen.

Luke 14-15

28th October

Turning Impossibilities into Reality

"So in the course of time Hannah became pregnant and gave birth to a son. She named him Samuel saying, "Because I asked the Lord for him" (1 Samuel 1:20).

Walking successfully with God demands that one gets to know the formulae He works with. Doing this can help us turn impossibilities into possibilities. Hannah was aware of the power of vows in walking with God. She was distressed for many years because of childlessness. In the midst of her distress, she knelt down and solemnly pledged that if she was to be blessed with a child, she would give him over to the Lord's service. God's acceptance of her pledge created a conducive environment for the impossible to become a reality. Our lives can be altered profoundly through making vows to God. Hannah made a fervent petition to God (1 Samuel 1:9-11). Her solemn oath was more than just words; it was a legally enforceable promise.

Vows honoured make the impossible possible. Hannah's vow ended her season of barrenness, making her a mother of not only Samuel, a servant of God, but also other children. In the absence of that pledge, Hannah might have been doomed to remain childless for the rest of her life. As we make our commitments to God by faith, we open ourselves to His mighty transformative power. No obstacle – however great or insurmountable – can resist the divine power activated by vows. God is reliable and always watches over His word to perform it.

Further Reading: Psalm 66:13-14
Prayer for the Day: Dear Lord, grant us wisdom to understand the place of vows so that we can walk in the supernatural, Amen.

Day 302 — Luke 16; Luke 17:1-10

29th October

Plunder the Enemy by Binding the Strong Man

"Or again, how can anyone enter a strong man's house and carry off his possessions unless he first ties up the strong man? Then he can plunder his house" (Matthew 12:29).

Through His redemptive work, the Lord Jesus made a way for us to have dominion over the powers of the enemy. He gave us power and authority to trample on snakes and scorpions without being harmed. Through prayer and making declarations, we have the power to bind and to lose (Matthew 18:18). We have the Lord's authority to bind every plan of the enemy and lose the will of God on earth as it is done in heaven.

Jesus unveiled the spiritual strategy of plundering the kingdom of darkness. We must first bind the strong man assigned to keep people in bondage. As we do this, we demonstrate God's sovereignty over all creation.

God has called us to be spiritual soldiers. We have the right to exercise the power He has delegated to us which sets the captives free, heals the sick, delivers the oppressed and encourages the downcast through the power of His word. Through the guidance of His Spirit, we can ensure that only the will of God is done in our lives as we bind all powers of darkness that are determined to derail us from serving God's purpose and attaining our destinies.

Further Reading: Matthew 17:21; Luke 10:19
Prayer for the Day: Heavenly Father, grant us discernment to identify the works of darkness in our lives and bind them, so that we may walk in the freedom that Christ purchased for us when He died on the cross. Amen.

John 11

30th October

Confront All Forces of Darkness

"The one who does what is sinful is of the devil, because the devil has been sinning from the beginning. The reason the Son of God appeared was to destroy the devil's work" (1 John 3:8).

Sin is often used by the devil to ensnare God's people hindering them from serving God's purpose. God detests sin as it contradicts His holy nature. He has already done everything He will ever need to do to save us and empower us to overcome all the evil in the world. Jesus' life, death and resurrection made room for us to walk in the dominion God intended from the beginning. Those who reject the Lordship of Jesus and choose to live outside His redemptive plan belong to the devil. They do Satan's will and follow in his rebellion against God. The Scriptures say that severe judgment awaits them as God will condemn his enemies.

However, those who are in Christ have been transformed to become children of God. Through the work of Christ, they are free to do God's will and serve His purpose. They partner with God to advance the kingdom of heaven on earth and in so doing push back the darkness imposed on many by the kingdom of the devil. We are the light of the world and must not allow our light to be put out by the sin and darkness in the world. We actually ought to shine God's light on all people for their salvation and deliverance.

Further Reading: Galatians 5:19-21; Matthew 5:13-16
Prayer for the Day: Today, I resist the devil and all his works in Jesus' name, Amen.

Day 304 — Luke 17:11-37; Luke 18:1-14

31st October

God Can Turn Curses into Blessings

"However, the Lord your God would not listen to Balaam but turned the curse into a blessing for you, because the Lord your God loves you" Deuteronomy 23:5).

God is sovereign and He can turn any curse into a blessing. His power is unlimited and His purposes cannot be thwarted. What He has blessed no man can curse, and the door he has opened no man can shut. Balak summoned Balaam commanding him to utter curses to Israel, with the intention of weakening and preventing her from fulfilling God's purpose and attaining her destiny. God's power prevailed and the curses turned into blessings. He confirmed that what God has blessed can never be cursed.

Likewise, we live in a world inhabited by enemies who desire and work for our downfall. Some people cast spells, use magic arts and ensnare God's people by their words. God opposes such and declares, "I am against your magic charms with which you ensnare people like birds; I will tear them from your arms; I will set free the people that you ensnare like birds" (Ezekiel 13:20).

As we serve God, we need not fear the evil words people speak against us to weaken us. As we walk in righteousness and align ourselves with God's will, He will shield us from all the curses thrown to us, and we will be showered with His blessings.

Further Reading: **Ezekiel 13:1-23; Isaiah 54:17**
Prayer for the Day: **Today in the name of Jesus Christ, I overturn all evil words spoken against my destiny. I walk in freedom because the Lord loves me and has showered me with blessings, Amen.**

Matthew 19; Mark 10

1st November

Exercise Your Authority

"Truly I tell you, whatever you bind on earth will be bound in heaven, and whatever you loose on earth will be loosed in heaven" (Matthew 18:18).

Christ has bestowed upon all believers great power and authority. Our words carry great power in the spiritual realm; we have divine power to make binding decrees, to put an end to the works of the evil one, and to enforce the will of God. The word of God in our mouths is just as powerful as it is in His mouth.

We need confidence in God to exercise the authority Christ has delegated to us. To enforce the verdict of the cross that purchased our salvation, freedom and guaranteed our inheritance, we need to stand firm on the authority of God's word. As we wage spiritual warfare, we need to be fully convinced that whatever we bind or lose on earth shall be bound or loosed in the spiritual realm. Our lives, families, businesses, careers, calling and ministry are meant to glorify God. They can be delivered from the grip of evil forces if we align ourselves with God's plan.

Our authority lies in conforming our words and actions with God's truth. The more we yield our destinies to God, the more we receive His backup as we exercise authority through the spiritual warfare.

Further Reading: James 5:16; 1 Timothy 2:5; Proverbs 21:30
Prayer for the Day: Heavenly Father, I thank you for the authority I have through Christ to bind and loose. May your plan prevail in my life. Amen.

Day 306 — Matthew 20-21

2nd November

Walk in the Hidden Path of Blessing

"but whose delight is in the law of the Lord, and who meditates on his law day and night. That person is like a tree planted by streams of water, which yields its fruit in season and whose leaf does not wither - whatever they do prospers" (Psalms 1:2-3)

The righteous delight in the Word of God and meditate upon it day and night. The Scriptures compare them to trees planted by life-giving streams. Such trees bear abundant fruit in due season, their leaves never wither and they enjoy great prosperity. On the contrary, the wicked do not have a firm foundation; they resemble chaff which is easily scattered by the wind. Those who neglect the word of God end up losing in this life and in eternity. They fail to realise the potential God has deposited in them and their godless living disqualifies the eternal life God gives to those who fear, love and serve Him faithfully.

Walking in the path God has set for us through His word makes us a mystery to the enemy. Forces of darkness that render people unfruitful have no access to us when we are hidden in the power of God's eternal word. His word is an anchor that safeguards our lives from harm and guarantees our fruitfulness. When we bear much fruit, our lives glorify Him and we become partners with Him in spreading the good news far and wide.

Further Reading: Proverbs 2:6; Proverbs 3:5-6; Isaiah 42:16
Prayer for the Day: Heavenly Father, guide me into the hidden path of blessings as I commit myself to continually delight in your word and meditate on it day and night. Amen.

Matthew 20-21

3rd November

Have Confidence in God's Plan

"For I know the plans I have for you," declares the Lord, "plans to prosper you and not to harm you, plans to give you hope and a future" (Jeremiah 29:11).

Having confidence in the plan God has for a person's life is greatly liberating. God is omniscient and a diligent planner. His design was that we walk in the path set for us which is good and profitable. Our lives should glorify the name of the Lord as we prosper from one level to another.

We should also face the future with confidence having the assurance that God is on our side. God's power gives us hope and faith as we see God's plan for our lives unfold progressively. We have two choices in life: worry and be anxiety or to walk in confidence in God. Worry leads to fear and uncertainty while confidence in God activates God's plan for our lives as He requires us to walk by faith.

From the beginning when God created man, He intended him to thrive by walking by faith. In the Garden of Eden, God taught Adam His ways and revealed His plan for his future. As long as Adam walked in God's ways, he was guaranteed of victory. However, he rebelled and was banished from Eden. By God's grace, He reconciled man to Himself and now we can attain our divine destinies.

Further Reading: Proverbs 3:5-6, Isaiah 26:3, Romans 8:28

Prayer for the Day: Heavenly Father, I have confidence that you have a perfect plan for my life. Take away worry and anxiety from my life, in the name of Jesus. Amen.

Day 308 | Mark 11; John 12

4th November

Strive to Know the Lord Intimately

"...I know whom I have believed, and am convinced that he is able to guard what I have entrusted to him until that day" **(2 Timothy 1:12b).**

An intimate knowledge of God helps us attain our destinies. This implies knowing who He is, what He can do as well as His ways. One of the most assuring attributes is His ability to guard what we entrust to Him until the day He will be manifested in His full glory. His word contains the revelation of the need to walk in the fullness of His will for our lives.

When we know God intimately, we become confident and walk in obedience to His word. Our lives are guided by the truth of His word and covered by His presence. With each step, the assurance grows and the cares of this world dissipate. Forgiveness flows effortlessly, prayer becomes effective and we are able to easily align ourselves with God's ways. Our future becomes secure and we live for God's glory.

Walking on this path keeps us safe from the enemy. Our temporal and eternal destinies are secure in Christ as we grow in the knowledge of our Lord and Saviour Jesus Christ. The word of God assures us that those who know the Lord shall be strong and do great exploits (Daniel 11:32b). Having little or wrong knowledge about God hinders most people from fulfilling His purposes in their lives.

Further Reading: Psalm 23:4; Philippians 4:6-7; Hebrews 11:6
Prayer for the Day: Heavenly Father, I entrust my life, dreams and fears to you. Help me to rest assured that you are able. Amen.

Matthew 22; Mark 12

5th November

Beware of the Way of Death

"There is a way that appears to be right, but in the end it leads to death" (Proverbs 14:12).

The path you choose can lead you to glory or destruction. The enemy schemes and strives to control the destinies of God's people by misleading them to follow the road that leads to death. Ironically, that road seems right but its destination is destruction. Seeking God fervently keeps us close to Him and helps us hear His voice clearly.

Paths that lead to destruction appear logical and appealing. The enemy can tempt you to seek revenge to assuage your past hurts. Unforgiveness leads to bitterness which puts one in a spiritual prison where the evil one then mercilessly destroys the life of a person ending up in eternal damnation. Such people normally miss out on all the blessings God intended them to enjoy. They end up having unfulfilled lives full of pain, struggles and turmoil.

By the grace and power of God, we can escape destruction and live fruitful lives as we let the Spirit of God guide us in making choices. We do not have to follow the path of destruction when we have fully been given abundant life in Christ.

Further reading: **Psalm 119:105; Jeremiah 6:16; Matthew 7:13-14**
Prayer for the day: *Heavenly Father, grant me wisdom to choose the right path that leads to life. Keep me away from the path of destruction in Jesus' name. Amen.*

6th November

Listen More than You Talk

'My dear brothers and sisters, take note of this: Everyone should be quick to listen, slow to speak and slow to become angry" **(James 1:19).**

Effective communication is key in relationships. As we walk with Christ, He requires us to abide by His word and to exercise self-control and regulation in our speech. We should learn how to communicate without sinning with the tongue. Apostle James, through wisdom as an elder admonished followers of Jesus to control their tongues so that they could only speak what is profitable and necessary. He instructs believers to emulate God by being slow to anger. James 3:1-12 underpins the significance of the words we speak. We gauge spiritual maturity through the way a person speaks. Unfortunately, many people are ignorant of what God's word says on the use of the tongue, and this makes them ensnare themselves and others through careless speech.

Small as it is, the tongue determines a person's success or failure in life. Many people are failures because of the limitations they impose on themselves through careless speech. Our tongues should be used for creative purposes and not for destruction; we should seek divine wisdom on how to use them to build our lives and those of others. To be an effective or fruitful Christian, we ought to do less speaking but more listening.

Further Reading: Proverbs 15:1; Ephesians 4:26-27; Proverbs 18:1; Colossians 4:6; Isaiah 50; 4

Prayer for the Day: Heavenly Father, grant me the grace to listen more than I speak so as I can be keen to hear your voice and not sin against You in the multitude of my words. Amen

Mark 13

Day 311

7th November

Partner with God by Raising Godly Offspring

"Didn't the Lord make you one with your wife? In body and spirit, you are his. And what does he want? Godly children from your union. So guard your heart; remain loyal to the wife of your youth" (Malachi 2:15).

Marriage is God's idea. In the Garden of Eden, He made a helper suitable for Adam. From then on, the human race has been perpetuated through relationships between men and women. Some of those relationships have been subjected to the will of God while others operate outside the confines of His holy will.

Through the security that marriage guarantees a couple, God desires a godly offspring. In ancient Israel, He warned His people against intermarrying with pagan nations who would lead them to the worship of idols. On many occasions, they were unable to exercise restraint and disobeyed His commandment. The consequences were disastrous as those who did so became idolatrous and attracted divine judgment.

Healthy families mirror God's will and are a fertile ground for rearing balanced children who are taught and do the will of God. Godliness is a great need in the society today. This can best be enforced in a secure home environment where children are brought up in the instruction of the Lord and nurtured to become well-adjusted adults.

Further Reading: Psalm 127:3-5; Proverbs 22:6; Deuteronomy 6:6-9
Prayer for the Day: Heavenly Father, I recognize the sacred duty of raising godly offspring. Help me do this by modeling a holy life for your glory, in Jesus' name. Amen

8th November

Our Peace is in Christ

"Blessed are those whose strength is in you, who have set their hearts on pilgrimage. As they pass through the Valley of Baca, they make it a place of springs; the autumn rains also cover it with pools. They go from strength to strength, till each appears before God in Zion" (Psalms 84:5-7).

Every believer faces the metaphorical Valley of Baca in his spiritual journey. This valley is not physical but is a spiritual reality we have to face at some point or other. It is full of challenges and trials and requires faith and fortitude to cross. Salvation does not insulate us from challenges but strengthens us to face them.

During our seasons of adversity, we receive God's blessings and are transformed from strength to strength until we appear in Zion. The challenges we face are stepping stones to greater levels of glory. They refine our character and equip us for more effectiveness in the kingdom of God. Those who have been tried and tested add value to the kingdom of God as their lives are a testimony of God's power and faithfulness.

Even though we are bound to face tribulations, we find peace in Christ. This peace surpasses all understanding and guards our hearts and minds even in the most trying moments. This supernatural peace makes others wonder how we remain calm in the midst of storms.

*Further Reading: **John 16:33; Philippians 4:7***
*Prayer for the Day: **Dear Lord, strengthen and guide me as I pass through this valley, and help me depend on your grace for my peace. Amen.***

Matthew 25

9th November

Have Faith Even When You Suffer Loss

"Naked I came from my mother's womb, and naked I will depart. The Lord gave and the Lord has taken away; may the name of the Lord be praised" (Job 1:21-22).

Our lives on earth are transient and worldly possessions last only a short time. Unfortunately, many people attach an inordinate value to material possessions and lose their faith when they lose their possessions. By so doing, they miss the peace, security and comfort God desires His people to have even when they face difficulties.

Job acknowledges the temporary nature of human existence and wealth. Despite the severity of his suffering, Job refused to recant his faith in God. His wife provoked him to curse God and die but he stood firm. He praised God and believed that all things come from and return to God.

Having faith in God equips us with divine strength which sets us apart from unbelievers. We are not immune to trials and tribulations but we are supernaturally empowered to overcome them. Our strength comes from our knowledge of the word of God and His character. He is faithful and ready to help us when we call on His name. The trials we face are an opportunity for spiritual growth. When perceived correctly, they enable us develop a deeper relationship with God.

Further Reading: Daniel 3:19-28; Ecclesiastes 7:2-3
Prayer for the Day: Dear Heavenly Father, in times of trials and tribulations, help me remember that you are my source of strength. Amen.

Day 314 — Matthew 26; Mark 14

10th November

Allow God to Refine You

"In all this, you greatly rejoice, though now for a little while you may have had to suffer grief in all kinds of trials. These have come so that the proven genuineness of your faith - of greater worth than gold, which perishes even though refined by fire - may result in praise, glory, and honor when Jesus Christ is revealed" ***(1 Peter 1:5-7).***

We relate with God by faith. His word says that without faith we cannot please Him and our seeking Him must be based on the foundation of confidence in His existence (Hebrews 11:6). To be effective and productive, our faith in God must be tested and refined. In God's wisdom, the best way to test the authenticity of a man's faith is subjecting it to different kinds of fiery trials.

Our faith is compared to gold. In its natural form, gold is embedded in rocks. It is mined, refined and purified through fire. Similarly, our faith needs to go through the refining fire of trials to become unshakable. Faith that has been refined is of great value in the sight of God. When we are tested, the impurities of our faith are cleansed and our spiritual resilience emerges. This process is usually slow, taxing and painful but is a necessity for spiritual growth. It results in "praise, glory, and honor when Jesus Christ is revealed" as scripture indicates.

Further Reading: *James 1:2-4; Romans 5:3-5; Isaiah 48:10*
Prayer for the Day: *Dear Lord, help me to see trials as an opportunity for my faith to be refined and purified for your glory. Amen.*

Luke 22; John 13

11th November

Our Speech Reveals the Contents of Our Hearts

"You brood of vipers, how can you who are evil say anything good? For the mouth speaks what the heart is full of. A good man brings good things out of the good stored up in him, and an evil man brings evil things out of the evil stored up in him" **(Matthew 12:34-35).**

The words we speak reveal the things we have stored in the innermost recesses of our hearts. If the deposits in our hearts are pure, we will speak pure words. On the other hand, if we have evil in our hearts, this will reflect in our words. When we speak harsh words, we do it because they are in our hearts waiting for an opportunity to be expressed. Small foxes ruin vineyards and hinder them from bearing fruit (Song of Solomon 2:15). These "small foxes" are hidden faults and character flaws that sabotage our spiritual growth and hinder our blessings. They are unnoticed until they are exposed when we face spiritual, social or mental pressure.

We need to identify the weaknesses and limitations that trouble our lives and partner with God to deal with them. The best place to begin is in the heart because it is the storehouse of our lives. The things we allow to take residence there determine the path of our lives. We need to address all the weaknesses we have in our hearts so that they do not make us engage in ungodly speech that can hinder the pursuit of our divine destinies.

Further Reading: Luke 6:45; Proverbs 4:23; Galatians 5:22-23
Prayer for the Day: Lord, give me the grace I need to work on my heart so that I can be transformed to reflect your image. Amen.

Day 316 — John 14-17

12th November

Maintain Integrity and Entrust Yourself to God

He committed no sin, and no deceit was found in his mouth." When they hurled their insults at him, he did not retaliate; when he suffered, he made no threats. Instead, he entrusted himself to him who judges justly" **(1 Peter 2:22-23).**

As we walk with God, we need to strive for integrity. Our words and actions should be in sync no matter where we are or who is watching. We also need to learn the art of entrusting ourselves to God at all times, in good and bad times.

Our Lord and Saviour set an example for us. After He was betrayed by Judas Iscariot, He endured mockery, ridicule and mistreatment from sinners. He knew His divine assignment and took all the beatings and negative words graciously; He endured the pain until He completed His assignment. Through His death, we have been reconciled with God and are now heirs of God's promise to Abraham. We also have the precious gifts of eternal life and daily access to God. As we walk with God, we are bound to face situations that test our integrity and our commitment to God. When such things happen, we need to learn from the examples God has given us in His word for our encouragement and strengthening.

Further Reading: *Matthew 5:38-48; Romans 12:14-21; Proverbs 15:1; 2 Samuel 16:5-12*

Prayer for the Day: *Heavenly Father, thank you for the example Jesus Christ has shown us when He responded to His persecutors with grace and humility as He trusted your justice. May my responses to trials reveal my trust in You. Amen.*

Matthew 27; Mark 15

13th November

Renew Your Strength in the Lord

"but those who hope in the LORD will renew their strength. They will soar on wings like eagles; they will run and not grow weary, they will walk and not be faint" *(Isaiah 40:31).*

We daily face situations and challenges that weaken and drain our confidence in God. Serving God, seeking His face and doing His will require inner strength that, just like physical strength, can be depleted and needs to be replenished. The word of God promises the saints that they can depend on God as a source of new strength. When they receive this inner strength, they are able to overcome challenges and attain their destinies no matter the intensity of the opposition.

Hope is a great anchor for the soul of every believer. It instills in us a sense of confidence in God's plans for our lives. Scriptures say that God has plans to give us a future and a hope; He arms us with strength so that we can serve His purposes better. False prophets, false Christs and false teachers have deceived many and diverted them from the truth of the word of God. As a result, the gospel has been mocked and many have lost hope. However, as God's dearly beloved children, we are safe in Christ. We can trust God to renew our strength as we wait on Him no matter the adversity.

Further Reading: 2 Samuel 3:1; Psalm 84:7
Prayer for the Day: Heavenly Father, I embrace courage and faith as I trust you to renew my strength to attain my divine destiny. Amen.

Day 318 | Luke 23; John 18-19

14th November

Have Confidence in God's Victory

Then one of the elders said to me, "Do not weep! See, the Lion of the tribe of Judah, the Root of David, has triumphed. He can open the scroll and its seven seals" *(Revelation 5:5).*

The Lord likens Himself to a lion. The lion's confidence and courage make it the king of the jungle. It reigns supreme in the wilderness and is not intimidated by the size or strength of its prey. The lion has an attitude of unwavering determination that makes it an invincible hunter. It is the will of God that every believer should be tenacious and determined. As we walk with God, we cannot avoid facing difficult or even life-threatening situations. However, we need not fear because by faith, we are able to overcome all of them and manifest God's glory. All things are possible for the man who has faith. Our faith in God needs to be anchored on His word and His unlimited power that prevails over all other powers. The fact that Jesus conquered all battles should strengthen us to fight the good fight of faith with confidence.

The words of our mouths and the confessions we make must align with the will of God. Our words reflect the contents of our hearts (Luke 6:45). If our hearts are saturated with fear, our words will be full of fear. However, if we fill our hearts with faith, victory and God's word, our words will be authoritative and powerful.

Further Reading: *Daniel 11:32; Habakkuk 2:4*
Prayer for the Day: *Lord, instill in me the lion's attitude of confidence and courage to conquer everything in Jesus' name, Amen.*

Matthew 28; Mark 16

15th November

Overcome Doubt and Double-mindedness

"Submit yourselves, then, to God. Resist the devil, and he will flee from you. Come near to God and he will come near to you. Wash your hands, you sinners, and purify your hearts, you double-minded" *(James 4:7-8).*

Double-mindedness is a great enemy as far as our faith is concerned. People whose mind is not singularly focused on God waver between opinions and fail to manifest God's power because God works through people whose confidence in Him is unshakeable. The enemy attacks those who are double-minded which leads to sabotaging God's plan for them and their destinies.

Apostle James wrote his epistle to the church as an elder. His advanced age gave him the advantage of the wisdom that comes with old age. Notable Biblical figures such as John the Baptist experienced doubt. When imprisoned, he sent his disciples to ask Jesus for confirmation whether He really was the Messiah. Similarly, in our journey of faith, we may occasionally question whether God, who has been with us all along, will continue to fight for us.

The spirit of doubt and double-mindedness targets the mind. It works alongside spirits of unbelief and fear. If unaddressed by the authority in the name of Jesus, a person's faith can be shaken. Scriptures admonish us to stand firm in faith. Our devotion to God displeases the enemy and his demons but we need not fear them because Jesus has assured us of victory both in time and in eternity.

Further Reading: Judges 6:25-32; Hebrews 10:35
Prayer for the Day: Heavenly Father, help us to stand firm in our faith and overcome every form of doubt and double-mindedness in the name of Jesus. Amen.

Luke 24; John 20-21

16th November

Embrace the Holy Spirit and His Power

"Not by might, nor by power, but by my Spirit," says the LORD Almighty (Zechariah 4:6).

The Holy Spirit is the Chief Executive Officer of the church of Jesus Christ. He is in charge of day to day running of the body of Christ and is intimately involved in everything that happens in the church. He came after Jesus ascended to reveal God to man and to act as a Helper to the followers of the Lord (John 16:7).

The secret to success in our walk and service to God is reliance on God's unlimited power. It is through His power that He performs great signs, miracles and wonders. Those who embrace the Spirit of God and relate reverentially with Him receive dynamic divine power and do great exploits. Our greatest role model Jesus was confident in His purpose on earth and fulfilled the will of His Heavenly Father without fear. As His followers, we need to have faith in God's power. We need to be confident that with Him on our side, we will triumph over worldly challenges.

God has entrusted each of us a divine vision and desires that we fulfill as He did to Zerubbabel. The assignment might seem daunting but with Him on our side, no mountain can stand on our way.

Further Reading: *Judges 4:1-24; Romans 9:10-13*
Prayer for the Day: *Lord, I surrender to You and ask for guidance as I embrace the vision You have for me and for the church. I am encouraged for I know that with You on my side, all things are possible, in Jesus' name, Amen.*

Acts 1-3

Day 321

17th November

Have Faith in God's Name as You Face Challenges

"Then David said to the Philistine, 'You come to me with a sword, with a spear, and with a javelin. But I come to you in the name of the LORD of hosts, the God of the armies of Israel, whom you have defied" **(1 Samuel 17:45).**

God takes delight when He operates in our lives in a way we can easily identify with. Every time He gave an assignment to those He called, He gave them the ability and empowered them to execute the mission successfully. When He called Moses to deliver Israel from Egypt, He used what was already familiar to Moses - a shepherd's staff which he used for many years as a shepherd. Similarly, to give Jael victory over Sisera, He used a tent peg, a tool with which Jael was accustomed to in her daily life.

In the same way, God uses what is in our hands to accomplish His purposes. He created each of us with unique abilities and strengths to solve specific problems. He knows that we carry solutions to the problems facing our generation because He custom-designed us for this purpose. We should therefore not underestimate our capacity. Our confidence should stem from the knowledge that God has configured us for a purpose and He will faithfully enable us fulfill His calling.

Further Reading: Exodus 4:1-17; 1 Samuel 17:32-50
Prayer for the Day: Lord, we thank you for the gifts and abilities you have given us. Help us recognize the tools in our hands and give us the confidence to use them for your glory in Jesus' name. Amen.

Day 322 — Acts 4-6

18th November

Shine in Darkness

"Arise, shine, for your light has come, and the glory of the LORD rises upon you" (Isaiah 60:1).

God teaches and prepares us for our destinies through progressive growth. This approach allows us to learn, experience victories and reinforce our faith. It equips us with the confidence we need to face challenging times. We must therefore hold on to faith until we prevail over all the challenges of this life and reign with Christ through eternity.

When all things around us seem useless, we can stand by faith as Children of God and witness the hand of God at work in effecting our divine elevation. Our faith is very significant in the physical and spiritual realms and enables us to shine in the darkness that covers the world. When we shine the light of God, we become beacons of hope for many. Those around us are inspired to trust God in their circumstances and by this, God's power and purposes are established around the world.

By the grace of God, we can reflect the light of God even in the hardest times in our callings, families, mandates and nations. Shining in darkness also implies inspiring hope in others in the domains God has positioned us. As others witness the confidence, courage, and divine favor in our lives, they too can be motivated to trust in God's faithfulness and His ability to provide and sustain them during challenging times.

Further Reading: *Matthew 5:14-16; Philippians 2:14-16*
Prayer for the Day: *Lord, grant me strength and confidence to face challenging times. As the darkness of the world grows thicker, may your light within us shine brighter. Amen.*

Acts 7-8

19th November

Have Assurance in the Face of Death

"It is better to go to a house of mourning than to go to a house of feasting, for death is the destiny of everyone; the living should take this to heart"(Ecclesiastes 7:2).

For many people, some believers included, death is a taboo subject. It is shrouded in fear and mystery that many choose to ignore it altogether. However, it is a reality we simply cannot wish away. We are all bound to face it and we feel its sting when we lose family members or those close to us. Solomon had divine wisdom and dealt with this emotive subject in his wisdom books. He encouraged his readers to ponder over their common destiny in death and to adequately prepare.

Instead of waiting for the day we depart from the earth with fear and uncertainty, we can prepare for it by doing what we need to do before the ordained day. The will of God is that we should be assured of our eternal destiny based on the understanding that death is not an end but the beginning of a new life with Christ in the presence of God. We can have assurance and calmness if we examine our hearts through the lenses of God's word that gives clear directions on how to prepare for our eternal home. Celebrations and feasts are part of our lives on earth, but we should not allow them to distract us from the deeper truths in the word of God.

Further Reading: Romans 14:8; 1 Thessalonians 5:9-10
Prayer for the Day: Lord, help me to prepare while in this life how I will spend eternity with you. Amen.

Day 324 — Acts 9-10

20th November

Understand the Value of Salvation

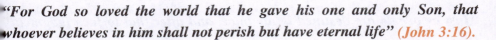

"For God so loved the world that he gave his one and only Son, that whoever believes in him shall not perish but have eternal life" **(John 3:16).**

As we draw closer to the end-times, the message of the gospel has been watered down. Many people have a wrong understanding of prosperity and they view the gospel as a means of making wealth. This is against God's original plan because He intended it to be used to spread His love for the salvation of humanity. God delights in providing all the material needs of His people as long as they prioritise His kingdom in everything they do (see Matthew 6:33).

True salvation is based on the foundation of God's love that was manifested through Jesus' sacrificial death. The anchor verse teaches that the ultimate purpose of Jesus' sacrifice was to give us eternal life. Material blessings are a by-product of spiritual blessings and should not be our primary focus. Jesus taught His disciples about the realities of our eternal destinies. The parable of the rich man and Lazarus serves as a reminder of the temporary nature of earthly wealth and the enduring value of spiritual wealth. The rich man lived in luxury while Lazarus lived in poverty. However, when they died, Lazarus was comforted in Abraham's bosom while the rich man was tormented in Hades. He understood the value of godliness too late and lost his eternal destiny by concentrating too much on material things at the expense of the spiritual.

Further Reading: **Luke 16:19-31; Hebrews 11:35**
Prayer for the Day: **Father, help me remember the real value of the salvation you have provided for me through Christ. Amen.**

Acts 11-12

Day 325

21st November

Prepare for Eternity by Investing in God's Kingdom

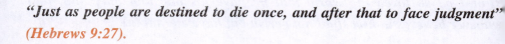

"Just as people are destined to die once, and after that to face judgment" (Hebrews 9:27).

The Bible provides us with profound wisdom and insights on our temporal and eternal destinies. We should take these lessons seriously because they will determine whether we will fulfill God's purposes or not. The word of God teaches that our lives on earth are short and compares them to a mist (James 4:14). We should invest in the kingdom of God as a matter of priority. Since we are certain that death is inevitable and that we shall all give account for all our deeds in the flesh (Romans 14:12), we need to learn what to do as we prepare to meet God.

We must make every effort to invest our time, energy and effort in propagating the gospel to all nations of the world. The Great Commission that Jesus gave His disciples applies to us and we should daily spread the word so that we can make disciples for God's glory. On the Day of Judgment, we shall all appear before God's throne and He will reward us for everything we did in the flesh. He is a just judge and will reward each man for His work. Jesus promises that His return is imminent and He has in His hands the rewards He will give to each of His servants.

Further Reading: 1 John 2:25; John 11:25
Prayer for the Day: Heavenly Father, help us to invest in Your kingdom every day as we prepare to spend eternity with You.

22nd November

Invest Your Treasures in Eternity

And he told them this parable: "The ground of a certain rich man produced a good crop. He thought to himself, 'What shall I do? I have no place to store my crops.' "Then he said, 'This is what I'll do. I will tear down my barns and build bigger ones, and there I will store all my grain and my goods. And I'll say to myself, "You have plenty of good things laid up for many years. Take life easy; eat, drink and be merry" (Luke 12:16-19).

Life is unpredictable and often, earthly achievements can distract us from the more important spiritual goals of being "rich toward God." Worldly possessions are not meant to be an end in themselves but to facilitate our service to God and humanity.

The anchor scriptures narrate the selfish and shallow life of the rich man. Jesus described him as a fool because he was only interested in temporary pursuit of wealth unaware that his life would end sooner than he thought. He stored up many goods for himself and neglected His eternal destiny. If we are not careful, we can easily become like the rich fool. Though material possessions are not evil in themselves, they can easily distract us from our relationship with God and our spiritual growth if we do not have a solid Biblical foundation of how to handle them.

Further Reading: Titus 1:2; 1 Corinthians 15:58; Hebrews 11:10
Prayer for the day: Dear Lord, help me to prioritize you above all else. Make me rich in faith and good deeds rather than in worldly possessions. Give me the grace to store up treasures in heaven in Jesus' name. Amen.

James 1-5

Day 327

23rd November

Fulfil God's Assignment

"I have fought the good fight, I have finished the race, I have kept the faith" (2 Timothy 4:7).

Knowing and wholeheartedly pursuing the purposes of God for our lives can inspire us to be confident and to have a sense of purpose. God created each of us with a unique destiny and for a special purpose. Our greatest fulfillment is in discovering and fulfilling the purpose for which God made us. Apostle Paul set a good example for us. Even though he was originally a bitter persecutor and enemy of the church of Jesus Christ, he became a zealous preacher of the good news when he came back to his senses. His life-changing encounter with Christ on the road to Damascus gave him a sense of purpose he was ready to die defending. In many of his epistles, he emphasized God's will for his life.

As we strive to fulfill God's purpose, we should understand that He works within us to accomplish His purpose (Philippians 2:13). The parable of the talents conveys a valuable lesson about the consequences of neglecting the tasks God has assigned us. The servant who received one talent and buried it was reprimanded by his master. His failure to carry out his assignment led to a tragic outcome. We should be faithful stewards of the tasks and resources God has entrusted to us. Temporary pleasures, accomplishments and comfort should not distract us from fulfilling our purpose.

Further Reading: *Matthew 25:14-30; Luke 2:26; Acts 13:36*
Prayer for the Day: *Dear Heavenly Father, grant me the wisdom and courage to pursue and fulfill my divine assignment, in Jesus' name, Amen*

Day 328

24th November

Secure Your Destiny with God Through Holiness

"Make every effort to live in peace with everyone and to be holy; without holiness, no one will see the Lord" *(Hebrews 12:14).*

The earthly and eternal destinies of many people are compromised because of failure to pursue peace and holiness. The Lord our God is the Prince of peace and desires that we emulate His example. We cannot claim to belong to Him if we are quarrelsome and given to bickering. The gospel message we have teaches peace and demands that we make every effort to live at peace with all men. God requires holiness from every person who confesses His name. Since He is holy, we must emulate His character by setting ourselves apart for His purposes. Without holiness, we cannot see God in our earthly lives and in eternity.

God hates sin and is displeased by the ways of the wicked (Psalm 7:11). To please Him and receive His help in attaining our destinies, we must train ourselves to be holy. Becoming godly is demanding but we must be ready to pay the cost so that our lives can have the impact God desires. To walk with God with ease and have fruitful lives as His saints, Demands that we learn to renounce all forms of evil and impurity and set ourselves apart for His purposes. This requires that we treasure His word and commune with Him every day so that His Spirit can empower us to live pure and blameless lives.

Further Reading: Matthew 7:21-23; Ezekiel 33:11
Prayer for the Day: Dear Lord, guide me into living a life of holiness with the confidence to do Your will.

25th November

Trust in the Lord with All Your Heart

"Trust in the Lord with all your heart and lean not on your own understanding; in all your ways submit to him, and he will make your paths straight. Do not be wise in your own eyes; fear the Lord and shun evil" **(Proverbs 3:5-7).**

The heart is the wellspring of the issues of life. Its state determines the outcome of a person's life. God desires that we trust Him with all our heart, for in doing so, our confidence in Him deepens, shifting from our own achievements and abilities. Acknowledging God in all what we do is a demonstration of surrendering to His will. Men's decisions in most cases are unfruitful especially when made using their own understanding and knowledge which is limited. They eventually become fragile and cannot be trusted as an anchor in times of need.

Solomon understood that being wise in one's own eyes is a sure path to destruction. It exposes one to pride which eventually leads to failure as pride comes before destruction (Proverbs 16:18). Proud people sin against God and themselves, missing out on the grace of God. Pride defies God's command to His people to humble themselves and willingly submit to His will. Submission to God makes Him instruct our paths which leads to righteousness. He orders our steps through the Holy Spirit, giving us an expected end which is our destiny.

Further Reading: *James 4:11-12; Matthew 7:1-2*
Prayer for the Day: *Dear Lord, help me trust You at all times and not rely on my own limited understanding. Amen.*

26th November

Embrace God's Servants for Spiritual Growth

"Whoever welcomes a prophet as a prophet will receive a prophet's reward, and whoever welcomes a righteous person as a righteous person will receive a righteous person's reward" **(Matthew 10:41).**

We cannot succeed in our spiritual journeys if we walk alone. We need other believers for fellowship and anointed servants of God to minister to us along the way. In His unsearchable wisdom, God chooses and anoints men to serve as His servants who guide, uplift and impart spiritual gifts into His people. Our ability to receive the gifts and graces they carry depends on our response to them.

The Lord allows His servants to minister to people in order to deal with pride in the body of Christ. His will is that we should love one another and humbly receive our fellow saints as we acknowledge the grace and gifts deposited in them. The body of Christ is meant to operate in harmony, respect and recognition of the gifts He has given His children out of His generosity and free will.

The Bible emphasizes the significance of the different ministry offices and callings. Their purpose is to edify and build up the body of Christ (Ephesians 4:10-12). The enemy knows this and advances schemes to discredit God's servants, thereby hampering the growth of the church. We must discern his devices and forcefully resist them.

Further Reading: *Ephesians 4:13-16; 1 Thessalonians 5:12-13*
Prayer for the Day: *Lord, open our hearts to genuinely recognize and receive your servants. Increase our discernment and shield us from the divisive tactics of the enemy. Amen.*

Acts 17; Acts 18:1-18

27th November

Divine Impartation is Affected by Perception

"All the people, even the tax collectors, when they heard Jesus' words, acknowledged that God's way was right, because they had been baptized by John. But the Pharisees and experts in the law rejected God's purpose for themselves, because they had not been baptized by John" **(Luke 7:29-30).**

Our perception of the human vessels God has chosen to work through determines the extent to which we benefit from the ministry given to them. Jesus highlighted the importance of receiving prophets for who they are. One can only partake of the grace upon a servant of God if the heart is open toward that servant. A tainted impression blocks the flow of divine virtues. The enemy knows the significance of God's servants in our lives and creates wrong impressions to destroy our connections with them, so that we miss out what we ought to receive from them.

In Jesus' time, tax collectors who were marginalized in society, recognized and justified God's work. The religious types such as the Pharisees were prejudiced against Jesus and missed out on the will of God. They refused John's baptism for repentance of sins.

It is imperative to maintain clarity of heart and mind so that we do not miss out on the move of God. He uses those He has chosen to bring revival. We must therefore respect God's servants and perceive them as He does, because they are His gifts for us.

Further Reading: Luke 7:31-35; Isaiah 55:8-9
Prayer for the Day: Heavenly Father, help me perceive Your servants as divine instruments assigned by You for my benefit. Correct my perception so that I do not miss out on my blessings in Jesus' name.

Day 332 — 1 Thessalonians 1-5; 2 Thessalonians 1-3

28th November

Demonic Impressions are a Snare

"For John came neither eating nor drinking, and they say, 'He has a demon'" (Matthew 11:18).

The kingdom of darkness opposes the kingdom of light and uses different schemes and tactics to do so. Many of them target the minds of people, hindering them from receiving the word of God meant to give them access to salvation, healing, deliverance, wealth and many other possibilities in Christ. As we process the truth in us, we should allow the Holy Spirit to be in control so that we are not polluted by demonic impressions. An impression is a clear and telling mental image. The devil blinds the minds of unbelievers from seeing the light of the gospel that is meant to manifest the glory of God (2 Corinthians 4:4). If the devil succeeds in planting evil seeds in the minds and hearts of God's people, he can hinder them from attaining their destinies. He can also obstruct their path to receiving help from the Lord through His servants.

Despite having a divine mission, John the Baptist faced harsh prejudices due to his self-sacrificial lifestyle. His attire, diet, and habitat became fodder for those seeking to undermine his divine authority. Many servants of God are subjected to similar judgment today. Their names and ministries are tarnished by enemies of the gospel, blocking the impartation of spiritual gifts, blessings and anointing.

Many believers are closely scrutinized and subjected to misconceptions. They need to be spiritually armed to discern and resist demonic impressions.

Further Reading: *John 1:19-28; 1 Peter 2:1-3*
Prayer for the Day: *Lord, shield our hearts from the deceitful whispers of the enemy. Grant us discernment to separate truth from falsehood in Jesus' name. Amen.*

Acts 18:19-28; Acts 19:1-41

29th November

Relate with Spiritual Leaders in a Godly Way

"Obey your leaders and submit to them, for they are keeping watch over your souls, as those who will have to give an account. Let them do this with joy and not with groaning, for that would be of no advantage to you" **(Hebrews 13:17)**.

God has structured His eternal kingdom in such a way that His servants are in charge of the souls of His people. They act as watchmen and shepherds who protect and feed His flock through the ministry of the word. In His wisdom, God chooses men from our midst and charges them to watch over His people. They become accountable for these souls, and they will be rewarded according to the work done. Believers should honour spiritual leaders, failure to which their temporal and eternal destinies will be negatively affected.

The enemy is well aware of this kingdom system and works tirelessly to pollute, kill, steal and destroy the godly relationships the saints should have with the overseers of their souls. Once he has succeeded, he sows seeds of hatred, discord, bitterness, and disunity. God's power and blessings do not thrive in a contaminated environment because where evil thrives, destinies are cut short or destroyed. We should avoid situations where we perpetuate false and malicious rumours touching spiritual leaders. Instead let us take time to pray for them and the ministries God has given them because we are all parts of the body of Christ.

Further Reading: 1 Timothy 5:17-19; Ephesians 4:11-16
Prayer for the day: *Father, guide me to recognize and fully embrace the spiritual leaders You have placed in my life in Jesus' name. Amen.*

Day 334 — 1 Corinthians 1-4

30th November

Thank God as You Pray for Your Faith

'How can we thank God enough for you in return for all the joy we have in the presence of our God because of you? Night and day we pray most earnestly that we may see you again and supply what is lacking in your faith" *(1 Thessalonians 3:9-10).*

As we walk with God, we need to pray daily. Some of the ingredients we must include in our communication with God are thanksgiving and making requests. Apostle Paul demonstrated this understanding in many of his epistles. He modelled a life of prayer as he prayed earnestly for believers and encouraged saints to pray without ceasing (1 Thessalonians 5:17).

Apostle Paul planted and nurtured many churches to a level they were established in the ways of God. Together with his ministry partners, he had great joy in the Lord because the saints had grown spiritually. He prayed for them day and night as he desired to meet them again and impart spiritual virtues into their lives.

When we approach God by faith and make requests to Him, He is faithful and grants us what we ask. He is a good father who delights in supplying the things we need so that we grow in faith for the glory and honour of His name.

Further Reading: Ephesians 4:11-13; 1 Corinthians 12:12-26
Prayer for the Day: *Lord, I thank you for translating me from the kingdom of darkness into the kingdom of light. I ask that You supply what is lacking in my faith so that I may grow spiritually.*

1 Corinthians 5-8

1st December

Rebuild Broken Relationships

"Without wood a fire goes out; without gossip a quarrel dies down (Proverbs 26:20)

The quality of our lives, manifesting our identity, fulfilling our purpose and glorifying God to a large degree depends on our ability to form and maintain healthy relationships. The enemy is aware of the great power godly relationships have on the lives of God's people and desires to destroy them so that their destinies are aborted. Very many people have been wounded by unhealthy relationships that made their souls sick rendering them unfit to serve God's purposes.

The sins of the tongue that kill relationships include gossip, false and malicious accusations, slander, lies and cursing among others. They act as a fire that spreads hatred, bitterness and other negative emotions that jeopardize relationships. This causes disunity that hinders blessings because God only commands a blessing where there is unity (Psalm 133:1-3).

The book of Proverbs highlights the role of a talebearer or gossip in fueling conflicts. A powerful illustration of the consequences of gossip is found in the life of David. He suffered distrust because of the words spoken about him. The exaggerated praises sung about him killing tens of thousands raised suspicion among Achish's princes. Even though Achish believed in David's righteousness, he yielded to the perceptions formed by others (1 Samuel 29:5). Like David, many people have suffered the aftermath of unverified reports.

Further Reading: 1 Samuel 29:1-11; Proverbs 11:13; 20:19
Prayer for the Day: Lord, help me recognize the snares of the enemy and avoid having my relationships destroyed by the enemy. In Jesus' name, amen.

1 Corinthians 9-11

2nd December

Be On Guard against False Testimony

"A false witness will not go unpunished, and he who pours out lies will perish" (Proverbs 19:9).

God delights in truth and commands us to be truthful in everything we do. Even though we live in a fallen world where sin has corrupted the lives of many, we can stand firm against all forms of sin including false testimony. We are prohibited from bearing false witness against others (Exodus 20:16).

False testimonies have destroyed the lives and destinies of many. Although a seasoned warrior, David often lamented how his enemies leveled false testimonies against him. They used sharpened arrows of their tongues to oppose and fight him. Our Lord and Saviour Jesus Christ was ensnared by Pharisees and the council, who sought and used false witnesses to justify his crucifixion.

False accusations permeate all realms of life: politics, churches, families, and businesses. Those who propagate them disregard their victims' sincerity, righteousness, and faithfulness, and only seek to destroy them. However, God does not leave us defenseless. He has given us His Spirit to help us identify our battles and face them confidently. False testimonies cannot stand against the power of truth and righteousness found in Jesus Christ. With the help of the Holy Spirit, we need to be vigilant and seek to walk in truth.

Further Reading: *1 Kings 21:9-10; Acts 6:8-15*
Prayer for the Day: *Heavenly Father, shield us from lies and false testimonies levelled against us by the enemy with the aim of tearing us down. Help us to focus on You for our deliverance.*

1 Corinthians 12-14

3rd December

Experience the Power of Persistent Prayer

"Remember Tobiah and Sanballat, my God, because of what they have done; remember also the prophet Noadiah and how she and the rest of the prophets have been trying to intimidate me. So the wall was completed on the twenty-fifth of Elul, in fifty-two days. When all our enemies heard about this, all the surrounding nations were afraid and lost their self confidence, because they realized that this work had been done with the help of our God" **(Nehemiah 6:14-16).**

Prayer wields an unparalleled strength in the spiritual realm. It serves as our channel to converse with God whose unlimited power is at the disposal of the saints who call on His name. No opposition can be strong enough to resist the power of a prayerful person especially when they pray in the will of God and walk in righteousness (see James 5:16).

Time and again the Scriptures encourage us to call on God in prayer as he delights in answering us (Psalms 65:2). When Nehemiah was rebuilding the wall of Jerusalem, he relied on God's power through prayer. He devoted himself to four months of prayer. Since he prayed in faith, he activated divine power that gave him grace and strength to accomplish the task in a record fifty-two days. This achievement silenced his critics and opponents who admitted that the work was done with the help of God.

Further Reading: Psalms 65:2; 1 Thessalonians 5:16-18
Prayer for the Day: Lord, may we always find the strength and tenacity to pray without ceasing, as You empower us with speed anointing in the assignments You have entrusted to us. Amen.

Day 338 — 1 Corinthians 15-16

4th December

Activate Divine Power through Prayer

'Therefore, confess your sins to each other and pray for each other so that you may be healed. The prayer of a righteous person is powerful and effective. Elijah was a human being, even as we are. He prayed earnestly that it would not rain, and it did not rain on the land for three and a half years. Again, he prayed, and the heavens gave rain, and the earth produced its crops" **(James 5:16-18).**

God has given us access to His unlimited power through the channel of prayer. Those who know how to pray in His will, in the name of Jesus and by faith can do all things. Signs, miracles and wonders accompany those who know how to activate divine power through communing with God in the place of prayer.

Elijah prophesied in Israel in a time of apostasy. The nation was turned away from the worship of the true God by Jezebel into the worship of Baal. However, Elijah resisted her firmly. He prayed that it would not rain for three and a half years and God heeded his prayer. After that duration, he prayed that it would rain and God heeded his call.

Apostle James points out Elijah's humanity to encourage us to be confident in God when we pray. Instead of retreating in fear and giving up when confronted by seemingly impossible situations, we should fix our eyes on the Lord and activate His power through prayer.

Further Reading: *1 Kings 17:1; 1 Kings 18:1; Luke 18:1-8*
Prayer for the Day: *Lord, give me the grace to pray with fervency and faith. May our prayers generate divine power in Jesus' name, amen.*

2 Corinthians 1-4

5th December

Sink Deep into God's Presence

"Deep calls to deep in the roar of your waterfalls; all your waves and breakers have swept over me" **(Psalm 42:7)**.

As we commune with God in prayer, we need to be aware that our prayer should have three dimensions: length, frequency and depth. To get hold of the deeper mysteries of God, we should learn to tarry in prayer. Scriptures indicate that many saints who did great exploits in the name of the Lord spent quality time in prayer. In addition, they prayed without ceasing. Persistence in prayer demonstrates that we have authentic faith and moves the supernatural to act on our behalf. A third element of prayer that is the subject of today's devotional is depth. There are shallow levels of prayer, and there are deeper levels in which God's power moves with great ease and effectiveness.

For our prayer to be effective and transformative, it needs to be empowered by the Holy Spirit. Scriptures say that we do not know how we ought to pray but the Holy Spirit intercedes for us through groans that cannot be expressed (Romans 8:26). Hannah's prayers for a son demonstrated the depth of her relationship with God. Like her, we need to allow the Holy Spirit to move us into deeper levels of intimacy with God as we spend quality time with him more often. As we strive for fervency in prayer, we must also pursue righteousness.

Further Reading: 1 Samuel 1:13; Isaiah 64:6-7
Prayer for the day: Heavenly Father, help me to have longer periods with You in deep communion more often. Strengthen my prayer life in Jesus' name. Amen.

2 Corinthians 5-9

6th December

The Grace of God Makes Us Righteous

"All of us have become like one who is unclean, and all our righteous acts are like filthy rags; we all shrivel up like a leaf, and like the wind our sins sweep us away" **(Isaiah 64:6).**

All the efforts we make to be righteous are vain if we are not justified by faith in Christ Jesus. The word of God teaches that no matter how hard we try, we cannot attain God's standard of righteousness because it is quite high. God regards all our attempts to become righteous by works as filthy rags. No matter how pure our intentions might be, they fall short of the immaculate standards of righteousness that our Creator aspires us to have.

No matter how much we try to do well and have a right standing before God, we cannot succeed on our own. Apostle Paul, who had an intimate walk with God, admitted that much as he struggled to do right, he still found himself doing evil: "For I do not do the good I want to do, but the evil I do not want to do - this I keep on doing" (Romans 7:19). This confession underscores the battle between human intent and sin's compelling pull. The singular antidote to this battle is surrendering completely to God. When we do so, He bestows upon us the righteousness of His dear Son Jesus.

Further Reading: Romans 7:19-25; 2 Corinthians 5:21
Prayer for the Day: Lord, I sureender my will, my struggles and my desire to do good into Your hands. Transform me from the inside out and let my actions be a reflection of Your righteousness. Amen.

2 Corinthians 10-13

7th December

Approach God's Throne with Confidence

"Let us then approach God's throne of grace with confidence, so that we may receive mercy and find grace to help us in our time of need" **(Hebrews 4:16).**

To attain our divine destinies, we need to call on the name of the Lord. As we do so, we need to know God's expectations of us, so that we can please Him. When our ways please God, He releases the help we need to move to the next level. Scriptures encourage us to confidently approach God because He will grant us our requests. When we seek God's face, we receive mercy and adequate supplies of grace to help us in every area of our need. The mercies of God are plenty and they exempt us from destruction and judgment. They are new every morning and they do not at any given time run out (Lamentations 3:22-23).

Grace refers to unmerited favour. As we seek God, He releases all the help we need to overcome the challenges of life. No human weakness or need is excluded from the provision of the grace of God. It holds the key to our increase, elevation and fulfillment of our mandate. The redemptive work of Jesus Christ on the cross guarantees us of God's help if we call on His name. This is through the power of the Holy Spirit within us.

Further Reading: Ephesians 6:10-18; 1 Thessalonians 5:16-18
Prayer for the Day: Lord, help me to approach Your throne with confidence that I may receive Your mercy and grace for my times of need. Amen.

Day 342 | Acts 20:1-3; Romans 1-3

8th December

Strive to Lay Hold of God

'No one calls on your name or strives to lay hold of you; for you have hidden your face from us and have given us over to our sins" (Isaiah 64:7).

Our lives are characterized by pursuit of different things. Some people pursue fame, others wealth, while the spiritually mature pursue the kingdom of God and His righteousness as a matter of priority. The word of God promises countless blessings to those who lay down their lives to pursue God's interests and do His will.

Seeking God with the intention of laying hold of Him is a spiritual exercise that requires effort, stamina and determination. We need to fulfil His requirements so that He can reveal His face to us by calling upon His name and making every effort to lay hold of Him.

Spiritual exercises that include prayer, studying the word and meditating on it builds our spiritual strength and transforms our lives. Since we are predisposed to sinning and gratifying the desires of the flesh instead of seeking God, striving to get hold of God is often a struggle. We must overcome the sinful nature and totally submit to God allowing His will be done in our lives.

Further Reading: *Luke 22:44; Isaiah 66:8; John 15:7*
Prayer for the day: *Father, help us to strive in prayer, to go deeper and birth the purposes and visions You have entrusted us. Help us to seek You with all our hearts. Amen.*

9th December

Defeat the Grasshopper Mindset

"We seemed like grasshoppers in our own eyes, and we looked the same to them" (Numbers 13:33).

God delivered Israel out of Egypt with an outstretched arm that disarmed their captors and stamped His authority as the sovereign of the universe. The ten plagues He sent to Egypt demonstrated His invincibility and exposed the futility of idols. By performing miraculous signs and wonders, He not only defeated the gods of Egypt but also wanted Israel to have faith in His power. Since it is impossible to please Him without faith, He gave Israel every opportunity to believe in Him without faltering.

However, like most of us, the Israelites did not fully understand God's ways and His power. Instead of trusting Him to deliver and settle them in the Promised Land, many feared and wavered through unbelief. They tested God many times and often spoke against Him. When Moses sent the twelve spies to scout the land, some of them returned with a negative report that misled the people. They viewed themselves as grasshoppers. This happened even after they came to the verge of possessing the Promised Land.

They felt inferior, fearful and doubted God's ability to help them. To attain our destinies, we need to fight and overcome every spirit of inferiority and be confident in God's power to fulfill every promise He has made.

Further Reading: Philippians 4:13; Romans 8:31; Hebrews 13:8
Prayer for the Day: Heavenly Father, we renounce the grasshopper mentality that belittles our ability In You. Help us remember Your past faithfulness, and rekindle our trust in Your promises in Jesus' name. Amen.

10th December

Make Progress by Being Spiritually Sensitive

"There is a time for everything, and a season for every activity under heaven" (Ecclesiastes 3:1).

Farmers discern optimal planting times for bountiful harvests; believers can likewise prosper by understanding their spiritual seasons. Unfortunately, many have missed God's timing even when He desires that we prosper in all aspects of our lives.

Those who are spiritually sensitive discern the times and respond to the promptings of the Holy Spirit. He guides them into profitable paths. The patriarchs for instance, walked with God by being sensitive to His leading. They discerned the time to separate themselves from their kin, offer sacrifices and move from one place to another.

Elijah discerned God's will and submitted to divine leading. When the brook that supplied water to him dried, he knew that his season of being in the wilderness was over. God directed him to a widow at Zarephath where his daily needs were met through miraculous provision.

The sons of Issachar had authority over their contemporaries as they discerned the times and understood what Israel should do. We too can know and understand our times in the process of becoming what God ordained us to be. As New Testament believers, the Holy Spirit lives in us and we rely on Him for help and guidance as we continue serving and walking with God. Let us all make the necessary effort to be sensitive and submit to the gentle and loving leadership of the Holy Spirit.

Further Reading: *Psalm 32:8; Jeremiah 29:11; Acts 17:26-28*

Prayer for the Day: *Lord, help us to be able to discern the times as we align ourselves with Your plan. Amen.*

Romans 11-13

11th December

Maintain Your Relationship with God

"For you did not receive a spirit that makes you a slave again to fear, but you received the Spirit of sonship. And by him we cry, 'Abba, Father.' The Spirit himself testifies with our spirit that we are God's children. Now if we are children, then we are heirs - heirs of God and co-heirs with Christ, if indeed we share in his sufferings in order that we may also share in his glory" **(Romans 8:15-17).**

The redemptive work of Christ made a way for us to become sons of God by translating us from the kingdom of darkness to the kingdom of light. God graciously fills us with the Holy Spirit who affirms that we are His. Through Christ, God adopted all who believe into His family, making them sons. These makes all genuine believers to be partakers of the gift of eternal life the same way Christ possesses eternal life.

Earthly children maintain their relationship with their parents, and we too need to maintain our relationship with God every day. Biological children endure the challenges their parents face, and believers too must endure the sufferings their faith in God leads them to. Scriptures teach that we enter the kingdom of God through many hardships (Acts 14:22). This means that no matter what we face in our walk with God, we must be ready to endure pain and sufferings as Christ did.

Further Reading: *Ephesians 1:18; Hebrews 11:27; 2 Corinthians 10:5*
Prayer for the Day: **Lord, grant us thee grace to always see ourselves as Your children. Strengthen our faith as we recognize our identity in You, in Jesus name, amen.**

Day 346 | Romans 14-16

12th December

Resist Spiritual Blindness and Deception

'The god of this age has blinded the minds of unbelievers, so that they cannot see the light of the gospel that displays the glory of Christ, who is the image of God. For what we preach is not ourselves, but Jesus Christ as Lord, and ourselves as your servants for Jesus' sake" **(2 Corinthians 4:4-5).**

Many people have their spiritual eyes and minds blinded by the devil and they are unable to see the brilliance of the gospel and the glory in Jesus. The devil uses different tools to hinder God's people from receiving and believing the word of God. These include societal norms, technology, deceptive mindsets and worldly systems. God has called and anointed us to exercise the authority He has delegated to us to break down these barriers and ensure that the light of the gospel shines to all people on earth.

We can learn the significance of the work of the gospel by studying the lives of the Israelites on their way from the Promised Land. Although Moses instructed them on the way they should walk and respond to His word, many of them did not heed and hardened their hearts. They rebelled against God, disobeyed His instructions persisting in unbelief despite witnessing firsthand God's hand at work in signs, miracles and wonders. As we walk with God, we need to steadfastly resist the deception and lies of the enemy so that they do not abort our destinies.

Further Reading: *Numbers 13:33; Lamentations 3:22-23; Titus 2:11-12*
Prayer for the Day: *Lord, I renounce every form of demonic deception and spiritual blindness in Jesus' holy name. Amen.*

Acts 20:4-38; Acts 21; Acts 22; Acts 23:1-35

13th December

Renew Your Mind by Seeking the Will of God

"Do not conform to the pattern of this world, but be transformed by the renewing of your mind. Then you will be able to test and approve what God's will is - his good, pleasing and perfect will" (Romans 12:2).

Our minds have the potential to continuously develop and be transformed as we seek and do the will of God. As we yield to Christ's leadership and submit wholly to the will of God, we become increasingly like Him as we discern His will with ease.

Without divine transformation through the power of the word of God, our minds easily indulge in carnality and delight in sin. We harbour falsehood ideas that resist and undermine the will of God. However, when we humbly accept the will of God, He is able to move us gradually from one level of glory to another. We are able to know His ways and to be strengthened in Him.

As we delight ourselves in Him, He reveals His pleasing will which is higher than His good will. As we mature in our walk of faith, we discern His perfect will that is best for us in all things. We are able to understand Him better and to hunger and thirst for deeper things in Him. He transforms us to vessels of honour and makes us carriers of His glory. We are able to minister to others because our lives are sold out to advancing His interests on earth, and having His will done on earth as it is in heaven.

Further reading: Proverbs 2:1-6; 1 Corinthians 2:16; Isaiah 55:8-9
Prayer for the day: Dear Lord, empower us to actively renew our minds, directing our thoughts towards purposeful actions that magnify Your name and better our world for Your glory. Amen.

14th December

Understand the Ministry of Angels

"Are not all angels ministering spirits sent to serve those who will inherit salvation?" (Hebrews 1:14).

The earth is not only populated by mankind. It also has spirit beings that are invisible to the human eye. These include angels and demons who are actively involved in the lives of mankind. They have power that affects the outcome of our lives whether we are aware of it or not. God assigns His angels to His people to minister to their needs while the devil works through evil spirits to torment and oppress people.

Advancing the kingdom of God is spiritual work that cannot be done without divine backing. This is why the ministry of angels is critical for believers. God is benevolent and He has not only given Himself in the Person of the Holy Spirit but also deploys angelic beings to offer us help and deliver His messages to us.

As disciples of Jesus, we can be sure that God will do anything that is necessary – including moving heaven and earth – to send us help in our times of need. When Jesus was fasting in the wilderness for forty days and forty nights and tempted by the devil, angels ministered to Him (see Mark 1:13). We have the assurance that God will always send us His help from His holy hill through angels when we call on His name.

Further Reading: Acts 12:1-10; Psalm 34:7; Psalm 91:11-12

Prayer for the day: Heavenly Father, I thank you that You have given us the ministry of angels to minister to us in our earthly lives and as we journey towards our eternal destinies.

Acts 27-28

15th December

God Appointed Our Times and Boundaries

"From one man he made all the nations, that they should inhabit the whole earth; and he marked out their appointed times in history and the boundaries of their lands" **(Acts 17:26).**

The Lord our God is the sovereign of the universe and determines where and when each man will live. He controls the affairs of the whole universe and decides where each of us will live and how long we will. God also predetermined the epochs in which we will live and wired us to face and overcome all the challenges of our times. He determined the assignment each of us should undertake, giving us grace and empowerment to fulfill His purpose. Every one of us is alive by divine design. Consequently, we should be aware that God has expectations as far as the assignments He has given us is concerned. This calls for us to work as unto Him with all our strength and might.

We must always be conscious of our purpose. David was aware of the purpose for which he was created and did his best to fulfil it. God commended him because he was singularly devoted to His will and served with love, diligence and righteousness despite his human shortcomings that sometimes got on his way of walking right with God. Similarly, we need to be cognizant of the fact that every position we hold and every opportunity we get is meant to help us rise to a higher purpose. At every point of our lives there is always a higher level and glory which we should aspire to be in.

Further Reading: Luke 10:20; Acts 13:36; Matthew 6:33
Prayer for the Day: Lord, give me the grace to recognize and fulfill my divine assignments. In the Name of Jesus, amen.

Colossians 1-4; Philemon

16th December

We are Guarded by God's Power

"who through faith are shielded by God's power until the coming of the salvation that is ready to be revealed in the last time" **(1 Peter 1:5).**

Our faith in God's sovereignty acts as a fortress. It defends us from life's challenges and guarantees our protection until Christ is revealed and we are transformed to be like Him. Through genuine faith in the word of God, our lives are safeguarded in Christ and no evil can destroy us.

God's power offers holistic protection – spiritual and physical. It acts as a barrier against illnesses, difficulties and every form of adversity. It gives us divine exemption so that we are not harmed by the circumstances and situations that destroy others. To be effective, the faith we profess in Christ should be accompanied by corresponding actions because faith without action is dead (James 2:26). The shield of faith is active and does not relent from taking steps that demonstrate its authenticity.

As believers working toward our divine destinies, it is not enough to simply have faith. Rather, we must allow that faith to shape our decisions, reactions, and lives. We should always bear in mind that the faith we profess is our defense, and we are not only protected but also positioned for divine exemption from the difficulties that others may experience.

Further Reading: Hebrews 11:1; Ephesians 6:16; James 2:14-26
Prayer for the Day: *Heavenly Father, fortify my faith that it may act as my steadfast shield through all the trials and challenges of life. Amen.*

Ephesians 1-6

17th December

Activate God's Covenant through Obedience

"But remember the Lord your God, for it is he who gives you the ability to produce wealth, and so confirms his covenant, which he swore to your ancestors, as it is today" **(Deuteronomy 8:18).**

The Lord our God is faithful and keeps all the covenants He makes. He does not take back the word He has spoken but remains faithful to His people no matter the circumstances. God made a covenant of blessings and provision with the patriarchs. His intention was that their descendants and all followers of Christ would become partakers of the blessings of that covenant. God's part of the covenant was that He would give them the power to make wealth and His people would reciprocate by doing His will.

As we walk with God, we need not fear that the vagaries of the world will negatively affect us. Through this covenant, we have access to the riches of God's wealth and storehouse and he promises that we will lack no good thing. A covenant is not merely an agreement. It is a divine alignment that guarantees mutual commitment and protection. The covenant you uphold has the power to elevate you beyond qualifications and create a path of increase and prosperity where there was none. Godly covenants invoke the power of divine favour that usher us into greatness as we obey God's word and do everything He commands us.

Further Reading: *Genesis 26:12-13; Malachi 3:10*
Prayer for the Day: *Lord, direct my path so that I am able to uphold the covenants I have entered with You. May my life reflect Your glory in Jesus name, amen.*

18th December

Live in God's Purpose

"Then the word of the Lord came to Elijah: 'Leave here, turn eastward and hide in the Kerith Ravine, east of the Jordan. You will drink from the brook, and I have directed the ravens to supply you with food there.' So he did what the Lord had told him. The ravens brought him bread and meat in the morning and bread and meat in the evening, and he drank from the brook" (1 Kings 17:2-6).

God has designed a unique path for each of us. Activating this divine blueprint can unlock His provision and protection in our lives. Those who align themselves with God's purpose receive divine backing irrespective of the opposition they may face from the kingdom of darkness.

Our anchor Scripture is about Elijah. He lived in the will of God and served His purpose despite facing great adversity. Israel had become apostate in his day and was suffering under the yoke of poor leadership. When Israel faced a severe drought as punishment for abandoning the true God, the Lord divinely provided for Elijah's daily needs faithfully. He did this miraculously through supernatural interventions because ravens – birds that are known for their high appetite – brought him bread and meat twice a day without fail. Like Elijah, David was devoted to God's purpose and he received divine protection and provision. When we truly align ourselves with God's will, we receive divine protection and provision, and God champions our cause.

Further Reading: Acts 13:36; 1 Samuel 19:1-6
Prayer for thee Day: Lord, help me discern and pursue Your divine purpose for my life. May I remain steadfast, fulfilling every plan You have for me. Amen.

1 Timothy 1-6

19th December

Make the Kingdom of God Your Priority

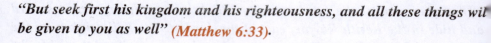

"But seek first his kingdom and his righteousness, and all these things will be given to you as well" **(Matthew 6:33).**

The kingdom of God operates on principles. To receive the benefits it offers, one must grasp and live by those principles. Matthew 13:11 indicates the privilege we have in understanding the secrets of the kingdom of God. We are blessed beyond imagination because we are able to access spiritual wisdom, knowledge and understanding that many people do not have.

We know God's will through His word. The teachings of our Lord and Saviour Jesus highlighted the need for us to take His kingdom seriously. However, instead of seeking the kingdom of God above all else, many people pursue selfish interests. They seek money, wealth, fame and comfort. We cannot attain our destinies and serve God's purpose without making His kingdom a priority in everything we do.

Besides, we also must strive to be righteous. Righteousness means having a right standing with God as He expects all believers to be righteous. Some examples of works of righteousness include giving to the needy and catering for the needs of the kingdom of God. In everything we do, we must make every effort to live for God's glory. Our words, speech and conduct must be aimed at glorifying God (Colossians 3:17).

Further Reading: 1 Corinthians 4:20; Romans 14:17
Prayer for the Day: Lord, help me to seek Your kingdom and righteousness above everything else. Help me to realise that everything else is secondary to seeking Your face. Amen.

Day 354 — Titus 1-3

20th December

Recognize the Source of Our Blessings

"May the peoples praise you, O God; may all the peoples praise you. Then the land will yield its harvest, and God, our God, will bless us" (Psalms 67:5-6).

Recognising that we are not self-made is a foundational truth we should appreciate. Various individuals have been involved in moulding and shaping us. Our parents, friends, relatives and other members of the society have played a part in our becoming who we are. Beyond these earthly connections, we have a friend who surpasses all – the Lord Jesus Christ.

Jesus is our ever-present friend and is highly instrumental in shaping our destinies. He has provided everything we need for life and godliness through His great and precious promises (2 Peter 1:3-4). He is our healer who delivers us from sickness and heals all our diseases. The leper who was healed glorified and worshipped Him with a loud voice, and he was made whole (Luke 17:15-16). When we respond to God with gratitude, we demonstrate our acknowledgement that He is the source of all our blessings and the favour we enjoy.

The Bible emphasizes the pivotal role of praise and thanksgiving in unlocking God's blessings. When we praise God from the depth of our hearts, the earth responds by granting us her riches. Our blessings increase so greatly that even nations cannot help but acknowledge God's hand in our lives just as they did with Abraham, Isaac and Jacob.

Further Reading: Psalms 67:7; 1 Thessalonians 5:18
Prayer for thee day: Lord, we humbly acknowledge that our accomplishments are not our doing but a product of Your great grace and generosity. Amen.

1 Peter 1-5

21st December

Believe God's Hand is Upon Your Life

"The LORD will keep you from all harm - he will watch over your life; the LORD will watch over your coming and going both now and forevermore (Psalms 121:7-8).

While we pursue our divine destinies, the Lord precedes us to make a way. His mighty hand works in our lives clearing the way and making a path where there is none. His power goes ahead of us graciously releasing the strength we need to move forward. His love and mercy shield us on every side securing us from the enemy and ensuring God's grand plan for each one of us is not foiled. Scriptures describe God's way of divinely exercising His power of releasing grace to preserve His people from all harm. He puts His holy angels in charge of our lives so that no weapon of the enemy forged against us can succeed.

The Psalmist was a beneficiary of God's grace and power. In many instances He acknowledges the hand of God in the lives of His people, and the many benefits gained as they obediently submit to His will. Thanking God is a way of acknowledging His help. It is a recognition of the role of the Holy Spirit in our lives because He is responsible for revealing the will of God to us and helping us do it.

Further Reading: Psalm 91:1-4; Isaiah 41:10
Prayer for the day: Lord, we stand in awe of Your mighty hand of protection and guidance. Thank You for walking with us every step of the journey.

Day 356 | Hebrews 1-6

22nd December

Recognize God's Mercies in Your Struggles

"Because of the LORD's great love we are not consumed, for his compassions never fail. They are new every morning; great is your faithfulness" **(Lamentations 3:22-23).**

The Lord reveals Himself as a compassionate God (Exodus 34:4-7). He understands the trouble and suffering His people go through. He comes in to intervene by alleviating the suffering of His beloved.

Jesus does not change and is overflowing with mercy, grace and love. Our circumstances, trials, temptations and hardships touch His heart because He also experienced the physical nature and is well acquainted with our humanity. This qualifies Him to serve as our High Priest. He was tempted in every way as we are and never sinned (Hebrews 4:15). This sets Him apart from humanity although He lived and died like any other man.

God's kindness and mercy have carried us through. He has preserved us in the face of struggles and protected us from being drowned by the world around us. Jacob faced adversity in his quest to have a family. He worked for seven years as a shepherd of his father-in-law's flocks. He was however short-changed as he was given Leah for a wife instead of her more beautiful sister Rachel. Since he was determined, he worked another seven years for the desire of his heart to be met. God gave him the perseverance He needed to work in the hardest circumstances where his wages were changed multiple times.

Further Reading: *Psalm 103:8-12; 2 Corinthians 12:9*
Prayer for the Day: *Heavenly Father, thank You for Your unfailing love and mercy. Open our eyes to recognize Your hand in our lives. Amen.*

Hebrews 7-10

23rd December

Win the Battle in Your Mind

"For though we live in the world, we do not wage war as the world does. The weapons we fight with are not the weapons of the world. On the contrary, they have divine power to demolish strongholds. We demolish arguments and every pretension that sets itself up against the knowledge of God, and we take captive every thought to make it obedient to Christ" (2 Corinthians 10:3-5).

Our minds are some of the most valuable assets God has given us. They are the epicenter of all spiritual battles, which we either win or lose, depending on our mindsets. The patterns etched within our minds can either unlock divine blessings or become barriers of accessing them. In his epistles, Apostle Paul reveals profound truths about the power of the mind. He states that our wrestling is not against physical foes but against mental strongholds. These strongholds are the arguments, beliefs and notions that defy the knowledge of God.

The greatest battleground in the world is in our minds. Our thoughts determine our actions and hence our lives, and unless we change our thinking, we may remain the same. Winning the battle in the mind opens doors to triumph in all areas of life. We do this by intentionally subjecting every thought to Christ's sovereignty. We thus have a divine responsibility of filtering the ideas we allow in our minds lest they lead us to defeat in spiritual warfare. Our warfare should be different from that of the world as it targets the enemy's powerhouse, and our minds should always align to God's word to tap His power to win.

Further Reading: *Isaiah 55:8-9; Philippians 4:8*
Prayer for the Day: *Heavenly Father, I acknowledge that my mind is the battleground and I need You to takee over my mind that I may win my battles. Amen.*

Day 358 — Hebrews 11-13

24th December

Transform Your Mindset for Lasting Success

"If the Lord is pleased with us, he will lead us into that land, a land flowing with milk and honey, and will give it to us" **(Numbers 14:8)**.

Our minds as a battlefield hold a great significance in the spirit realm. The kingdom of darkness contends for our minds with a view to enslaving us through ungodly thought patterns. If we are not careful and watchful, we are likely to suffer defeat even when God's desire is for us to walk in victory and dominion.

A successful walk with God entails aligning our thinking patterns with His perfect will. This is because as we walk by faith, He often requires us to do things that the rational mind cannot easily comprehend.

As Israel planned to enter the Promised Land, God commanded them to send spies to scout the land He was about to give them. He desired to enlarge their vision and prepare them for the great inheritance He intended for them. However, majority did not have this vision of possessing the land. They spoke against God. Only Joshua and Caleb had total faith in God's plan and promise. Caleb insisted that God had the power to fulfill every promise He had made to them, provided that they believed Him. His mind was aligned to God's will.

Further Reading: Romans 12:2; Ephesians 4:23
Prayer for the Day: Dear Heavenly Father, I open my mind to the transforming work of Your Holy Spirit so that my mindset may conform to Your will. Amen.

25th December

Trust God for Leadership and Provision

"The LORD is my shepherd, I shall not be in want" **(Psalm 23:1).**

God has given us His word to serve as a manual for our lives. Just like a product manual, the Bible contains promises, guidance, and wisdom essential for our success. Scriptures contain the rules by which we should follow, to please God and enjoy abundant lives. Sadly, many people overlook this and miss the many benefits it is meant to confer on those who accept and believe its message.

Since the Bible reveals the character of God, it is meant to offer us guidance on the path we should follow. As fickle human beings, we do not have the ability to make profitable decisions or the right choices without divine help and guidance. This is why reading, studying and meditating on the word of God is a necessity for every person who desires to live a fruitful life.

The Psalmist compared man to sheep. Without a shepherd, they are exposed to many dangers. They are weak and do not have a means of defending themselves from danger. However, when they are under the care of a committed shepherd, they are protected from harm and their nutritional needs met. Similarly, God takes care of the needs of His children. By faith in God, we are able to live with the confidence and awareness that God desires our success as this attracts honour to His holy name

Further Reading: Joshua 24:15; Proverbs 3:5-6
Prayer for the Day: Heavenly Father, Your word is my guide to success. Help me embrace its promises and wisdom in Jesus' name. Amen.

Day 360 — 2 Peter 1-3; Jude

26th December

Recognize God as Your Ultimate Source

'And without faith it is impossible to please God, because anyone who comes to him must believe that he exists and that he rewards those who earnestly seek him" *(Hebrews 11:6)*.

The essence of faith is in believing that God is real and that He is at work in one's life to reward their diligent pursuit of Him. We cannot please God without faith in who He is and in what He can do. Scriptures say that He is favourably disposed to those who accept and believe in His word. As we seek His face, we should be fully convinced of these truths.

When we walk by faith, we perceive God as our Father. Fathers play an indispensable role in the lives of their children. They are progenitors, providers, protectors and teachers. The same way earthly fathers do their best to meet all the needs of their children, our heavenly Father faithfully meets our needs when we fully commit to pleasing Him.

The fact that He is our Father implies that we originate from Him and everything we have or desire can only come from Him. God's wisdom is unsearchable and He sovereignly chooses how to provide for our needs. Irrespective of the channel He uses to bless us, He is the ultimate source of all good gifts. Acknowledging and relating with God as a Father accords us many privileges, and puts our hearts and minds at rest.

Further Reading: Luke 11:11-13; Matthew 6:25-34; Psalm 121:1-2
Prayer for the Day: Heavenly Father, I acknowledge You as my ultimate source. Grant me the ability to relate with You as my father even as You become my provider in Jesus' name. Amen.

1 John 1-5

Day 361

27th December

Embrace God as a Father

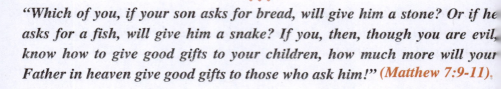

"Which of you, if your son asks for bread, will give him a stone? Or if he asks for a fish, will give him a snake? If you, then, though you are evil, know how to give good gifts to your children, how much more will your Father in heaven give good gifts to those who ask him!" (Matthew 7:9-11).

Jesus taught many times about the great and immeasurable love of our heavenly Father. The Lord desires to take care of all our needs out of the abundance of His wealth and goodness. His provision cuts across spiritual, material, psychological and social needs. He gives us grace, finances, mental power as well as social connections so that we can live fruitful lives. As a Father, God sustains us through all the challenges we face. His greatest desire is that we grow our relationship with Him until we attain the stature of Christ.

In our relationship with God, we should always strive to get rid of every trait that is likely to strain our fellowship with Him. He is holy and despises hypocrisy and thus, we should always approach Him with genuine hearts.

In many of His teachings, the Lord Jesus rebuked the Pharisees and teachers of the law for their empty religious practices. He warned us against the yeast of the Pharisees which is hypocrisy (Luke 12:1). When we deal with God as a Father, we acknowledge His omnipresence and are aware that we cannot hide anything from Him.

Further Reading: Jeremiah 29:11; Psalm 139:1-4; James 1:17
Prayer for the Day: Dear Father, I come before You acknowledging your loving care. Help me approach You with genuine reverence for You are my Father. Amen.

Day 362 — 2 John; 3 John

28th December

Revere God and Embrace His Majesty

"A son honors his father, and a servant his master. If I am a father, where is the honor due me? If I am a master, where is the respect due me?" says the Lord Almighty **(Malachi 1:6).**

Understanding God's holiness is vital in having a fruitful walk with Him and attaining our divine destinies. God is majestic and glorious. He cannot be compared to anything in creation because He is clothed with great power and lives in unapproachable light (1 Timothy 6:16). Although He is highly lifted up, He loves us deeply and desires the best for us. He does not despise any of us (Job 36:5) but He expects us to reverence Him in everything we do. He is the King of kings and the Lord of Lords.

Like many people in past generations, we run the risk of getting accustomed to God's presence and majesty. Those who do so despise His power and glory. The sons of Eli were meant to be priests who would teach Israel how to reverence God and worship Him in truth and spirit. However, they despised the name of the Lord and were destroyed. God judged them for misrepresenting Him by making Israel view Him as contemptible through their wicked character. Scriptures teach that God's name should be great among the nations (Malachi 1:11). We need to be careful and guard against becoming familiar with God, as this would hurt and hinder us from receiving divine help to fulfill our divine purposes.

Further Reading: Psalm 99:3; Psalm 22:3; Hebrews 12:28-29

Prayer for the Day: *Majestic Father, you are the King of kings and Lord of Lords. I approach You with reverence, recognizing Your magnificence and sovereignty. Take all the pre-eminence in my life. Amen.*

Revelation 1-5

Day 363

29th December

You Cannot Hide from God's Presence

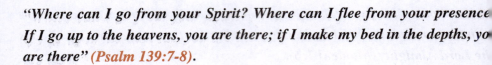

"Where can I go from your Spirit? Where can I flee from your presence? If I go up to the heavens, you are there; if I make my bed in the depths, you are there" **(Psalm 139:7-8)**.

Geographical location cannot limit God. He can be in all places at the same time: He is omnipresent. His Spirit is in the entire universe although He only manifests in certain places after man meets the conditions He has set.

The Psalmist was constantly aware of the promise of God's abiding presence. He knew that no matter where he went, he could not escape the presence of God. Jesus promised His disciples that He would grant them the presence of God wherever they went. The Bible contains multiple promises of the presence of God which we need to believe and activate in our lives (see Hebrews 13:5-6).

Just before He ascended to heaven, Jesus promised His disciples that He would return to them through the Holy Spirit who now makes His dwelling in the hearts of those who love and obey the Father (John 14:21-23). From the Day of Pentecost, believers have the abiding presence of God in their hearts. He works in and through them to accomplish God's purpose and glorify His name among men. The assurance of the presence of God in believer's life through the Holy Spirit makes all the difference, providing everything needed in life and eternity.

Further Reading: Hebrews 12:14; Psalm 51:10; Matthew 5:8
Prayer for the Day: Gracious Lord, thank You for Your presence in my life. Grant me grace to walk in true salvation and enable me maintain Your presence in Jesus' name. Amen.

Day 364 — Revelation 6-11

30th December

Strive to Fulfill what is Written About You

"Your eyes saw my unformed body; all the days ordained for me were written in your book before one of them came to be" **(Psalm 139:16).**

God's will for our lives goes beyond our immediate needs; it is a comprehensive plan beyond our earthly lives. When we pray for God's will, we do not merely ask Him to meet our desires, but to help us align with His purposes for our lives. His perfect will caters for all our physical and spiritual needs.

It is awe-inspiring to realize that God's plan for our lives was set in motion long before we were born. In His foreknowledge, God planned the direction we should follow and the works we should do for His glory. He documented all these details and desires that we cooperate with Him for their manifestation. The things God ordained for us are progressive. His word says that He established the borders of the land His people would occupy, and promised to strengthen them until they conquered all that territory (see Exodus 23:28-31). Similarly, God has set the boundaries we should reach with His help.

God's plan is superior to our own aspirations. Seeking His will helps us discover our purpose, gives us direction and assures us of His guidance along the way to our earthly and eternal destinies.

Further Reading: *Jeremiah 29:11; Matthew 6:10; Romans 8:28*
Prayer for the Day: *Heavenly Father, I surrender my plans and desires to Your will. Help me trust in Your purpose even when it differs from mine. Guide me along the path You have ordained for me, and grant me wisdom to discern Your will in every situation in Jesus' name. Amen.*

Revelation 12-18 | Day 365

31st December

Travail is the Price of New Beginning

"Who has ever heard of such things? Who has ever seen things like this? Can a country be born in a day or a nation be brought forth in a moment? Yet no sooner is Zion in labor than she gives birth to her children" **(Isaiah 66:8).**

The Lord our God is unlimited; He can do anything He desires without breaking sweat. His power has accomplished great things in past generations and will continue doing so in future. Scripture highlights how God's power works, and does the seemingly impossible by bringing forth a nation in a moment. It indicates that Zion bears her children as soon as she enters labour.

The process of giving birth is demanding and time-consuming. To manifest God's plan for our lives, we must seek Him with all our hearts. With this partnership, God causes great things to happen. Doing this requires that we count the cost of what we desire to see manifested, and be ready to pay the price. We can demonstrate our spiritual maturity by being ready to do everything God requires of us so that His purposes can be fulfilled. A man who desires to build a tower must first count the cost to see if he has enough resources to accomplish the task (Luke 14:28-30). We too must pay the price to accomplish God's purposes on earth. We birth revival, destiny and purpose through travailing in the Spirit. May God grant us the tenacity to travail until we birth God's purposes on earth.

Further Reading: *John 12:24-26; Matthew 26:36-46; Luke 18:1-8*
Prayer for the Day: *Lord, grant us the courage to pay the price of birthing Your purposes on earth. Help us realize that birthing requires sacrifice, earnestness and empowerment by Your Spirit in Jesus' name. Amen.*

Day 366 | Revelation 19-22

Epilogue

Thank you for dedicating your time this year to the reading of Nuggets of Destiny Devotional. We trust that your journey with the Lord has been impactful and transformative. May the Lord respond to each prayer you have lifted up to Him and foster an everlasting relationship with you.

Other Books by Apostle John K. William

1. Spiritual Maturity
2. Ten Principles of Success in Ministry
3. Manifesting Your Glory
4. Dealing with Foundations and Altars
5. Ingredients of Success
6. Battles of Life
7. Choosing the Best Marriage Partner
8. Serving God
9. Making Impact through the Power of Prayer
10. Spiritual Hedge
11. Spiritual Race
12. The Treasure of the Gospel
13. Great Questions of Destiny
14. The Weight of a Matter
15. The Power of Acceptable Sacrifice
16. Can God Trust You?
17. The Beauty of a Transformed Life
18. Pursuing Your Destiny
19. God's Scoring Board
20. Sin as Cancer
21. Pillars of Walking with God
22. Wealth without Wings
23. Setting Your Standard
24. Provoked to Greatness
25. Spiritual Diagnosis
26. Commitment as a Key to Success

27. The Life of an Eagle
28. Becoming a Spiritual Builder
29. Spiritual Capital for your Destiny
30. Benefits of Fasting
31. Divine Exemption
32. Possibilities in Christ
33. The Seven Mountains of Influence
34. The Power of Praise and Thanksgiving
35. Taking Care of Your Spiritual Health
36. The Story of My Mum
37. Nuggets of Destiny Devotional - 2021
38. Nuggets of Destiny Devotional - 2022
39. Nuggets of Destiny Devotional - 2023

New Titles by Apostle John K. William

1. The Potter's Touch
2. Destroyers of Prophetic Destiny
3. Setting Your Standard (Revised and Updated)
4. Partakers of the Divine Nature
5. The Principle of Substitution
6. Relationship with God
7. Dealing with Stubborn Limitations
8. Discover, Recover and Manifest Your Identity